# Software Perspectives

*The System is the Message*

# Software Perspectives

*The System is the Message*

Peter Freeman

*University of California, Irvine*

Addison-Wesley Publishing Company

*Reading, Massachusetts • Menlo Park, California • Don Mills, Ontario*
*Wokingham, England • Amstersdam • Sydney • Singapore*
*Tokyo • Madrid • Bogotá • Santiago • San Juan*

Title page photograph courtesy of Orange County Performing Arts Center, Costa Mesa, California. Photo by Valerie and Prasad.

*Library of Congress Cataloging-in-Publication Data*

Freeman, Peter, 1941–
Software perspectives.

Bibliography: p.
Includes index.
1. Computer software. I. Title.
QA76.754.F75 1987 005 86-32135
ISBN 0-201-11969-2

The material in Appendix A was drawn with permission from Kerola, P., and Freeman, Peter. "A Comparison of Lifecycle Models," *Proceedings of the 5th International Conference on Software Engineering*, pp. 90-99, San Diego, 1981.

The quote on p. 33 of Chapter 2 was taken from *Zen and the Art of Motorcycle Maintenance* by Robert M. Pirsig. Copyright 1974 by Robert M. Pirsig. Reprinted by permission of William Morrow and Company.

The opening quote on p. 165 of Chapter 7 was taken with permission from Robert E. Kelley, *The Gold Collar Worker: Harnessing the Power of the New Work Force*. Addison-Wesley, Reading, Mass., 1985.



ABCDEFGHIJ-HA-8987

To Mattie Hull Robinson
—mother, teacher, guide—
who has shaped my perspective on the world.

# Preface

Do you have difficulty in communicating your software needs to technical people?

If you *are* a technical person, do you have difficulty communicating to your customers the reason why development is taking a long time?

Are you trying to manage or guide an activity that is dependent on developing software?

As a senior technical person, are you frustrated by your inability to control the technical development of a software system adequately?

Whoever you are, do you *really* understand what software is?

If any of these questions strike a responsive cord, then this book is for you.

It is about the underlying nature of software, its quality, and the processes used to create it. Its message is very simple: The complex of elements and factors that surround the activity of creating software *themselves* form a system, providing us a means—the systems approach—of successfully dealing with the development activity and its products.

Thus, this is a book for *anyone* who wants to understand—or improve—software systems and the processes used to create them. You may be a manager; or a programmer; or the owner of a small business; or someone trying to understand what the DP department has done to your request for a new program; or the head of a large corporation; or the proverbial "intelligent layman" interested in knowing more about one of the most challenging technical tasks in today's world. A broad range of people, yes, but with a common need: how to understand and deal with the development of software-intensive systems in a coherent and systematic manner.

A deep technical understanding of software is neither necessary nor wasted in reading this book. Strange as this may seem, it is true because much of the content of this book concerns connections between different elements of the environment surrounding software. If you are technically strong, then this book will help you better connect your technical skills and knowledge to the organizational/ human issues that are also an important part of software development. If your personal knowledge and strength lie in areas other than the technical details of software, then it will help you better connect your skills and knowledge to the technical processes of software development.

Likewise, you do not need to be a manager to profit from the perspectives on software development I have tried to provide here. For example, there is an extensive discussion of the nature of software; that is not normally something found in a book for technical people. While you may be tempted to skip that—or worse, dismiss the whole book if it has something so *trivial* in it—I suspect that you will find that it confirms and perhaps even expands your conceptualization of this stuff we work with every day.

By now, you should understand that this is not a textbook or "how-to" book. It is a description and explanation of the process of creating systems that are largely software, presented in a way intended to be useful to technical and nontechnical people alike. As a friend of mine, a very knowledgeable systems expert, noted, this book contains things that can't be found elsewhere.

As Fred Brooks did in *The Mythical Man-Month,* I have tried to share a set of experiences and insights that I have gained in 25 years of work with software. My perspective, however, is somewhat different: I have worked as a programmer, participated in the design of complex systems, and continue to be involved in many of the technical as well as managerial details of software development through my work with a range of consulting clients; in addition, I have been active in leading-edge software research and advanced graduate education at the same time. My underlying motivation is to distill the concepts and principles that underlie all these activities so that we can do a better job tomorrow. That has been the theme of my research in the university, it is the objective of my lecturing and writing, and it is the essence of this book.

Whether you are directly involved in the process of developing software, or are simply interested in what the person across the hall is struggling with, there is something here for you. The value of this book is not limited to technical people or their managers. Anyone—vice presidents, board members, functional managers in other areas, students—who has an open mind and a desire to understand a challenging intellectual task that is engrossing to thousands and impacting millions will find something of interest here.

Acknowledgments are difficult for me because there are so many. My greatest debt is to my wife Barbara, who urged me to write and then gave me constant and invaluable support while I did; her unflagging faith was the pilot light that burned steadily. Literally thousands of students, clients, acquaintances, and colleagues have taught me what I know about systems and my gratitude to them is as deep as they are numerous. My thanks also to the several people who waded through a rough, early draft and provided excellent feedback, most especially Roger Pressman. I have drawn freely on the experience and insights of Jerry Hoskins, and the assistance and perspective of Chris Pidgeon. I appreciate the help of Robert G. Babb II who offered comments on the second draft. My thanks to all. Jim Yates's insight and encouragement are a continuing touchstone, without which this would be a very different book.

The financial and institutional support of the University of California, Irvine, the National Science Foundation, the IBM Software Engineering Institute, IBM do Brasil, Université de Genève, and Institut Européen d'Administration des Affaires made possible the sabbatical during which most of the research and writing were done. Michel Lissandre of IGL, Paris, provided the final form of the SADT diagrams.

Finally, but certainly not least, this book would not exist without Susie Dunaway, who managed my affairs, and Lynn Caverly-Stauffer, who did the excellent job of formatting and production, and kept track of me during a three-continent sabbatical.

*Laguna Beach, Calif.* P.F.

# Contents

# Prologue

# Prologue

*It is a foolish thing to make a long prologue, and to be short in the story itself.*

*— Second Maccabees 2:32*

As with systems work, it is important to understand the ground rules under which a book has been written. This prologue addresses four topics that will help you profit from your reading: the general organization of the book, terminology, my assumptions about your background, and the context of my background.

### *Organization*

Several years ago I set out to write a textbook that would tell you everything you needed to know about software development. What I soon discovered, which should have been obvious in the first place, is that what we know about software systems development is evolving much too fast to permit it to be frozen into a classic textbook that will remain largely unchanged for years. That is not to say that one can't write a good textbook at this stage (there are several[P.1]) only that they will age quickly.

> *The superscripts refer to notes, organized by chapter, in the back of the book. The notes provide references, side comments, further explanation, and other material not necessary to a first reading. I suggest you ignore them for now.*

National Football League Properties, photo by David Boss

In this book, then, I have tried to capture three things that will help you understand not only what you observe and experience, but will encounter in other books and papers: realities, concepts, and precepts. These are not simply listed, but rather are presented in the context of an underlying view that *systems work is a system itself.*

It is important to be realistic, to understand what really is, to sort out fantasies and wishes from what is factual. That is often difficult in the present world of software, and is especially difficult if you are a newcomer to the field. I present those realities that I have seen demonstrated enough to be sure of, for example, that carefully *designed* systems are easier to maintain and modify than those that are not. The ultimate reality is captured in the title, however—that it *is* possible to make sense of software systems development, *if* you adopt a systems viewpoint.

Concepts (or ideas or abstractions), if drawn from specifics, are essential to formulating strategies, organizing technical work, making decisions—in short, doing the work of and managing the technical process. While managers typically have a good set of concepts to guide their work and technical people a good set to guide theirs, one of the primary gaps of knowledge in the software field is created by each group not understanding the others' concepts. My focus here is on bridging that gap.

If we understand the realities and concepts of our world, we are in a position to formulate some precepts, or rules of actions, that impose a certain standard of action. Where possible, I have tried to provide you with those precepts that I have seen followed successfully. For example, a highly successful precept in many organizations is to always apply some explicit inspection process to every software workproduct (specification, design, program, and so on) before declaring it finished.

In tune with the underlying message, the book is organized around a description and explanation of the parts of a development system. Where possible, I have provided some analysis of why things seem to work the way they do, given guidance or perspective on strategies and approaches that seem to work (or not), and commented on what I have observed being done (or not done) in many development situations.

The book is organized in a straightforward way: Chapter 1 explores in a way useful to neophytes and experts alike the question

"What is software?" while Chapter 2 addresses the all-important issue of how to define software quality. (In some ways, the remainder of the book is then concerned with how to achieve it.) Chapters 3 and 4 present the central concept that I use to organize knowledge about software development—the software development system (SDS)—and Chapter 5 discusses its overall operation as seen in the development process (Appendix A expands on this last topic). Chapters 6 through 9 then discuss four of the six major elements of the SDS (policies, people, procedures, and tools) and the relationships among them. The other two elements, objectives and information, are discussed throughout. Chapter 10 discusses the relationship between the SDS and the people, organizations, and technologies that make up its environment. Chapter 11 concludes the body of the book by identifying some trends and directions in the field of systems development.

Notes containing expansion or explication of topics in the text are collected in Appendix B (so you won't be distracted by them). A glossary and bibliography round out the book.

### *A Few Terms*

Let's start with a term that permeates this book—"system." Although one can provide precise, technical definitions, the meaning I employ here is the intuitive one: a collection of things related in a way that forms a coherent whole. In dealing with systems, there are always two questions: What are the elements? and What are the relationships between them?

"Software" will be used largely in a generic sense to refer to collections of programs, individual programs, designs or specifications for programs—in short, any of the information that directly relates to the instructions and control data (but not the application data) that is loaded into the hardware to produce desired outputs. I will use "program," "design," "specification," and so on when I mean those specific items of software; the meaning should usually be clear from the context.

Without going off into a long philosophical treatise, let me note that this is a very broad definition. Certainly for some purposes (for example, defining languages for software development) one must be more precise, but here I want to focus on the overall process of reaching development objectives. In that context, it is important to include all the information and workproducts that bear on reaching our objectives.

Another nondistinction I will employ in many cases is to equate "system" and "software." There are some obvious exceptions to this equation: On the one hand a single, 50-line program is not a system; I think your common sense will guide you to be able to apply what I may be saying about systems to your single program situation (you will find that a surprising amount of what is true for systems is true for individual programs).

On the other hand, there are certainly systems that are not software; indeed, one of the tenets of system development is that to the extent possible you should proceed with the early stages of design without worrying about whether it will be realized in hardware or software. As with scaling down to small situations, common sense should guide you in scaling up to systems that include hardware and other nonsoftware elements.

There is another reason for closely identifying software and system, however. In many situations today, the systems we are developing are certainly "software-intensive" in that software is the critical or dominant element. Further, because of its complexity, if you can deal effectively with the design of a software system, then you can probably also deal with the design of a larger system containing other elements. Indeed, some of the techniques for dealing with software development are now being used in the development of the overall system or systems that may be realized in hardware (for example, VLSI design shares a lot with the design of a pure software system).

> *Software development is an instance of systems development. Much of what we know about one applies to the other.*

Finally, it is important to recognize explicitly (and keep separated) that I am using the word "system" in two very distinct, but related ways. I will often refer to the system being developed—the software—or even just to "the system." My reference is to the product being produced.

On the other hand, the underlying conceptual framework and key to controlling development revolves around the idea of "software development system," a collection of objectives, policies, people, techniques, tools, and information that form a *system for producing systems*. I may sometimes abbreviate "software development system" to SDS to reduce confusion (and save space), but I have resisted the temptation to create a new term to stand for SDS since I don't want to lose the close identification with the inherent understanding we all have of what a "system" is.

### *Who Are You?*

Even when writing a book intended to serve the needs of a broad class of people, as I have here, an author must make some assumptions about the potential audience. In general, I have assumed that you are interested in understanding or improving the process of creating software, very likely because you are interested in improving the quality of the software produced. There are at least four categories of people I hope will read this: technical professionals, managers directly concerned with software development, managers concerned with other aspects of organizational activity but who must interact with the development activity in some way, and others who are simply interested in what is going on in an active and challenging segment of our culture. There are others, such as students, teachers, and consultants, who can identify closely with one or more of these categories as well.

The senior technical person will gain some insight into what his or her management does (or doesn't do) and thus be able to work with that part of the team better. The junior technical person can gather some idea of why the world is organized the way it is, even if sometimes he or she has little opportunity to change it.

The technical project manager will find many points of interest here. Of special interest to this person will be the principles relating to the use of technical methods and tools. All technical people will gain deeper insight into the nature of software and the processes used to produce it.

The general manager (a person perhaps two or three levels above the individual project manager) that is responsible for development activities may find the principles presented here as useful as anyone. Indeed, it is this person (responsible for organizing the overall process, allocating resources, and seeing that it all continues to run) who often has the greatest opportunity for utilizing the ideas discussed here. This person in many cases (if not most) has "come up the ladder" and thus has also served as a junior technical person, technical leader, project manager, and so on.

There is another type of general manager emerging in many organizations today—the person who has a technical background, has come up through the ranks, but is not conversant with software and its problems. Typical is the executive in an engineering or technology-based company where, until recently, software was something that the people in the DP center dealt with. The rapid growth of importance of enabling technologies such as computer-aided design and manufacturing (CAD/CAM) and computer-integrated manufacturing (CIM) is forcing issues of software development strategies to the top of such organizations; in addition, many technologies and processes that once were based on some other technology (electronics or fluids, in the control area, for example) are rapidly becoming computer-based, which again means heavy involvement in software.

Utilization of this book is not limited to those concerned directly with managing or performing the development activity. Anyone (executives, board members, or simply the intelligent layman) who has an open mind and a desire to understand one of the most challenging intellectual tasks in today's world will find something of interest here.

No deep understanding of computers, electronics, mathematics, or programming is necessary. If you have some or all of this background, then you will interpret things in that context and perhaps be able to make connections that others will not. An ability to think logically and to keep separate means and ends, to be able to identify parts and connections, *is* required.

Likewise, no deep understanding of management or organizations is necessary. If you do have a stronger background in this area, then, as with the technical person, you may be able to take away a deeper set of insights. An ability to understand that management is necessary and even productive in every situation is required.

### *Who Am I?*

I don't have all the answers. No one does. But I do have a set of experiences and a background that helps provide me with a certain perspective.

My starting point is the technical side. I have designed and built complex software (scientific applications, operating systems, research programs in artificial intelligence). My graduate training is in computer science and I am still an active researcher attempting to advance our understanding and capabilities in software engineering.

As a professor of computer science and lecturer to professionals I try to educate students in basics (such as computer architecture) and their applications (for example, design methods for complex software systems).

I have been able to gain some insight into the application of software technology through extensive lecturing and consulting in industry, in addition to my direct experiences. This has brought me into close and continuing contact with those trying to use the new technology (and the old) to build software ranging from small one-person, two-week projects to those that can only be measured in kiloyears of effort. Through this contact, my own use or participation in the use of techniques, and assistance to those most vitally concerned with improving their software development systems, I have developed a set of observations of what works and what doesn't work.

I have been in the software field continuously since 1961. I have seen some significant improvements in software technology (along with the obvious improvements in hardware technology) but am increasingly frustrated by their slow adoption. It is not just that they are research ideas which must be translated into usable form; I am speaking of those techniques that are in use today (and have been for a number of years in some cases) by some organizations but that are still ignored or rejected by others, not only to their economic peril but to the safety and convenience of the public at large.

We don't have to wait for breakthroughs. There is much available today. Nowhere is it written that we must all repeat the mistakes of our predecessors. Yet that seems to be what many are trying to do.

Much has been written [P.2] about the challenges of information technology to mankind in general and to the relative position of national economies in particular.

There is indeed a new wave of technology coming, but we must learn to perform, manage, and utilize software development if we are to understand and control whatever comes next—because it clearly will be software-like in nature and thus subject to many of the same problems and solutions.

CHAPTER

# 1

# Psst, What *Is* Software, Anyway?

CHAPTER

# 1

# Psst, What *Is* Software, Anyway?

*Be not ignorant of any thing in a great matter or a small.*

— *Ecclesiasticus* 5:15



The Bettman Archive

## 1.1 It's OK to Ask

Five or ten years ago, intelligent people were not ashamed to ask "What is software?" Today, with stories about it appearing regularly on the covers of newsmagazines or on the front pages of daily newspapers, most people hesitate to ask what they fear is a stupid question.

It isn't and they shouldn't!

Indeed, many of the people that are daily concerned with software should be asking this question. All too often, they do not have a sufficient understanding of what software is to permit them to deal with it in an effective manner.

The problem is not that people don't know that software is just another name for computer programs—most third graders as well as older people now know that. The recognition that people often lack is that software is *more* than just programs and that there is one overriding characteristic of it that *MUST* be attended to—the fact that it is a system.

Before looking more deeply at the process of creating software, it will be helpful to explore some of the aspects of software itself. As the old adage puts it, "To master your enemy, you must know him!"

> *Most of us can profit by enquiring more deeply about the nature of software.*

## 1.2 Isn't Software Just Programs?

Only if you are a complete literalist, absolutely not believing in abstractions, programming on your own personal computer, and never coming back to programs you wrote last year, is this true. The question is not simply what software *is*, any more than the question is simply what the trade policy of a nation *is*. Rather, it is how you think about it and what role it plays in a larger context that are the important issues.

From the perspective of a computer, yes, of course, software is a set of programs that tell it what to do. But the perspective of a computer is rather limited and has little to do, directly, with what we want computers to do for us. That is why thinking about software just as programs leads to so many problems, both in their creation and use.

Perhaps the most common misconception in the software field is that productivity is measured by how many lines of code are produced in unit time. The common joke in many software development shops is some form of "Quit trying to figure out what you are doing and write some code!" While there may be times (few, in my estimation) when such an order contains some degree of truth, such comments, invariably based on an underlying and strongly held belief, belie a view that it is only programs, in the narrow sense of *executable* programs, that can be used to measure progress or that represent productivity output on the part of a developmental staff.[1.1]

What this leads to quite often is an attitude on the part of management and technical people alike that the only important thing is the production of code. This focus, clearly understood in psychological and pragmatic terms, conditions the entire environment to focus on the production of code.[1.2] The result, time and again, is the production of mountains of code that cannot be integrated to work as a system, or the building of a system which does not satisfy the needs of the customer even though it may work well technically.

What, then, is software if it is something more than just programs?

## 1.3 Software Is . . .

The brain and soul of a computer, not just a coat of paint

The embodiment of the functions of a system

The captured knowledge about an application area

The collection of all the programs and data that are necessary to make a computer a special-purpose machine designed for a particular application

All of the information (documentation) produced during the development of a software-intensive system

All of these characterizations contain some important elements of truth that will help you better understand the world of software even if you are already deeply involved (mired?) in it. Let's look briefly at each in turn.

For years, the belief in many organizations, especially those that manufactured computer hardware or other sophisticated electronic equipment that included computers (for example, military systems) was that software was something that was added on after the system—the *hardware*—was built; in short, it was viewed as a coat of paint that was put on the hardware after the real system design had been done. As people keep rediscovering, general-purpose computer hardware does nothing without software.

An often-heard debate is whether systems design should be driven by the hardware constraints or the software requirements. Worse, it sometimes is not even a topic for discussion, with the result that an inappropriate choice is made.

Usually, but not always, the hardware characteristics are permitted to drive the overall design. This can lead to severe problems later when features of the hardware that are inappropriate to the *system* constraints must be compensated for in the design of the software (if possible). By analogy, this would be like choosing a French restaurant because it is close, irrespective of its menu or type of service, and then ordering a quick-service Chinese take-out. If it can be made to happen, it won't be easy (or cheap)!

I witnessed a slow, agonizing example of this in an organization rebuilding a large application system. The decision was made (perhaps implicitly) to rebuild it on the same type of hardware. As the design of the rebuilt application system proceeded, software decisions about the database management system were then constrained by the hardware choice. This, in turn, resulted in such a great expansion in the requirements for disk storage that ultimately (after lots of new hardware had been obtained) the entire project had to be scrapped because the expanded configuration could not physically fit in to the operations facility. A careful *system* design in the first place could have identified or even sidestepped some of the problems by calculating the resources needed to implement the system under alternative assumptions about the hardware.

Two realities of software development are illustrated here. First, hardware considerations all too often drive the development process out of a mistaken belief that they are the dominant cost and most inflexible design element; while they may be, one cannot really say without looking at the overall system. Second, the "debate" as whether a particular effort should be hardware- or software-driven is a red herring; neither is the right approach because only with a systems approach that takes into account and evaluates both elements appropriately can a system be produced that meets the functional and operational requirements of the customer.

Software provides the active portion of the system, the part that makes the system seem "alive"; hence, the characterization of it as the brains and soul (or heart) of a system. While it is obvious that the underlying hardware is an essential ingredient of any computer system, the nature of general-purpose computer systems is precisely that they can do anything (and, thus, nothing) that a particular set of software instructs them to do.[1.3]

The second characterization above captures a viewpoint that is crucial to creating a successful software system: the focus on the functions of an application system, not on the functions of the underlying hardware. After all, carrying out a set of application functions is ultimately the purpose of any computer system. Taking this viewpoint helps to direct attention to the instrumental objective of building any computer system—to achieve some goals in a wider sphere (such as reducing inventory costs, controlling a machine, or creating a new service to sell).

Leonard Sayles and Margaret Chandler in their perceptive study of the NASA program that landed the first man on the moon point out how important the overall objective set by President Kennedy was to the success of the program.[1.4] It was an objective that often served as a forcing function to get things done in order that the objective could be met. They also point out, however, that while having a clear main objective is important, it does not help very much in deciding what to do next on a detailed level.

The last two characterizations start to provide that detailed guidance. One of the reasons that it is unproductive to think of software as only consisting of programs is that, at least implicitly, this usually connotes only the procedural part of programs, leaving out the all-important data portions. For this reason, it is sometimes useful to focus on the fact that the software that makes up the application functions is composed of both data and functions.

There is a fine line here: Is a large database, that is, the data in it, not the programs that access it and process the data, software? Generally, the database itself is viewed as being outside the realm of software (but certainly not outside the realm of computer science, nor of systematic ways of building the collection of data) while the data that define a database and its accessors is a part of the software. This carries with it a connotation of software being an active and general-purpose element that is not tied to a specific set of facts (as would be the case with the data stored in an actual database).

I once saw a good example of ignoring the data portion of a system—and the development problems that can result. A group was developing a complex system that included tables that would be used to define the characteristics of an individual installation of the system. The design team was not familiar with the application area and felt that the design of the tables would be simple and belonged in the province of the application specialists since it was just data; consequently, little attention was paid to data during most of the design phase.

As the early versions of the system were brought up for testing, it was discovered that the tables were not only unexpectedly large and complex, but that the efficiency of the system depended critically on their design. A serious delay in the development of the system resulted while the data portions of the system were belatedly designed. The failure to understand the structure of this data component of the system and treat it equally with the process portions nearly resulted in disaster.

When focusing on the development process, all the information that is produced during development is of interest. The success of an effort to build a software-intensive system is thus directly tied to how well one deals with all of the information present, much of which is something other than directly executable programs or their imbedded data. Hence I am led to the conceptual generalization that software is all the information produced during development.

> *Software is many things, but all are simply aspects of information.*

It may come down to a matter of semantics: some would like to reserve the name "software" to refer just to programs (and perhaps data); if so, then there is a lot of other information that is very central to what software developers do that must be accounted for and named in some fashion. If we include all the information relevant to a piece of executable software in the generic definition, then we will have to deal with that information in the same rigorous and systematic way that we must deal with executable software. This is essential to successful development, since if it is not done information is lost or altered, introducing errors.

A common example is the widespread tendency to not maintain software designs. A system is built from some sort of design document, but as modifications are made to the code, these are not recorded in the design. Later, if major changes are contemplated, they can only be made intelligently by considering the design—which is unavailable because it has not been treated in a rigorous and systematic way.

## 1.4 What Does This Mean in Practice?

It is just as counterproductive to include every scrap of information in the definition of software as it is to restrict it to only executable code. At a gross level, we can differentiate among several important classes of information that are involved in producing software (Fig. 1.1): *software representations* (representations for short), *software engineering knowledge* (development information), and *domain-specific knowledge* (application information). Because it is important to have a well-grounded understanding of these classes, let's take a deeper look at them before proceeding. (While the following discussion may seem technical, it is really just a logical description and will provide you some important characterizations.)

*Software representations* include programs, detailed designs written in a program description language, architectural designs represented as structure charts, specifications written in a formal language, system requirements expressed in a combination of notations, or any one of hundreds of other possibilities.[1.5] In short, any information that in some direct way represents an eventual set of programs and their associated data may be included in a software representation.

The definition of a consistent set of representations and specification of how to achieve them is currently one of the primary issues facing software development professionals and the organizations for which they work. It is one of the troubling realities, however, that they frequently do not recognize the importance of representations.

It would, of course, be simpler if we had different terms for those objects that are executable and those that merely describe executable objects. But we don't. Reserving "software" to describe only executable objects—and having no other widely accepted term available—

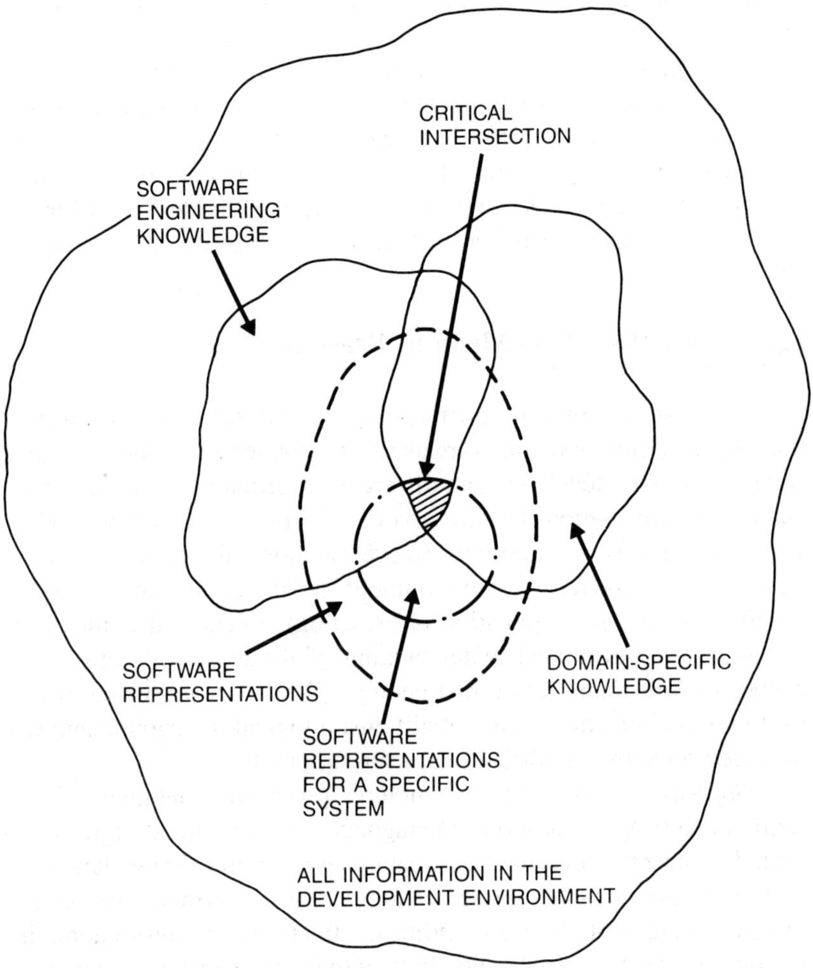


FIGURE 1.1 Software Information

puts us back in the situation of focusing too much on the executable objects in their *final form* and not enough on the earlier descriptions. Hence the breadth of my definition.

The second class, *software engineering knowledge*, is all of the information that relates to development in general (for example, how to use a specific design method) or information that relates to a specific development (for example, the testing schedule on a project).

The information of this type includes project-related information, software technology information (methods, concepts,techniques), knowledge about similar systems, and the detailed information relating to the identification and solution of technical problems on the system being developed. More general information (for example, the notice of this month's professional society meeting or the next office party) is in the larger set that we are not concerned with in any explicit way.

The third class of information that is essential to creating software is the *domain-specific knowledge* about the application area. The examples are everywhere: understanding of a physical process to be controlled, accounting rules, procedures for updating and changing employee records, and so on. While this information is clearly essential to creating software, discovering it and putting it into a useful form is usually the province of an applications specialist such as a process control engineer or an accountant or a business systems analyst.

As we have applied computers to ever more complex situations, however, it has become evident that our understanding of the application domain is quite often the biggest stumbling block to creating effective software; at a minimum, communicating the understanding of the applications specialist to the computer specialist has increasingly been identified as a key problem. Progress has been slow at improving this interface, as we will explore in more detail below.

Some "solutions" provide tools to the applications specialist so that he can directly build the software. Thus the motivation for many of the "fourth-generation" languages, prototyping schemes, and program generators. While they are very powerful for some situations and certainly permit us to break down the communication barrier between applications specialist and computer specialist in some cases, they do not solve all problems.

Specifically, there are situations in which there is simply too much to be known in each domain (the application domain or the computer domain) to permit one person to master both; a specialist is required in each, with good communication paths between them. That is the thrust of some of the modeling techniques such as structured analysis.

Let's return to the classes of information defined in Figure 1.1 and look at their overlap. As the diagram indicates, the overlap is generally small. For example, although we have quite a bit of knowledge about how to develop software (software engineering knowledge), such as principles for organizing programs, most languages (software representations) directly incorporate very little of this software engineering knowledge. That is one reason for the interest in and high hopes for the new programming language Ada™[1] which was designed specifically to incorporate software engineering knowledge in certain areas.[1.6]

The intersection between software representations and domain-specific knowledge is also small. A language such as FORTRAN obviously embodies some very general information about the domain of scientific calculations; COBOL embodies some information about business data processing; Ada was intended to contain some information about the domain of embedded systems. The problem is that the amount of information is very small in order to permit the languages to be applied to the largest possible range of applications.

At the other end of the spectrum, we are starting to see some highly specialized languages that incorporate a great deal of information about an application. Languages for the control of a particular piece of equipment are of this sort, as are the program generator packages that are based on an underlying model of some specific application. These languages presently cover only a very small part of the total range of applications, but research is under way to make it easier to produce application-specific languages.

An even smaller intersection exists between software engineering knowledge and domain-specific knowledge. We have very few principles in software engineering that specifically address how to build applications of a particular type (for example, hotel registration systems). To some extent, that is OK since we do have some specifics that cover entire classes of applications (for example, real-time systems or database systems). However, this knowledge is woefully inadequate at present.

As you might expect, the smallest overlap between classes of development information occurs when we try to find information in each class that is relevant to a specific system. This intersection is absolutely critical to the successful creation of software since it conceptually contains all the information necessary to bring the desired system into being.

---

[1]Ada™ is a trademark of the U.S. Department of Defense.

There are some strategic implications of this state of affairs. Creating software representations (new languages) that do not help us to better utilize domain knowledge and/or software engineering knowledge belongs in the area of pure research, that is, exploring the implications of language design principles for their own sake. That is quite important for the long term and certainly should be supported. It is important to recognize, however, that to gain more immediate benefits it may be best to focus on new languages that can better help utilize the domain and development knowledge we now have.

> *Control of information is at the heart of controlling development—and representation is at the heart of information control.*

In terms of pragmatic software development, it is important to manage the balance between the different forms of information in the development environment. A group that is heavy on software engineering skills but does not have effective access to domain-specific (application) knowledge will have great difficulty building the systems needed by the customers. On the other hand, a group that thoroughly understands an application area but that is short on software engineering know-how stands in danger of foundering on the complexity of the software they try to create. Underlying both is the necessity for effective ways of representing the information so that the overall process can be managed.

## 1.5 Why Worry About Information?

The answer is that information is the essence of software. If it is not managed correctly, it will rapidly become confused and lost, with predictable impact on the software.

In reality, this often happens. The situation is similar to that in hospitals 100 years ago. As discoveries were made about the role of various micro organisms, people realized that many of the things they had been doing in hospitals were very dangerous; as a result, major attention was suddenly paid to practices (such as the sterilization of instruments) which previously had been ignored. We are just beginning to appreciate more fully the role of many kinds of information on the process of producing executable software, and thus to treat it with more respect.

At present there is a poor balance between naturalness and formality in handling development information. Many technical personnel focus only on the executable forms of software, leading to problems. For example, much good information about the structural aspects of a piece of software is lost during development. Initially, this may not pose a problem, but eventually it usually does since this is precisely the information that is needed to help preserve the integrity of the software during *evolution* (typically called maintenance, although it incorporates three kinds of change: repair, adaptation, and enhancement). This is similar to an organization that divides itself into departments and then loses all information about which employees belong to which departments; reorganization will be very difficult.

Belady and Lehman, in their pioneering studies,[1.7] found that structural information (definition of subunits such as modules and the interfaces between them) was essential to maintaining technical and managerial control of a software system over time as it undergoes change. In spite of a wave of techniques incorporating "structure" in their names (programming, design, analysis, testing), it is still common to find software produced with little attention paid to its physical structure and even more common to find that after initial development, no coherent record of the system's internal structure is maintained.

Management, on the other hand, too often assumes it is all technical information to be left to the technicians to be handled; again, valuable information for management, such as the reasons why a particular feature is requested by the customer, may be lost. Their response, once the importance of information is realized, is sometimes to mandate that everything be saved—leading to a very "formal" system, laden with paperwork and attendant problems.

We should strive to be more relaxed and intuitive about the information in the development environment, while still preserving in usable form relevant parts of it. For the present, however, while we are still discovering which information is most important and learning how to deal with it, we must be more explicit. To that end, let's look at software, in the general sense, and see what happens to it over time.

## 1.6 Pragmatic Forms of Software

You are probably familiar, at least vaguely, with many of the forms software takes:

- Programs in machine language
- Programs in higher-level language
- Specifications
- Needs statements
- Requirements
- Architectural designs
- Detailed designs
- Data formats
- Collections of programs
- Programs being tested
- Finished programs
- Systems in use for production

as well as some of the other forms of information which I include under the generic term "software":

- Analysis of requirements
- User documentation
- Maintenance documentation
- Change requests
- Modification specifications
- Error reports
- Performance measurements

and so on!

I often encounter one of several reactions when I start to discuss the forms of software: People who are deeply involved, in the technical development process want to argue for their particular definition of some of these elements; those not so deeply involved want to be given an explicit definition of each form and be told which they should use; some who are involved, but not directly, in the technical development, couldn't care less and want to get on to consideration of what they consider to be the critical issues. It is like analyzing an election; everyone has a different viewpoint.

All of these viewpoints are understandable and, in their place, appropriate. Here I want to encourage a different viewpoint for the purposes of improving your understanding of the underlying principles of good software development: that of an observer of the development process who is trying to see what forms this slippery substance called software takes during its journey from idea to production system.

This viewpoint can very quickly lead to arguments about the relative merits of different sequences of steps that are taken in developing software (usually labeled as arguments about the best lifecycle to use). We will come back to some of that later, but again, let's delay the arguments about specific approaches until we understand a little better the underlying nature of what we are dealing with.

The concept of a lifecycle has been adopted in the world of software to indicate the stages that software goes through. As in biology from which we borrow the term, a piece of executable software goes through a set of stages that are more or less dictated by the nature of the animal (and to some extent by the techniques we have for bringing the finished product into existence). Roughly, software goes through the following stages:

Concept development (definition)
Technical creation (development)
Product for use (operation)
Object of further development (evolution)

The methods, tools, and techniques that are used have little impact on this basic, overriding sequence. We must start with an idea of what the system will do, then we create it, use it, and, quite likely, modify it. In each form of the software, we have a representation of the final object which will be loaded into some hardware to create the desired behavior.

It is important to understand that there are variations on this basic sequence that may be extremely important. Just as children engage in limited adult activities so that they can learn, it is often critical that software be exposed to some operational stresses while it is being developed in order that we can learn at the earliest possible moment whether it will stand up to its ultimate "adulthood" or not. We understand more clearly now that software development cannot always have a completely strict progression, but may need to cycle through stages in an iterative fashion. Software prototyping, for example, is one expression of this basic concept.

At this point, I am trying to keep from becoming too specific (I know this is frustrating to some of you, but as in the technical design of software it sometimes pays not to rush too rapidly to the final point) in order to provide a broad perspective on the nature of software. I find that the following description (with examples) of the forms of software is useful:

1. Development Prologues
   - Needs statements
   - Analyses of needs
   - Requirements statements
   - Analyses of requirements
   - Data element definitions
   - Functional specifications
2. Technical System Descriptions
   - Technical specifications
   - Architectural designs
   - Detailed designs
   - Database structures
   - Data descriptions
   - Executable programs
3. System Aggregations
   - Collections of programs
   - Systems of programs
   - Interface definitions
   - Integrated hardware/software systems
   - Integrated human/hardware/software systems
4. Installed Systems
   - Reference (baseline) systems
   - Versions
   - Production systems
5. Performance Data
   - Efficiency measurements
   - Error reports
   - Effectiveness ratings
   - User ratings

Let me repeat: My purpose here is not to provide absolute, technically perfect definitions of software artifacts. Rather, I am trying to provide some abstractions that will help you gain some perspective on what is going on around you. Let's look briefly at each of these categories.

> *Software information can be put into one of five classes.*

It is clear that something comes before the technical development of software—a memo from the boss, a concept for an application sketched on the back of a napkin, a detailed statement of the functions that are needed in a system, analysis of the needs and stated requirements, and so on. The general nature of this information is that it focuses on the functionality of the system, its usage in some instrumental setting, its relationship to other systems—in short, looking away from the underlying physical hardware (one of the things that goes awry in development is that technical descriptions are sometimes mixed in with this kind of information before a clear understanding of the external aspects of the system is gained). I have labeled this "development prologues" to emphasize that it is information that comes before the technical development. Yet, in all of it we can glimpse some aspect of the eventual system. Development prologues are like the editorials and speeches and articles that precede some governmental action, such as passage of a new law.

"Technical system descriptions" are the familiar artifacts found in designers' offices, on programmers' desks, scribbled on blackboards (or, the programmer's favorite, whiteboards, which provide the extra dimension of easy coloring). There shouldn't be much of a problem understanding this class. It is worth noting the overlap that exists in practice between development prologues and technical descriptions in the area of specifications. Indeed, a good set of specifications is precisely the bridge between the outward-looking development prologues and the inward-looking technical descriptions since they can be considered both at the same time. Continuing the analogy, technical system descriptions are the laws and regulations.

"System aggregations" are technical artifacts, too, of course, but I have separated them to emphasize the change in focus. Up to the point where we have individual components (running programs in the case of software) our focus is on those individual pieces. In building large systems, however, the battle is barely begun once the pieces exist because then we must integrate them into a working system. This

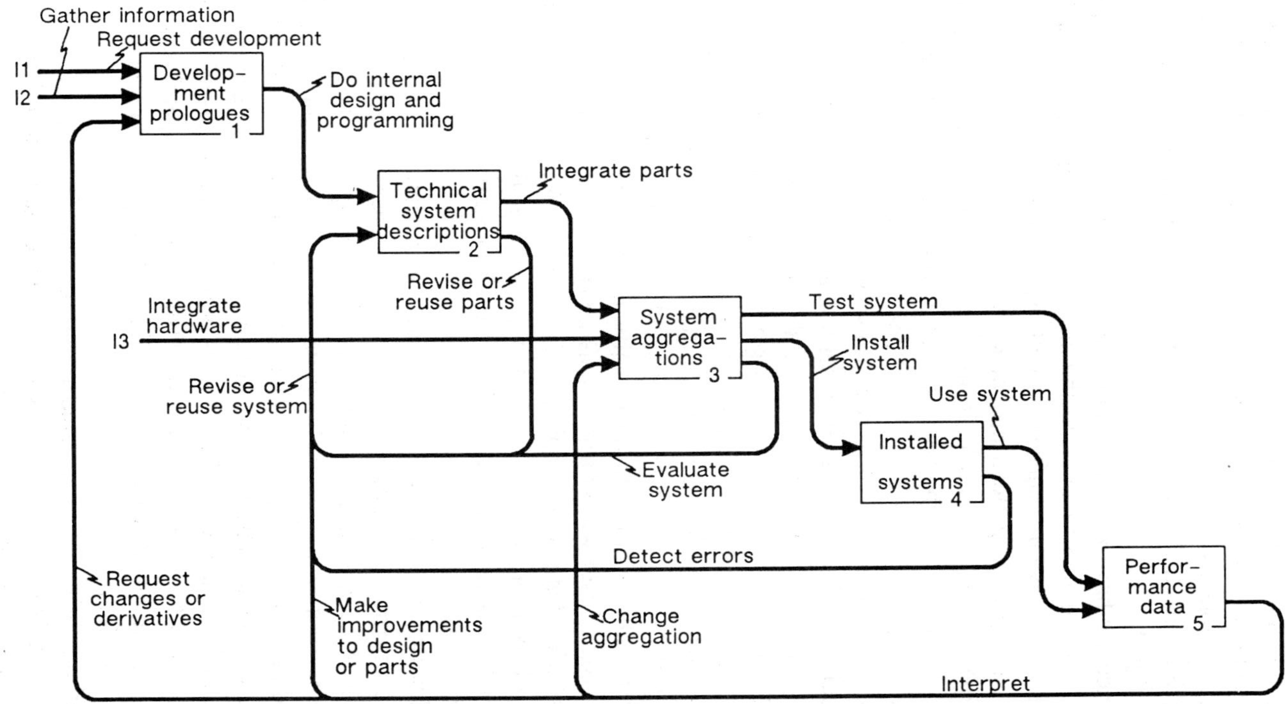


FIGURE 1.2 Forms of Software

activity not only takes a large amount of effort in most cases, but it has fundamentally different concerns. Hence I think it is useful to look at the aggregations as a different type of object. In the analogy, system descriptions are the collections of laws and regulations pertaining to some subject.

Once we have a system built and ready for use, the focus again changes, so I have shown a fourth class of system objects: "installed systems." Now we are concerned with entire systems, not individual pieces but the aggregations that make up the total system. We treat them differently so again it is useful to separate them. Installed systems correspond to the laws actually being used and interpreted.

The last class I have shown, "performance data," may be the hardest to accept, since I have now transcended artifacts which we can all recognize as in some way representing at least a part of an executable system and entered the realm of abstractions. Instead of descriptions of systems, this class contains measurements and other data that characterize the system in use. In the analogy these are the statistics and observations collected on the results of using the law.

Figure 1.2 shows some of the activities that use—and, thus, interrelate—the different forms of software. Each box represents one of the classes of software forms discussed above and the arrows represent activities that may be applied to these forms. Arrows entering the left of a box represent activities that *create* that form of software; arrows that exit to the right of a box represent activities that *use* that form of software.

Although the left-to-right layout suggests a sequence of activities, the diagram models equally well other sequences of activity. For example, the arrow labeled "Interpret" emanating from box 5 could well represent what often happens—performance data from an installed system are analyzed, leading to a request for a revised or new system. In another instance, we may be interested in describing the sequence of evaluating a system that is built, but not yet installed, and on the basis of the analysis revise the design of the system and produce a new integration (described in the diagram by the connections between boxes 2 and 3).

Ultimately we are interested in the results of development. The best use of this diagram, then, is to help understand the relationship between the different forms of software. This simple model is obviously at a very high level of abstraction and would have to be made much more detailed in order to be used in any very precise manner. On the other hand, we can use it, even at this level of abstraction.

For example, although this diagram was drawn for the situation where there was no concurrent hardware development (resulting in the arrow on box 3 showing the integration of hardware), if we needed to structure our environment to take account of concurrent hardware and software development, we could use this as a basis, adding appropriate representation of the activities that would tie together the developing forms of the hardware and software system to see if we had structured the environment properly before actually setting it up.

I will come back later to a viewpoint that is implicit in this characterization of the forms of software: that it is useful to consider the development of a software-intensive system as a set of transformations that carry one form of the system into another. First, though, there are some other properties of the object of interest—software—that we should consider.

## 1.7 Software Is *Not* Easy to Change!

One of the enduring siren songs of software entices us with the message that it is easy to change. Countless managers and unwitting programmer accomplices have looked at a working piece of software and been seduced into believing that they could easily make some changes to improve it or transform it into something else. Little did they realize the agony, frustration, and destruction of good relationships (for example, with their customers) that lay behind that seemingly benign and simple encounter!

This two-faced situation—on the one hand lines of code are very easy to change, while on the other systems can be incredibly difficult to alter successfully—comes about because of the underlying fact that software is a *system.* It is the thousands of interwoven dependencies and interconnections that pull us down into the tarpit, not the individual pieces.

Consider a modern manufacturing plant. A complex system by anyone's standards, physical facilities, supply deliveries, power, labor rules, and hundreds of other things (both hard and soft) must work together properly to create a productive environment. Yet almost none of these elements are easy to change. Power systems are expensive and require long lead times to build, alteration of labor rules may require years of bargaining, suppliers may be scarce for certain parts, and so on. Consequently, we are not so tempted to change the manufacturing system. (Indeed, this difficulty of change has probably been perceived as harder than it is by some, hastening the decline of certain industries.) The underlying mechanisms of the system are hard to change and hence we don't lightly undertake systemic changes.

Oh, that we had less pliability in software!

Technically, it is the unforeseen consequences and hidden relationships that kill us in software. We think that a minor change in the screen format of a presentation will improve its readability (undoubtedly true), so we ask the programming staff to make the change (they have indicated it is only a minor change to one module of code). The change is successfully made.

Unfortunately, the change involved expanding slightly a table used by the module, pushing the system size above the scheduling limit for small programs, meaning the program now gets significantly less rapid service, resulting in a response time of the program to requests from the user at the terminal that is now nearly three times as long! Since the program is used to generate information to support a telephone marketing representative while on the phone, the system is now useless.

And, of course, the programmer making the change finished at 8 P.M. on Friday night, deciding to leave documentation until he returned from the two-week camping trip to the wilderness on which he left the next morning at 5 A.M. Thus a seemingly minor change in a program led to a major change in the performance characteristics of the program resulting in several weeks lost productivity. This is a rather obvious example of an unintended design consequence—one that can be readily seen and understood. Others are not so evident.

An engineering firm that designs plants built a parts-inventory system to keep track of spares for their plants. An important customer was promised a copy of the system, but the entire system had to be rebuilt at great expense to accommodate the customer's parts-numbers which were one digit longer. A design decision (or lack thereof) concerning the internal representation of part-numbers in the original design of the system resulted in it being essentially unchangeable years later.

In building software we do not yet have the coherent conceptual basis that we have in other pragmatic disciplines. Physics underlies electrical and mechanical engineering, giving us a way of predicting consequences and understanding relationships. Chemistry underlies chemical engineering. Biology supports medicine. Because software is all man-made and interpreted by finite and deterministic machines (computers), we believe that we can ultimately understand the underlying science of computers and hence be better able to deal with consequences and connections. At present, though, we are much closer to medical doctors (who have only an imperfect understanding of the underlying nature of the human body) in having to prescribe actions with only a partial understanding of the results to be expected. Even worse, we have much less experience than the medical profession!

> *The siren song of software flexibility has seduced many well-meaning professionals.*

As though our inability in many situations to understand design consequences and system linkages were not bad enough, there is another dimension that causes perhaps even more trouble and expense in the long run. That is the web of connections between the different aspects (or forms) of software discussed above, the chain of representations extending from needs statement to specifications to design to code to test results. The technical problem is one commonly called the *design-updating problem.* What usually happens is that even when a careful chain of system representations has been built, once the system exists, changes will be made to the programs without *reflecting* those changes back into changes in the design and the specifications. The result: The more abstract representations of the system are quickly made useless, so that future changes to the system must be made using only the program listings (or an equivalently low-level representation). In building construction, this would be like building without plans or standards and keeping no record of where pipes and wires were installed after the initial construction so that future changes to the building required walls to be torn out simply to find out where the wires were.

What are the implications of the reality of software being hard to change? There are two, in general terms. First, build the system as though it will last forever, enduring many changes along the way. Second, control of and changes to any system must be made very carefully. Let's look a bit more at the first implication (the second will resurface later).

## 1.8 Old Code Never Dies

This is a reality that many people and organizations learned years ago. Yet because the average length of experience of people in the field seems to be dropping (due to the rapid expansion of the use of computers and hence of people's involvement in creating software) it is a lesson that people constantly learn anew the hard way!

Software lives forever for any number of reasons, good and bad. The most obvious and pervasive reason is that once built and in productive usage, there is inertia that must be overcome if it is to be changed or replaced. The users like it. The boss likes it. The customers like it. It doesn't matter that it is slow, prone to errors, needs to be expanded to take care of new functions, and so on. The software has become a part of their lives and all they want is that it be fixed up a bit—certainly not replaced or changed in any major way!

The relationship between software and the people around it (users, customers, managers, operators, and so on) is not unlike the relationship between people that find themselves associated for historical reasons (e.g., in a marriage, working situation, neighbors) which may have little bearing on their present situation. It takes a tremendous amount of effort to change the situation and break the relationship to the software! The result: The software lives on and on and . . .

There are often economic reasons why software doesn't die, beyond those stemming from its intimate role in the production process. Software of any magnitude costs quite a bit to create in the first place (and, worse, it usually can't be considered a capital cost). If it has been used very much, then quite likely considerable money has been spent on it over the years to repair, adapt, and enhance it with new functions; it is not uncommon to find that three or four times the original development cost has been spent in this way. That turns out to be a large investment, generating the expected inertia on getting rid of it (even if the users agree that it is time to replace it).

Finally, it is not uncommon to build a piece of software for a "quick" application, one that supposedly will last for a limited time after which the software will be thrown away, only to find that the application is so productive that the decision is made to continue it—together with the use of the quick (and dirty) software!

The moral is: You must expect that software will never die. Build it as though it will continue far beyond your own retirement, will be adapted to run on new equipment, enhanced with new functions, repaired to take care of those pesky special cases, and generally outlive those that created it. There are obvious counterexamples—truly one-shot situations, applications for equipment that is about to die, functions that are eventually outmoded—but it is better to err on the side of too much preparation for the future rather than too little.

| *Software, like unwanted relatives, is difficult to get rid of.* |
|---|

## 1.9 Software As a Product

The history of computing has fostered the view that programs are highly mathematical in nature, created by genius mathematicians to solve esoteric problems understood only by them and a few others. Indeed, that was the nature of many early programs and the people that created them. As computers were applied to a wider variety of tasks, people started to realize that in fact computers are very general symbol processors, not just number crunchers. That view has now become dominant because of the large amount of nonnumerical (or, at least, involving only very simple arithmetic) work that computers do and because of the advent of the personal computer used by millions of people for very ordinary tasks.

Another view, clearly a corollary of the first, was that software was not a product in the sense that one described it, packaged it, worried about inventory control and derivative models, marketed it, sold it, maintained it, and removed it from distribution when outdated. That view, too, has changed radically in the past 20 years, although the change has not been as pervasive nor as well heeded as the change in view regarding the essential nature of a computer.

Starting with the first "unbundling" of software from the price of the hardware in the late 1960s, software has gradually come to be seen as a product; in the past five years, the explosive growth of the personal computer field has made it abundantly clear to most (although not all) people that software can indeed be treated as a product.

Interestingly, many of the "software millionaires" are not old-line professional programmers, but rather people who quickly grasped in various contexts the need for a particular software product, created it, packaged it, and got it to the market first. Indeed, many of the most successful software products are not very sophisticated in technical terms (there is a lesson there, too).

Creating the idea for a product is not the same as building it. Neither is marketing and selling it the same as building it. In building a real product, one must pay careful attention to serviceability, reliability, customer tastes, cost of producing it, and so on. These aspects of what it means to make a product are only starting to be understood and taken into account by the development community. I think this is why many of the biggest successes in the software product field have been created by nonprofessionals.

At times the product ignorance of some technical people is actually a blessing. When building the software itself, it is important to focus on the technical characteristics and find the best technical solution within the constraints of the product parameters. If everyone is focusing on the product parameters, it may be more difficult to achieve a satisfactory technical solution.

Perhaps the most important thing is to keep the product and technical aspects of software in balance. All software is ultimately a product for someone else (perhaps just the builder using it in a different context), so it is important to deal appropriately with the product aspects. On the other hand, all packaging and no content is even worse than all content and no packaging (which can usually be more easily remedied).

Viewing software as a product quickly leads to many implications for the development process:[1.8] How we are to determine requirements from an anonymous set of users, how the design and implementation process can be speeded up, how we handle changes after it is released, and so on. Some of these issues will be discussed later in the context of individual parts of the development system.

> *Treat software as a product as well as a technical object.*

In this context, it is important to recognize one of the main product characteristics of software, namely, that it is essentially packaged knowledge.

## 1.10 Software As Knowledge

*The third [principle of painting] is, that the representation should so conform with the objects as to give their likeness.*

— Hsieh Ho *The Spirit of the Brush*

A view of software that I find especially appealing (perhaps because of its grandiose overtones, but, I prefer to think, because of its all-encompassing nature) is that software is an embodiment of knowledge. Any program certainly contains a large amount of information about a process and the data that are relevant to carrying it out. Programs also contain structural knowledge that indicates the relationship between different processes (programs) and their associated data, knowledge about the relationships among classes of data, and other information as well.

If programs, the end result of the chain of representations that we call software, contain knowledge about the outside world, then certainly the earlier versions—the designs and specifications and requirements—also contain knowledge. Indeed, one of the realities of software is that these forms of the system often contain valuable information which is lost before we get to the executable versions!

Whatever you may think of the grandiloquence of this view, it is well worth your pondering. If software is knowledge (I am not wasting many words to convince you of what seems so obvious), then the argument for taking great care to capture and manage properly the information that exists in the software development environment certainly takes on a new importance. Likewise, it adds weight to the plea, often heard, that more attention should be paid to the activities that come before the actual coding of programs. Those activities are producing something at least as valuable as plans for programs—knowledge. This is one of the primary motivators for software reusability.[1.9]

Programming—in the narrow sense of laying down sets of instructions that tell a machine precisely what to do—is comparable to writing a research report. It produces a representation of knowledge that has been acquired before the writing began.

In this context, it seems clear that what we are doing in the early stages of software development is uncovering and organizing knowledge. First, and most importantly for the larger picture, we are producing knowledge about the application; then, during design, we move on to producing knowledge about how to deal with the application with the computer.

The interaction between these two discovery processes (and the methods used) is complex and not well understood. Even less clear is the relationship between these processes, data description techniques, knowledge-based work in artificial intelligence, and traditional disciplines (such as philosophy) concerned with knowledge as an abstract entity. This is an area that I believe eventually is crucial to the success of software development (and thus computer application in general).

> *Software development people were implicitly doing "knowledge engineering" long before it became a hot topic. First-rate computer applications are almost always based on an incisive (and often original) understanding of the knowledge in a particular application.*

## 1.11 What Then *Is* Software?

Clearly, software is many things. It is different things over time, different things to different people, and different things depending on what you intend to do.

That is not all bad. Anything that is complex is not only open to many interpretations but *should* be viewed in different ways for different purposes. The trick is to pick the right view for the task at hand.

If you are concerned with establishing the right balance between analysis activities and program construction, then the "software is knowledge" view may be most relevant. If you are concerned with the overall organization of software development, then the "software is a product" view will be helpful. If you are concerned with providing the technical tools to aid development work, then the "software is a series of transformations" view will help. If you are a generalist trying to understand the essential nature of this activity, then the "software is knowledge" view may appeal to you.

The one view that will be highly unproductive for you to take, however, is that software is just like a lot of other things and hence merits little special consideration or thought!

CHAPTER

2

# In Search of Quality

CHAPTER

# 2

# In Search of Quality

*It is quality rather than quantity that matters.*

— *Lucius Seneca Epistles*

2.1 Why Worry About Quality at All? (introduction)

2.2 Doesn't "Quality" Just Mean the Software Works? (what quality means)

2.3 But We *Are* Producing Quality Software! (current state)

2.4 Steps Toward Quality (action)

2.5 Impending Doom (and Opportunity)! (the future)

## 2.1 Why Worry About Quality at All?

Quality should be the driver of the entire development system.

It usually isn't and there are going to be some real problems (and opportunities) for many organizations in the near future because of that. The problems are loss of business, loss of staff who refuse to be a part of a poor quality operation, and legal liability for poor performance or damage due to a product lacking in quality. The opportunities should be clear: High-quality products do well in the marketplace.

As the protagonist in Robert Pirsig's *Zen and the Art of Motorcycle Maintenance* discovered, quality is one of the more elusive things in life; you know it when you see it, but it can be difficult to define and even harder to create.[2.1] In the business of creating software, we know how to define it and how to achieve it to a degree much greater than is typically found in practice.

Quality is critical to the entire process. Inherent in the concept of a system is that there are some objectives of operation that it is intended to reach. Quality—in a broad sense—should characterize the objectives for a software development system, so that we must worry about quality at least for structural reasons.

There are some pressing economic reasons for emphasizing quality as well. The pressure of the marketplace demands that we focus on producing products that are differentiated by quality; there is no reason to believe that pressure won't apply to software-intensive systems just as much as is does to automobiles, stereos, and cameras. (Indeed, the success of Visicalc and other personal computer software was due in large measure to the fact that they provided certain quality characteristics—ease of use, stability, good fit to actual needs of users.) One of the lessons of Peters and Waterman's *In Search of Excellence,*[2.2] for example, is the importance of focusing on quality.

The external economic pressures for quality software are evident to all but the most tunnel-visioned and need little explanation. The structural reasons to use quality as a driver for the development system, while strong, may not be as evident. People tend to focus on what they are told is important; if you don't emphasize, up front, the importance of quality, then you won't get quality. Technical design is a process of decision making and there must be some concrete objectives against which to make the decisions; if quality is set as an objective in a way that can be tested, then the technical design process will often be easier.

The purpose of this chapter is to define software quality and show you how, in outline, to achieve it.

## 2.2 Doesn't Quality Just Mean the Software Works?

*But if you can't say what Quality is, how do you know what it is, or how do you know that it even exists? If no one knows what it is, then for all practical purposes it doesn't exist at all.*

— Robert M. Pirsig *Zen and the Art of Motorcycle Maintenance*

Today, for most situations, yes.

If you believe that is the way it will always be or has to be, then you probably believed that American automobiles would always be preferred by Americans or that IBM would never get into the personal computer market. They weren't and they did—both, at least partly, for reasons of quality. In the mid-1970s, quality in automobiles for Americans suddenly took on some new dimensions—maintainability and fuel economy—and American-produced cars were found to be sadly wanting. Quality in computing in the early 1980s also took on some new dimensions—attention to the functional user, flexibility, and ease of access. Those dimensions were fitted nicely by the personal computer and IBM, always focused on quality, had no choice but to provide their customers that choice in quality.

There are several important lessons in these examples. Quality oftentimes is in the eye of the beholder; Detroit has learned this lesson painfully as the eye of the car buyer has changed. Software people sometimes argue that software quality cannot be defined, perhaps because they recognize the arbitrariness and fickleness of the customer and the difficulty of satisfying his critical eyes. While that may be a reason for not providing a definition, it certainly is not a valid excuse.

More relevant to the task of establishing and achieving software quality, however, is the recognition that there are different dimensions of quality and thus that the definition of quality is sensitive to the context in which it is being used. This is basically what happened to the American automobile industry. People still liked big luxury cars, but in the changed context of high energy and repair prices, those characteristics of quality were overtaken by other factors.

IBM has long understood another important aspect of quality—that it is composed of a number of factors and that when one is dealing with a complex product, no one factor will predominate. Thus IBM provides a total package of service, training, equipment, and software, while stressing those factors that are of top priority to their customers at any point in time.

> *Contrary to popular belief, software quality can be defined and achieved. Definition is the subject of this chapter; achieving it is the subject of the rest of the book.*

## Quality Defined

In spite of general agreement that software quality is important, very little can be found in the literature concerning its definition. Most of what there is can be captured by the common definition:

> **Quality** is conformance to requirements, where requirements come from the customer, the user, standards, regulations, good practice, and so on.

There is almost nothing like Boehm's early study[2,3] that tries to say something concrete about what software quality is beyond the very general type of definition given above.

It appears sometimes that we are caught in a catch-22 situation. Technical people don't spend much time worrying about what quality is because they have many more pressing problems and because they believe that the customer/user/marketplace must ultimately define what they want quality to mean (true); the customer/user/marketplace, on the other hand, hardly knows where to begin in defining quality, is usually not organized to effectively make and impose definitions of technical quality, and thus doesn't do it.

The fact that more or less the same set of quality criteria have been with us for almost 15 years indicates that we don't really need to spend much time searching for new criteria. Yet why isn't quality given more attention?

There seem to be two reasons: On the technical side, it is usually not clear to many of those involved in development how to measure these various criteria, nor how to achieve them. On the customer's

| BASIC QUALITY | EXTRA QUALITY |
|---|---|
| functionality | flexibility |
| reliability | repairability |
| ease of use | adaptability |
| economy | understandability |
| safety | documentation |
| | enhanceability |

FIGURE 2.1 Dimensions of Quality

side, it may be partly a matter of simply not knowing what to ask for. Before looking at some of the issues of attaining quality, let's make sure we understand what the generally accepted quality dimensions are.

Let's start by breaking quality into two categories that make it easier to tie down a definition in a specific situation. It is useful to distinguish between *basic quality* and *extra quality*; Fig. 2.1 lists some dimensions of each type of quality. If you think the distinction between them is rather arbitrary, it is. Furthermore, it changes over time and with the situation!

This distinction is based on what is essential and what, to some extent, is "extra" (in the sense, that if you don't have it in your system you may still be able to compete to some extent). Reliability of operation is today *basic* in a piece of software; 10 years ago that wasn't always true because we were willing to accept unreliable operation over no operation at all. Adaptability to new situations for a piece of software is still *extra* in that its absence usually does not impair near-term acceptance.

What do system developers commonly[2.4] understand by these terms?

**Functionality** The software can perform, in a normal fashion, the functions that are required by the task for which it is intended.

One of the primary quality problems is that a piece of software may conform to the requirements *as stated* but when put into use the customer finds that those functions are not sufficient to make the software useful. For example, a financial reporting system may not be able to compare totals for a period to totals in comparable periods in the past.

**Reliability** The system must be able to perform its functions consistently and as intended. Even under abnormal conditions, it must continue to perform as much as possible, and without giving erroneous outputs under the guise of correct operation.

Software that cannot be counted upon to provide correct results or that is prone to blowing up under random conditions is generally considered worthless by most users; yet software is still delivered which will crash if inputs are given to it that were not planned for, which produces incorrect results under some normal conditions, or which causes side effects that prejudice its operation (or the operation of other software) the next time it is used.

**Ease of use** The system should permit the users to work with concepts and terms familiar to them, learn to use it with a minimum of training, and provide easy access to information about operation as it is needed.

An inventory management system that required the user to define blits, blats, and widgets for each schnarbe would be laughable. Yet, at a slightly less gross level, much software requires the user to learn a new vocabulary. Unnecessarily complicated user interfaces, among other things, may generate the need for considerable training to use what are otherwise functions that are known to the user. Systems that have no on-line help facilities and/or have huge, ill-organized manuals are definitely not easy to use.

**Economy** Software should do its job with a minimum of resources.

This means not only the obvious machine resources of processor cycles and memory space, but also peripherals, disk space, and supporting software. For example, a project management system which requires a large and ponderous database management system for support probably will not be very economical.

It is important to keep in mind that economy refers to the amount of resources needed to get a piece of the user's work done, such as producing a report or establishing the right parameters for a factory operation. This is different from efficiency, which usually refers to how well the system's hardware resources are being utilized.

Likewise, cost is not properly a part of the complex of factors that we label "quality." It has its own, well-understood metric, and should not be confused with other factors. Indeed, it is not uncommon for a high-priced system to have low quality or for a high-quality software system to not be particularly high-priced. That was one of the main drivers of the personal computer revolution; people suddenly found that high-quality software did not have to be high-priced and that many of the high-priced systems weren't of such high quality when compared to other possibilities.

**Safety** The software's operation should never permit harm or destruction to occur in the realm over which it has control.

As software systems have come into use in many life-critical situations, their quality has increasingly been judged on their ability to avoid catastrophic behavior, no matter what. Missile control software, for example, is rated on reliability; however, a separate dimension is to rate it on its ability to avoid permitting the missile to land on an innocent city even if the normal operation for some (unknown) reason fails.

While it may vary a good bit, it is fair to say that software without a good rating on these basic quality criteria will not long remain competitive; even if it is not a commercial product, it will not be effective in the context in which it is being used.

Beyond these basic criteria, the extra quality criteria are exactly that—criteria which, if present, provide a software product an extra measure of quality.

**Flexibility** A system is considered flexible if it can handle a range of different inputs.

For example, a compiler that accepts only syntactically correct programs is not very flexible; neither is an employee information system that can accept only the employee's ID number instead of also being able to accept some other identification (such as his name and department).

**Repairability** The ability of a system to have errors fixed.

This ranges from easy to almost impossible. If a piece of software is written in a way that is closely tied to a particular machine, no documentation is provided, the internal structure of the system is messy, and it uses its hardware resources to a maximum, then it may be very nearly impossible to repair it. On the other hand, a system that is well-designed and documented may be very easy to repair.

**Adaptability** The ability of a system to operate under a range of conditions.

Flexibility refers to a system's ability to work with different forms of a problem; adaptability is similar, but refers to a system's ability to work under different conditions. Typical situations are that you want to operate some software on a different hardware configuration (perhaps with less memory or a different type of video terminal), under a new operating system, or perhaps in an entirely new execution environment (different hardware and operating system, only the language is the same). An adaptable system poses a minimum of difficulty in these cases.

**Understandability** A system is understandable if it is possible to comprehend what it does and how to use it with a minimum of effort.

We have all had the experience of trying to use a system or even some mechanical artifact and of having to struggle to comprehend what it does (i.e. what its outputs are) and how to get it to do it. In the case of software, difficulty of understanding stems in part from the basic design of the system itself. If commands are poorly named, if simple operations require many discrete functions or if several operations normally separate are bundled in one system function, or if the same operation (for example, reading from a file) is done in different ways in different contexts of the system, then typically it is much harder to comprehend and use the system.

**Documentation** The extent to which information about the system and its usage is captured and clearly presented.

Software documentation has long been among the worst aspects of computing. Even with the pressure and example of consumer-oriented software which must have good documentation in order to survive, much software is still poorly documented. Functions are not completely explained, or worse, are incorrectly explained. Simple operations may require pages of explanation. Ordinary questions that every user has may not be addressed at all while obscure functions rarely used consume reams of documentation. The list goes on.

Documentation is clearly relevant to the understandability of a system, but it is entirely possible to have a well-documented system that is still fundamentally difficult to understand or vice versa. As software increasingly becomes a black-box product purchased and used by people who neither know nor care about its internal operation, documentation is increasingly a prime quality factor.

In the case of both understandability and documentation, there are issues of the quality along these dimensions relative to the internal aspects of the software. The maintenance programmer, for example, must be able to understand *how* the software works in order to fix it; this is affected by both the technical design of the system as well as by the state of the documentation. I have not focused on that aspect here because the first concern must be the external qualities; nonetheless, it is just as important to the overall viability of a piece of software in the long run.

**Enhanceability** The ease of adding new capability to an existing piece of software.

The eternal story of software is that as soon as a system is declared finished, someone immediately sees some important new ways in which it can be enhanced. This usually means adding some new functions (e.g., having the process control system also capture data relevant to a broader, factory-wide automation system) or being able to process additional data (e.g., having a project scheduling system for construction deliveries also schedule work crews). The underlying technical issues are usually dominant (how well the system is designed, constructed, and documented), but it nonetheless is a quality factor that is important to many customers.

> *Quality is a multidimensional concept that can be defined, and made specific to individual situations.*

It should be obvious that these (and other) quality factors are not all equally important. Safety may be unimportant in the context of a financial analysis system, while it may be paramount to a control system for a nuclear reactor; conversely, economy may be highly important to the financial analysis system if it is to compete against other products, while it may be relatively unimportant to the situation of the reactor control system.

Thus, ultimately, quality does have to be defined for each situation. Before we address that more directly, however, there are some other aspects of software quality you should understand.

## Internal Versus External Quality

The quality factors discussed so far have primarily been related to the external, or observable, quality of a piece of software. Reliability is patently obvious if it is not high; functionality usually takes only the least experienced user to judge; enhanceability and repairability will be very obvious to the manager responsible for allocating resources to those two activities. In short, one does not have to examine the internal technical details of a piece of software to evaluate external quality.

The *internal quality* of a system is important, too, however. Ultimately, much of the external quality of a system depends upon the internal quality. For example, the enhanceability of a system is directly related to how well structured the internal design is (i.e., the size, definition, and relationships between modules and subsystems) and even the functionality may be related to internal factors such as completeness and consistency of the technical design, not just the oversight of the functional designers of the system. (It is not uncommon for a system to fail to provide important functions because the technical implementation of a complete specification was incomplete or inconsistent, causing some functions to be dropped.)

Internal quality factors include such things as completeness, consistency, parsimony, traceability, rationality, structure, paradigm, and quality of algorithms and representations, as well as understandability and documentation as discussed above. The nature of these factors is not well understood in the abstract. For example, even for something as simple as completeness, I know of no thorough treatment of all the ways in which software can be incomplete at its various stages of development, let alone an effective way to measure or test for completeness.

Developers are not concerned about there not being an abstract theory of completeness, of course; the problem, though, is that without the conceptual understanding, we typically do not have the checklists, textbooks, standards, and tools necessary to help us produce software that is complete in important technical details. For more complex factors such as the type of paradigm used to organize the system (e.g., is it a finite-state machine, a message passing organization, a set of cooperating independent processes, etc.), we have only some intuition in most cases that the choice of one value over another is somehow related ultimately to some of the external quality variables of interest.

Discussion of internal quality parameters is well beyond our scope here, but it is important to recognize that those concerns exist. Further, once the external quality parameters for a specific situation are set, it may well be that the focus must be on the internal factors as the way of achieving the external levels.

### Process Versus Product Quality

Software is not the only field in which concern about the quality of the end product is translated into concern about the quality of the process that produces it. Fields as diverse as automobile manufacturing, metals production, and electronics go to great lengths to insure that their processes are of high quality in order to achieve desired product quality levels.

In software, even more than most fields, we must take this orientation since we have no raw material input to our product which might affect quality. In short, the software development process is *the* determiner of quality.

Unfortunately, this sometimes permits developers to lose sight of the product quality measures we have been discussing. While we must indeed focus on the process (the subject of most of this book, for example), the impact of that focus on the product quality parameters must always be kept in view. That is, after all, the purpose in worrying about the process!

An underlying truth of building quality software, is that it must be done step by step. Let's consider a simple analogy. It is quite obvious that if one manufactures a product, say an automobile or a TV set, each aspect of its manufacture must be quality-controlled if the final product is to be of the highest quality—the design must be effective and efficient, the parts must be of high quality, the process of putting it together must guard against misassembly, the testing processes must reliably weed out defective units, the packing and shipping must guarantee that the unit is not damaged, and so on.

Software is no different. The requirements must be carefully checked to make sure that the system that is needed (not necessarily *wanted*) is clearly specified by the requirements definition from which the designers will work. This is perhaps the area of greatest loss of quality in a broad sense, because quite often the requirements as given to the designers do not accurately mirror what the eventual customers will need and want.

Design checking, in spite of techniques oriented directly toward improving the quality of designs, is still not widely practiced. Structured design,[2.5] for example, was specifically formulated to provide a means of checking and improving the quality of software designs while they are still designs and before they become hard-to-change code. Yet it is employed by only a minor fraction of all software designers and then, quite often, the quality improving aspects of it are not fully utilized.

IBM's design inspection techniques[2.6] are precisely intended to apply this principle of continual quality checks all along the path of producing a software system. While one can imagine even better means of assuring design quality, the widespread application of these techniques by IBM is ample evidence of their cost-effectiveness. Common sense would indicate that they might be valuable to others as well. The surprising thing is that so few are availing themselves of these relatively low-cost quality improvers!

Code inspections, another part of IBM's software quality program, are a much older concept. Indeed, at heart, they are essentially the old "desk checking" that was often practiced when machine time was expensive and access difficult. Nonetheless, they are still valuable when used appropriately and form another part of the "continuous quality checking" approach.

The principle should be clear: Quality must be built in, step by step.

## Measuring Quality

In most technical fields, it is common to define quality parameters quantitatively: Parts per million pollution, mean time to failure, expected hours of service before repair, average time to repair a fault, breakdown voltage, peak operating temperature, load factor, and so on. That is not yet commonly the case with software products and is only beginning to be the case with the software process.[2.7]

The lack of standard measures for software quality, or even their total absence, should not be interpreted as a signal that one does not need to try to define them quantitatively. Once the appropriate quality factors are chosen for a particular development situation, it is imperative that a quantitative, objective way of measuring their values be established and used consistently.

I have not provided such definitions here because, quite honestly, they don't exist except for one or two areas such as reliability. But if I were managing a large software project or buying a large amount of software, I would define some measures, no matter how trivial, and apply them to help me determine objectively the quality of what I was getting.

For example, I might define "ease of use" in terms of the time needed for a "standard" user to learn to use the system to a defined level of capability and the time needed to answer a generic set of questions (with some weighting between these two measures that made sense for my situation). I might then try to normalize my measures by applying them (in statistically significant numbers) to several existing systems for which there was some agreement as to their general level of ease of use. This would provide a basis for evaluating my new system along this dimension. (In point of fact, this dimension is being explored and can be broken down into a number of technical parameters that can be measured[2.8]; thus there is some hope that in the future we will be able to have some standard measures for quality factors of this sort.)

The fundamental objective is to make all the quality criteria being used in any specific situation *operational,* that is, measurable. You must be able to ascertain objectively that the criterion is met; whether it can be measured with a metric that has a range of values is less important than the question of objectivity.

Before we address putting some of these concepts into practice, let's pause and ask what the current situation is in practice.

## 2.3 But We *Are* Producing Quality Software!

I doubt it.

Until quite recently, almost all software at best met basic quality requirements only, and in many cases not even some of them (such as reliability). The quest for quality software in a more advanced, competitive vein is quite new and only occasionally a real factor in most development situations.

Are things really that bad?

Yes and no. I don't mean that all software produced today is full of bugs, unreliable, and inefficient (although that is still an accurate description of some software). Many organizations today regularly produce software that works, more or less to specification, more or less on time. But we certainly do not produce as much quality software (in the basic sense) as we produce quality hardware. (I don't have any figures, nor do I know anyone who does, at least figures they will make public—but there are too many well-known cases of poor-quality software to waste very much time trying to decide whether or not we need, in general, to improve the quality of software.)

One of the reasons that we haven't had quality software is that in many cases the systems we were building were "existence proofs"; that is, we had never built a system of that type before and the whole emphasis was on showing that we could do it at all, never mind second-order features like reliability or economy. That has been and will continue to be the story of computing in one way. We are continually finding new applications and every time we do some new software has to be created, throwing us into a "discovery design" situation in which the focus must be on finding a way—any way—of creating the desired functionality.

That situation has started to change, however, not because we have a smaller number of new applications (quite the contrary), but because we now have an increasing number of situations in which we know the basic algorithms and structures that are needed and can focus on features of quality other than functionality. The advent of the personal computer and the consequent market for software has been a major factor in focusing attention on quality. Most of the applications on personal computers are not new (at least in general terms); what is new is the usage by naive users, the need for reliability to permit mass marketing, and other factors that directly lead to a focus on quality.

Some organizations correctly perceive that quality of software is just as important as the quality of the underlying hardware and have started to focus on ways of achieving that quality (I will outline some below). Unfortunately, many organizations pay only lip service to quality and haven't yet taken effective steps to achieve it; some don't even show any signs that they understand the problem exists.

Quality is rarely the issue of highest concern to most software managers and certainly isn't to most people responsible for building the software. Nor is it the case that these people don't care. Rather, they are working in a context in which quality hasn't been made a real priority or in which even though they do a quality job (as is usually the case at the level of creating individual programs), they have no control over the quality of the finished product of which their work is only a small part.

Even if the emphasis is there, most people don't really know what to do to bring about the desired quality. So what can you do?

## 2.4 Steps Toward Quality

In spite of this depressing state of affairs, there are some things that seem pretty clear as to how you should proceed once you decide to be serious about quality; these are things that are now being practiced successfully by some groups.[2.9] There are three steps you must take: Define what quality means for your situation, establish the means of producing it, and set up the mechanisms for tracking it.

### Defining Quality

The abstract definitions discussed above are good only if put to use. To put them to use, you must pick the two or three factors that are the most critical to your situation. That will normally be clear or, at least, dictated by the environment in which you are operating.

If not, ask what single quality will make your system most attractive to your customers, or what quality they would least like to lose. Don't guess if you don't know; ask them. (If you are the customer, ask yourself.)

Do this for several iterations until you have a set of quality parameters. Try to prioritize them or assign value to them. Imagine you have a thousand dollars of your personal money to spend to buy software quality; how much would you spend on each factor? Use the answers to set up a weighting scheme among the different factors.

For example, suppose you are preparing to have a financial management system built for your company. You decide that the three quality factors of most importance are functionality, ease of use, and adaptability; compared to them, the others don't count. In terms of ranking, you decide that to have a set of functions that covers your applications well is worth \$600, ease of use is worth \$300, and adaptability is worth \$100. Then you can rate the overall quality of the system built for you by weighting the actual measurements taken by 0.6, 0.3, and 0.1. (Appropriate normalizations of the measurements may have to be made in order to fold them all into a single measurement.)

This number isn't going to mean much by itself, of course, unless you have measured some similar systems. Over time you can collect such ratings and start to build up a history for comparison. In the near term, the value of a number like this is that it tracks the quality of the system as it is being developed.

In order to make measurements, you must have defined the quality factors in operational terms as we noted above. Even if the measurements seem rather trivial, if they have some correlation to the property you are measuring, then they will provide a way to track over time the characteristics of interest.

In the the example above, this might be done by defining "functionality" as a percentage coverage of an ideal set of automatable functions derived from a study of the financial operations of your company (an undertaking that may have beneficial side effects), defining "ease of use" in terms of the inverse of the length of time it takes a "standard" user to learn a core set of operations with the system, and defining "adaptability" as a count of the number of places in the system that a feature of the underlying hardware and operating system is used in a specific, nonisolated way.

You may already be concerned that just this definition process, let alone the measurement process, is going to cost something extra. That is true in the short run, but almost always false in the long run. First, there may be some actual payoff to thinking hard about what quality is in your situation (such as thoroughly studying the space of possibilities or introducing a number of operational staff to the concepts of the system at an early stage); second, the ability to evaluate the system's quality at different stages of development and provide a definable target for improvement will almost always lead in the long run to software that is of higher quality and thus lower overall cost (when considering evolution and operation).

So the first step toward quality involves three things: picking those quality factors that are important for your situation, establishing relative weights for each, and defining operational ways of measuring each factor.

## Producing Quality

Let's start by distinguishing between quality *control* and quality *assurance*. Quality control is concerned with inspecting the results of a process to make sure that they meet stated quality standards. In software, quality control is the province of testing activities, and just as in the manufacture of automobiles, testing of software does not *produce* quality software.[2.10] Quality assurance, on the other hand, is concerned with assuring that quality products are produced. In software, this means being concerned with the process by which the software is produced.

Those that are successfully producing quality software today are focusing on the *process* of creating software. That is why software engineering is gaining in importance in so many situations; people are improving the process in order to improve the quality of their product.

A fundamental tenet of quality assurance (in general, not just in software) is that a quality process is needed to produce quality products. Obviously, there are other factors (people, raw products, underlying technology), but the process is the place to start. This book is directed primarily toward the process since that is what the software development system embodies; thus most of what is covered here can be interpreted as steps toward a quality process.

> *Quality is not just a vacuous buzzword. It can be defined and used as a driver for greatly enhanced work of all kinds—technical and nontechnical alike. What's more, some are already doing that for software.*

There are several general issues regarding the process that are worth noting, however.

***Objectives*** Psychological studies[2.11] confirm the importance of focusing people's attention on specific objectives as a way of conditioning their output. If we want to insure that the output of the SDS is a quality product then we must make sure that one of the inputs to the system is a set of operational, quality objectives. This not only focuses people's attention, but provides some specific aid to the design process.

It is clear that quality must be designed into software, not tested in. Yet, many organizations still create software systems with no quality objectives to guide their processes at any level, then wonder what they can do to create better quality systems.

***Requirements*** There are some lessons from the study of excellent companies[2.12] that can be applied to software. The concept of staying close to the customer is slowly being learned by software people the hard way, but the success of the software entrepreneurs who stay close to their prospective customers and consequently produce software that is seen as very high quality by the people that count—the customers—is driving home the lesson.

***Leadership*** A similar lesson which could be applied well in many software situations is that the executives must stay close to the action. Two contrasting situations I am familiar with illustrate this point very well. Two executives of similar age in different organizations have been allowed (or forced) by their respective organizations to take very different paths. One, a programmer on a large system in its early days, has moved up to a position of responsibility and has lost essentially all touch with the technology. His personal knowledge of software development has not progressed much beyond 1970 and his decisions (some of them rather disastrous) show it. The other, while also at a high level of responsibility, has maintained a detailed knowledge of current development techniques and new ideas in computer science (that sometimes makes *me* blush). The guidance he provides to the projects under his responsibility clearly seems better.

While there are personal differences between people, I know that in the first case the organizational structure encourages great distance between the executives and the work. In the second, care is taken to make sure that this separation cannot build up. The difference in the quality of the software produced in the two cases is remarkable.

***Responsibility*** A third "excellence" lesson that can be applied to software production is the concept of making everyone responsible for the results that the organization produces (and letting everyone share in the rewards). There are many techniques of emphasizing everyone's responsibility for quality and these are being applied (successfully as far as I can see) by some organizations in the software area. There are some specific techniques, such as reviews and inspections, that are quite helpful in this regard that I will come back to later.

***Type of Organization*** I am afraid that we have a structural problem that will make it rather difficult to apply this last lesson. Most groups that develop software in the United States are organized much like a laboratory (some are even called that). The general atmosphere is one of a scientific lab in which everyone is trying to discover something by applying experimental techniques. It is certainly true that there are situations in which this sort of "discovery design" is necessary (for example, building the software for a highly advanced technical application such as control of satellite communications). But in this kind of environment, paying close attention to quality standards, documentation, configuration management, and other good engineering practices is not natural.

Contrast this to a factory in which a product is being produced on a regular basis. In that environment, it is more natural to focus on making sure that each product is produced with high quality. The Japanese are applying this concept in some of their "software factories" to achieve higher levels of productivity and quality in "routine design" situations in which the software being produced is neither unique nor totally new.[2.13]

Let me hasten to note that I am not advocating creating software factories, with the connotation that would have to many. (If I did, most programmers or designers reading this would immediately burn the book!) Indeed, we often need some discovery design and I certainly don't think software production can be completely routinized (although large amounts of it could be in some situations). What is needed in many instances, however, is more discipline and focus on turning out quality products and less of the attitude that we are all in the lab together mixing chemicals to see if we can get the desired reaction.

None of these precepts are sufficient to turn your operation into a "quality shop" over night. However, they *are* being used in some important cases to raise significantly the quality of the software being produced. There are many specific techniques that flow out of these more general precepts; some of them will be discussed later, while others must still be discovered.

### Tracking Quality

The third step in achieving quality is to be able to check whether or not the products actually have it and in what quantities. A tracking system for measuring the quality of both product and process is essential for a successful software operation. Properly defined, implemented, and measured, quality measures can be an invaluable tool for management and technical personnel alike. Without the third component—quality control (comparing with expectations)—much of the value of a quality effort is lost.

## 2.5 Impending Doom (and Opportunity)!

The current emphasis on quality is well known, so it doesn't take a prophet to see that emphasis finding its way into the software arena as soon as we get past our infancy (in which we are preoccupied with just learning to walk). That emphasis is already starting in the more mature and forward-looking organizations.

It is important to recognize that this isn't just a trend which will pass in a few years. Quality in surgical instruments is not a trend, because quality is absolutely essential to their proper operation. Software is essential for the application of computers and for that reason alone, quality software will always be essential.

There is another reason, however. The world today is not that of even just a few years ago. One of the unmistakable trends is toward more flexibility in almost everything we do; people want multiple options or colors or styles in their products; relationships between people, groups, and even machines are complex and best described by networks rather than trees or hierarchies.[2.14] It is the computer that will allow this and make it possible. It not only is going to appear in all our appliances (as it already has) but will become involved in our lives in many ways that we can only dimly understand at present. That level of involvement will drive the need for quality software even beyond economic factors.

While that may be a bit further down the road, the immediate economic challenges are going to cause a rapid shift in viewpoint in the software field within the next few years with respect to quality.[2.15] Today almost all software is produced in a laboratory atmosphere with little or no attention paid to quality. It would not surprise me if 10 years from now the dominant atmosphere was one of producing quality software first and foremost. I won't attempt to offer any data for this shift—such changes are generally not predictable in a straight-line forecasting manner—other than the structural arguments I have given above.

> *Some significant competitive advantages await those who organize for quality.*

That leads me to suggest impending doom for those that are not prepared to make the shift to a quality focus in software and, conversely, impending opportunity for those that have the software development systems set up and operating to take advantage of a new state of affairs in which quality is the norm. What's better is that even if you follow this forecast and I turn out to be wrong, you will still be ahead because you can never go wrong with quality!

CHAPTER

# 3

# The Key: Software Development Systems

HENRI
PELERIN

CHAPTER

# 3

# The Key: Software Development Systems

*The discoveries which have hitherto been made in the sciences are such as lie close to vulgar notions, scarcely beneath the surface. In order to penetrate into the inner and further recesses of nature, it is necessary that both notions and axioms be derived from things by a more sure and guarded way; and that a method of intellectual operations be introduced altogether better and more certain.*

— Sir Francis Bacon *Aphorisms Concerning the Interpretation of Nature and the Kingdom of Man*

3.1 The Key (introduction)

3.2 What Is an SDS? (definition)

3.3 The Systems View (Churchman's five aspects)

3.4 Using the Key (an example)

3.5 Some Essentials (essential characteristics of a system)

3.6 Doing It Right! (second example)

3.7 Making the Key Transferable (motivation for generalization of next chapter)

## 3.1 The Key

Conceptually, a key is something that reveals, clarifies, makes clear, uncovers, or otherwise is central to understanding—just as a physical key reveals by permitting us to open a door. I suspect you may be looking for a key to any of several situations:

- You are manager of a small software group in an organization that has just landed a big contract; you must rapidly expand your group's capabilities to support the new activity with greatly increased volume and quality of work. Should you add more people? Buy tools? Provide methodology training? Bring in new supervisors? Use a different language?
- You are CEO of a firm providing a computer-based service. Efforts to upgrade the software on which your business is built have been long, costly, and unsuccessful. You need to decide whether to continue trying to upgrade or not. If you do, how can you organize the effort in order to be successful?
- You are an educator or trainer of people in the software field. You have some sense of the kinds of jobs people go into, but wonder what mix of courses and educational experiences to offer to improve your students' chances of professional success.
- You are involved with the automation of large manufacturing plants. Which traditional groups in the company (data processing, engineering, research) are the appropriate ones to do the job? Can any one do it by itself? If there are several players, how do you organize them?
- You are head of an organization with a large computer operations component, including significant amounts of systems development and procurement. The support they have given you so far has been adequate to the task, but qualitative changes in the way the organization does business suggest that qualitative changes may be needed in the systems development activity. How do you tell? If changes, are needed, what are they? How can you bring them about? How can you tell the changes are working?
- You are simply interested in how increasingly complex systems with large amounts of software in them get built. How do hundreds of people work together for several years? How does a simple idea, like having computer support for the calculations

performed by your company's people in the course of their work, turn into a massive project? Why does it take so long?

Whatever your situation, if you are dealing with the development of software-intensive systems in any way then you probably need a key from time to time to help you understand the complexity of the situation with which you are faced. For me, that key has always been the concept of a *system.* It is a way of looking at things that provides the right perspective to permit a jumble of elements to fall into place and to permit me to answer questions such as those above.

> *All of the factors bearing on the development of software in a specific situation form a system.*

The idea is to view the whole mess as a system, treat it as a system, work with it as you would work with a system, and expect it to perform like a system. This system, which I call the *software development system* (or SDS for short), exists in some form any time someone produces software. Success (or failure) seems ultimately tied to the properties of the particular SDS (while not discounting the importance of politics, serendipity, or acts of God in the larger picture!).

The primary purpose of this book is to present this key concept in a way that will permit you, whatever your interest in systems, to use it to answer questions, make decisions, and understand. If we think of a system as a physical entity, then we can take (at least) two points of view: from within and from without.

Much of this book takes the *inside* perspective. What are the parts of an SDS? How do they work? How do they fit together? How can we make them work better? First, though, let's look at the SDS from the *outside.*

## 3.2 What Is an SDS?

You probably know what a system is, but let's begin with a brief review.

The dictionary[3.1] captures the important aspects of a system in its non-technical definition:

> **System** 1. An assemblage or combination of things or parts forming a complex or unitary whole: *a mountan system; a railroad system*. 2. Any assemblage or set of correlated members. 3. An ordered and comprehensive assemblage of facts, principles, methods, etc. in a particular field: *a system of philosophy.*

The technical usage of "system" carries the connotation of an input-output relationship; that is, in the technical world a "system" usually refers to a collection of elements that take some set of inputs and by working together harmoniously produce some desired set of outputs. For our purposes, then, let's use the following definition:

> **Software development system (SDS)** A collection of elements working together to produce software-intensive systems that meet given objectives.

Specifically, there are six classes of elements, depicted conceptually in Fig. 3.1 and detailed in the following chapters, that make up the SDS:

1. Objectives
2. Policies
3. People
4. Procedures
5. Tools
6. Information

It is the combination of particular items belonging to these six classes that produce our software systems and cause our problems! The definition is quite broad because we need to get above many of the specifics of systems development in order to see the relationships and characteristics that work or cause problems. This also permits us to transfer what we learn in one situation to another.

## 3.3 The Systems View

For some people, the approach to understanding development activities introduced here will seem very obvious; it is simply the "systems view" applied to the system development activity itself. To others, even though the concept of taking a systems approach to a

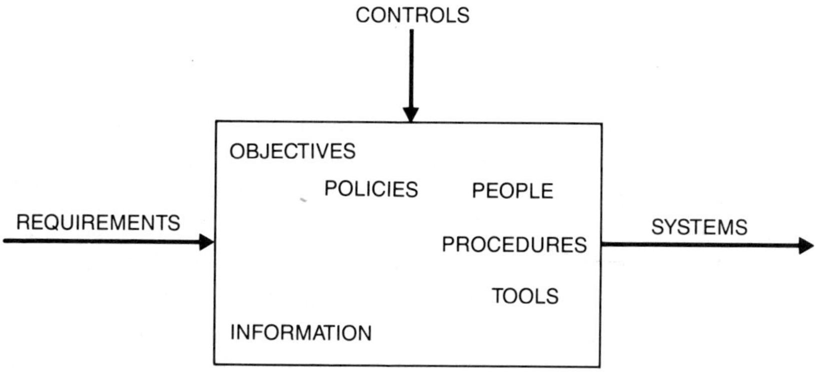


FIGURE 3.1 The Software Development System (SDS)

complex activity may be new, it may seem rather simple. To some, it may seem that we are simply adding more complexity to an already complex situation.

I guess having two out of three right is not bad!

The subtleties of a systems view or systems approach (depending on whether you are viewing or acting) are substantial, however. Many people today work with complex systems and, to some extent, understand their inner workings. That should not be confused with understanding or using the systems approach.

Churchman,[3.2] one of the fathers of this approach, has long advocated applying it to a number of situations. He suggests an approach to understanding a system that can be characterized by asking and answering five questions:

1. What are the objectives for the system (and how do we measure their attainment)?
2. What constraints define the environment in which the system exists?
3. What are the resources the system can draw upon?
4. What are the components of the system?
5. How is the system managed, especially in setting it up and establishing its objectives?

Answering these questions for SDSs is not an easy task. Rarely are there simple choices of elements, but we are beginning to understand some strategies for choosing them and some broad differentiations between classes of answers. For example, we know that methods that combine good management techniques with good technical procedures are better than those that don't, even if the technical method alone may be better in its treatment of technical issues in isolation.

The definition above answers the first question of what an SDS does in general, but obviously not in specific terms. And it certainly does not give us a handle on how to measure the performance of the SDS. For example, should we set up separate maintenance and development groups or combine them into a single group? And how do we measure their performance when they have such different constraints and detailed objectives?

The dynamic growth of computing means that quite frequently the objectives for the development organization are neither well defined nor well understood; further, they often tend to change rather rapidly as computing is utilized in more ways and becomes more critical to the operations of the organization. This causes problems on both sides: The development personnel do not have a clear picture of their role, thus making their task more difficult; at the same time, those that must interact with them in some way are confused because they do not clearly see what it is the development people are supposed to do.

Answering the second question (external constraints) is an organizational issue in many cases and one that all too often is avoided by development organizations. Rather than just accepting the givens (whether it is the charter of the development department in Big Corp. or your own personal skills), we must learn to view the SDS as part of an even larger system and be willing to consider changing the boundaries.

As the new kid on the block, system development organizations are often engaged in territorial wars (at least) as they try to establish their organizational legitimacy. Even in organizations where systems development is well established, there is often a constant flux of external constraints due to the changing nature of the development activity itself. As system development matures as a discipline, one of the most important things that must be done is for system professionals to assert their position on issues of system development. All too often, development activities—and the professionals that carry them out—are either too highly restricted (because it is felt they are just low-level technicians) or too loosely supervised (because no one else feels competent to judge what they are doing). Both situations are damaging and need to be avoided.

> *Churchman's basic questions provide an effective way of understanding your software development system.*

Consideration of the third aspect (resources) is best done for an SDS in the context of the components of the system. However, expanding the resources that can be applied to specific components is one of the most important things that can be done in building a development system. For example, enriching the pool of highly qualified managers available to participate in development can be very effective.

The answer to the fourth question (components) is both simple and complex. Simple, because we can easily see that objectives, policies, procedures, tools, information, and, most of all, people make up the environment of software development and thus must be the components; complex, because we don't understand very well yet the proper nature of those elements. The heart of this book—the next six chapters—explores what we do know about them.

There is a subquestion: What are the appropriate relationships between elements? This is the hardest question to answer and the one we have the least information about. Most software environments are relatively new and even in those that have existed for more than a few years the extremely rapid change in technology effectively changes many of their parameters every few years. The result is that in most cases there has been very little opportunity to study the relationships between elements. Nonetheless, in some of the more mature development organizations some important connections are beginning to be understood.

If you can answer the first four questions, even tentatively, then the last should be easy. The problem, however, is that sometimes managers try to answer the question of how to manage the SDS without taking the time to try to answer the first four questions; the result: confusion, frustration, and lack of results!

Now before you rush away to apply (or damn) this systems concept, be aware that there are some subtleties and refinements that must be considered. As a start to understanding them, let's look at some examples of software development systems before we look more thoroughly at the individual components.

## 3.4 Using the Key

There is little point in having a key if it is not used to unlock something. So let's begin with two examples and see what it means in each to view a development situation as a system.

### The Setting

Imagine that you have just been placed in charge of running the data processing division of a large service company. (You had previously been general manager of a smaller division of the company in a different area.) The company provides a mature service product and has been profitable for many years; it is considered a leader in its field.

Several attributes characterize your new division:

*It has a mature and stable internal structure.*

It includes four sections, one each to operate the computer center, run a data-entry operation, distribute information, and develop and maintain software systems. The relationships between the sections are well established, as are their ties to other parts of the company.

*Day-to-day operations run smoothly.*

The function of each section is well defined. They are able to run in noncrisis mode most of the time.

*There is a rapidly increasing load of development work.*

In addition to the normal increasing use of the computer by many groups within the company, two things have placed great pressure on the development group for new software: Business based on the main product of the company has increased rapidly and the capacity of the existing software/hardware combination has almost been reached; replacement with a new system has been planned, including a massive development effort of replacement software. In addition, marketing groups within the company are eager to offer new services, each of which will require significant new software development.

Even though the organization and its activities are mature, there are a number of problems in the division, almost all associated with the development group:

- Late delivery of software
- Large backlogs
- Poor quality software
- Users dissatisfied with delivered functionality
- Poor relationships between the development group and others
- Inability to complete a very large project.

The last problem dominates the others.

*The software development group consists of about 100 professionals.*

These range from three college students working in an intern program to several very experienced systems programmers that have been with the division since it started. The group seems to be well organized, with supervisors and managers that have worked up from inside and know the company and its systems well. Considerable time and money has been spent in recent years on training and development tools. The staff, although with the company on the average for longer than the typical software group, seems dedicated and current.

An effort to replace the existing mainline software has been underway for several years. The intent is to increase capacity and facilitate new product development. The effort, however, has repeatedly slipped behind schedule and there is now a serious question of whether it should be built at all.

In short, from an organizational perspective, the software development section is not doing what is needed and is creating conflict into the bargain. You were brought in primarily to do something about the situation, to turn software into an asset instead of a liability. Since it is a mature organization, seems to be structured like similar groups in other companies, has a stable group of professionals, and has been investing in training and tools, the reasons are not immediately obvious.

## The SDS

You suspect that the problems listed above are actually only symptoms of some underlying causes. Following your earlier training in systems work, you decide to view and to analyze the entire development situation as a system.

Specifically, that means asking Churchman's five questions:

1. What are the objectives of development and how can we objectively measure their attainment?
2. What constraints define the environment in which development takes place?
3. What resources can we draw upon to achieve development objectives?
4. What are the logical and physical components available for development?
5. How is the activity managed, especially with respect to establishing its objectives?

Before sketching answers to these questions, it is important to note a a very important subtlety in our phrasing of these questions: We have not taken as given the boundary of the established four sections of the department and framed all our questions in terms of the development section *as a given.* We are going to ask these questions about the development *activity.* Also, note that we are not directly addressing the symptoms listed above; rather, we are going to first try to understand the underlying system before coming back to address the symptoms and their causes.

### *What Are The Objectives?*

Let's start by looking at the inputs and outputs of the development section. Determining what function is performed (or should be performed) in the right way is important. (American railroads are often held up as an example of groups that did not provide the right answer. They answered that their function was "to provide rail transportation," instead of "to provide transport from point to point," and thus lost out competitively to trucks and other transportation systems.)

The current inputs are formal requests for development. Such requests must be submitted in a standard format that runs to several pages for the smallest project; they must be formally reviewed and approved by the manager of the submitting entity; and a quota system has been established (to help alleviate the backlog problem) that restricts the number of requests that may be submitted from each group in a given quarter.

The substance of each request is a proposal for undertaking a formal development to produce the required software. The desired software is described in terms of inputs, outputs, and the specific functions to be carried out; the proposals do not include much (if any) information about the environment in which the software will be used, nor about the general problem the system is to solve. A modified form of the development proposal that is somewhat shorter is used for requesting changes to existing systems. In theory, these are the only inputs to the development group.

The outputs of the development group consist of software for operation on any machine that the data center has in its inventory and operations manuals that are supplied to the machine operators. A brief user description is prepared for the department that requested the system in the first place and, if it is an interactive system, a brief user's manual is prepared. After a short period of testing by the development group using data supplied by the commissioning department, the system is declared operational and the project ended. Any future changes must then be requested in the form of changes. Only rudimentary user training or consulting is provided by the development group.

An accurate description of the function the development group provides is: "Process formal development requests and produce systems that satisfy those requests." The only performance measurements of the group are based on how many requests are processed per year (weighted by the effort each takes) and the number of lines of code produced and put into production (but not necessarily used).

This formal system was set up some years ago to help control things when the company grew beyond the original group of 25 that created the first product. From the development section's perspective, they are able to reduce their interaction time with other parts of the company in this way and have a consistent way to measure their performance from year to year. They have come to believe that processing the requests in their in-basket and producing lines of code is their function.

From the rest of the organization's perspective, however, this is not at all thefunction that the development group should be carrying out. Rather, they believe it should be providing software to solve problems, however and whenever they are defined. Thus we have out first clue: *The disparity between perceptions of the objective of the development group.*

### *What Are The Givens?*

For reasons that are lost to antiquity, the development section believes firmly that it cannot "enter" the user's territory; it perceives that it is only permitted to do what the users request via the formal development request mechanism. It believes that it has no control over what the users request, yet those requests, in their form, number, and content, obviously have great impact on the functioning of this particular SDS.

That is a classic definition of the "environment" of a system—something the system has no control over but which has impact on the operation of the system. In this case, however, what is in the environment of the SDS need not be. The reasons for such a distinct separation no longer exist. The users understand that they need help in defining their problems better before technical development is begun and they recognize that this must come about through closer cooperation with the developers before a large development effort is completely defined and begun.

Further, they are aware that because of the advent of personal computers, packaged software, and application generators, that many of their computerization tasks could be handled by their own personnel without resorting toa formal systems development effort. The boundary between the SDS and their departments prevents this; however, again this is for reasons that are no longer valid.

In short, it seems clear that *the boundary between the SDS and its environment is suboptimally defined.*

### *Are There Enough Resources? (And Are They The Right Ones?)*

A quick check with some friends in other companies indicates the size of the development section is about standard for the amount of systems they produce (measured simply in lines of code produced). Likewise, there is no reason to believe that the individuals in the department are particularly unproductive.

A closer inspection, however, indicates that some critical resources are missing: there is no one in the development group that is knowledgeable in the new end-user application technologies (because they haven't been needed within the professional development group). Further, the training and upgrading of tools that has been undertaken

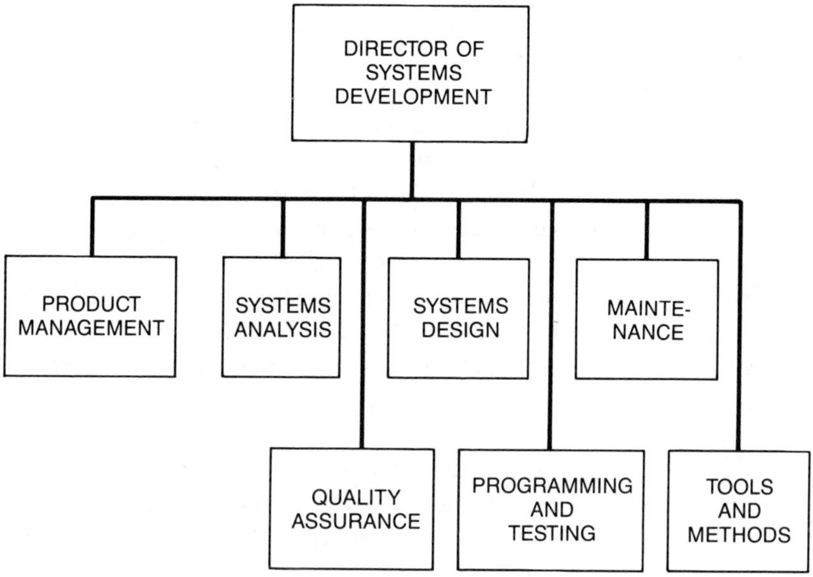


FIGURE 3.2 Organization of a Development Group

has all been directed toward the needs of the professionals dealing with the computer, not toward building strength in requirements analysis that would permit the developers to understand more easily the needs of the users. On top of that, a chance meeting with an old buddy suggested a casual inspection of the type of projects being undertaken; what you found was that 85% were some sort of database system. When you asked to talk to the database experts (on the hunch this might be an area causing bottlenecks) you were told there weren't any—everyone did their own database work.

In short, it appears that your SDS has at least two critical resource needs. *There is a severe lack of database expertise* and *little knowledge of requirements analysis and other end-user–oriented tools and techniques.*

### *Are the Parts Right?*

At this point you decide it is time to dig deeper into the development section itself. You ask to see how it is organized and are given the organization chart in Fig. 3.2.

This structure seems to be favored by the section's management because the functions of each department can be related to the task of processing a request for development. When work begins on a task, it is broken down into segments (design, programming, testing, and so on) and assigned to each department in turn by the cognizant project manager. There are clear definitions of function—the design department is supposed to design systems, the test department tests them, etc.

Is it possible a member of a department may be focusing on the wrong thing? Designing the system to the well-defined point that it can be passed on to the programming department may be easy to comprehend, but it does not necessarily mean that the design is a good one for the user.

Perhaps we are looking at the wrong thing altogether. What are the components of a software development system? Are they identical with the departments? Are they the individuals? What about tools? Design methods? Standards? Policies?

Tools, such as language translators, editors, and test generators, must have some impact on development. If they do, aren't they part of the development system? What about policies? For example, a policy that every program must be unit-tested before being integrated into a new system is bound to make the results of development different from the absence of that policy (unless everyone just automatically does that anyway, which is doubtful).

A quick investigation turns up the fact that there are no consistent policies of this sort. The design group uses the notations they think best, the programming group utilizes the language they consider the best (even though the testing group grouses that it makes integration harder). This confirms your suspicion that *the components of the SDS are not just the departments in the section, and that some important elements may be missing.*

### *What Is It That We Are Managing?*

At this point it is clear that the management of the development section has abdicated one of its primary responsibilities—setting objectives for the development system. The objective, to process requests for development, was set long ago, an organization evolved to meet it, and management spends its time dealing with the consequent problems.

It seems most of their time is spent in meetings with the users who are generally angry about the lateness of their systemsor the fact that they don't meet their needs once delivered. Another large chunk of their time is spent dealing with personnel problems and making sure that each department's budget is carefully followed.

Your analysis: *They are managing the wrong system and not paying attention to the true nature of their development system.*

## Making Connections

At this point you start to have a picture of the underlying development system in your new department and some of its problems. Even though a much more thorough study of it and comparison with norms is needed, this quick inspection *from a systems perspective* is sufficient to help you start to identify some causes of the problems with the department that you were handed when you walked in. For example:

The *disparity in objectives,* especially the fact that the group is not focusing on an objective that has any relevance to the customers, typically leads to poor quality in the work as judged by them. The developers are more concerned with completing formally defined tasks and overlook simple factors such as the technical quality of the work and how well the systems they produce meet the customer's needs. The focus on organizational work-flow objectives also probably is aggravating the late delivery problem by introducing delays and extra work associated with an overly bureaucratic way of getting work done.

The fact that there are *improperly defined boundaries* between the development group and its customers could well be causing several problems. Apparently there is very little customer involvement in the development process, for example, which would make it very difficult to know what they really want; that, in turn, could easily cause the customers to be dissatisfied with the functionality of the systems they receive. In the case of the large, complex project that the group is unable to complete, this boundary problem may be especially critical; such projects generally need a range of skills working on them and if the customers/users are excluded from the work of the development group, then this can rapidly lead to constant rework due to changing misunderstood requirements. And, it goes without saying, if there are problems with the way boundaries are drawn around the development group this could be causing the sour relations between them and other groups.

The *lack of resources* noted in your quick inspection of the SDS may well be much more pervasive, but even what you saw could lead to several of the observable problems. If most of the software produced uses a database intensively and there is no real database expertise represented in the group, then it is not unlikely this causes a lot of tasks to take longer than they should, in turn resulting in backlog problems. Lack of much expertise in requirements analysis is a clear cause of the customers not getting what they need. The undersupply of both of these resources will show up especially in large projects, aggravating the problems with that aspect of the group's work.

Without carrying out a more complete comparison of your group with accepted norms, you discovered that some things such as standards, policies, and tools are almost totally missing. This *absence of important elements* could well result in lowered quality (because expectations are not set for the quality of technical work) and late delivery (because tasks such as testing and system generation are not supported properly by tools). Again, these deficiencies will be especially problematical on large projects simply because of the numbers of people working on the project and the large amount of code, specifications, design documents, and so on that must be handled.

By this point, a pattern should be emerging: The software development system is not performing properly. The fact that the management of the group is *managing the wrong thing* should be no surprise. This means they are not controlling some things that can easily lead to poor relations, late delivery, stalled projects, and large backlogs.

As Fig. 3.3 portrays, these underlying problems with the SDS in your new department are very likely contributing to the list of problems (really, symptoms) you were hit with when you came in. Sometimes it is rather easy to detect problems with a system; for example, the fact that your group is focusing on a set of internal work rules rather than on solving the customer's problems is a pretty obvious structural problem. Other times, what the system should be like requires more comparison with norms; for example, knowing that the group should be using more development tools may not be obvious unless you are familiar with current practices in the field. Providing the perspective and framework necessary to start to make those kind of judgments is the objective for the remainder of this book.

But first we should complete the process started here.

Statcut.

American Red Cross

Blood Services
Greater Upstate New York Region

Syracuse Location:
636 South Warren Street
Syracuse, New York 13202-3368
(315) 425-1666

Albany Site:
Clara Barton at Hackett Blvd.
Albany, New York 12208
(518) 462-7461

City/State Albany, N.Y. 12205

(Initials)

Dear Carmella Tedesco:

We sincerely appreciate your willingness to donate blood, and are grateful for your support of this vital community activity.

However, we are obligated to follow the federal guidelines concerning blood donations, which require that you be temporarily disqualified from donating blood until (date) 3/16/90 for the following reason:

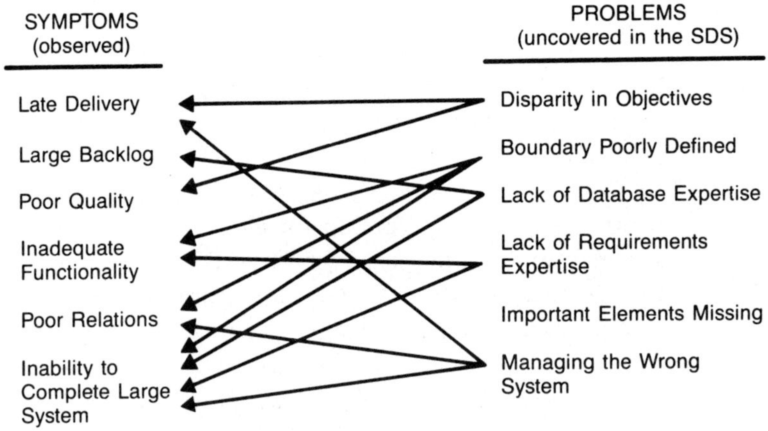


FIGURE 3.3 Symptoms and Problems

### *Fixing the System*

So far we've done two things: first, probed the underlying system, *as a system,* to get a picture of how well it is working; second, made some connections between underlying systemic problems and the symptoms (problems) we were hit with when we walked in the door. The next step should be obvious: Do something about them.

Describing the complete cure would rapidly put you to sleep, at least partly because there are a number of issues of politics and organizational behavior that must be dealt with (I'll come back to some of those later). But the way to start is easy to describe: Attack the systemic problems, letting the effect of appropriate measures on the observed symptoms tell you if you are being successful.

One can't do everything at once, so some priorities have to be set. Pick the highest payoff-to-cost items first,[3.3] get at least two things going from the start that will have short payoff times, and get underway at least one longer-term improvement item. For example, making some assumptions about how hard it is to do certain things and what the payoffs will be for this particular SDS, I would do the following in the order shown (obviously some things can be done in parallel, depending on budget, people resources, and so on):

1. *Hire one or two database experts.* Their job would be to work with all the application programmers to improve their

usage of the database and to introduce new techniques that will permit more rapid and accurate building of data-intensive applications. I would expect an almost immediate improvement in the length of time it takes to build small applications.

2. *Run an in-house requirements analysis training course.* I would have a 1-day version for everyone in the group to sensitize them to the need for and difficulty with effective requirements analysis. I would then carefully select the 10 best people, including managers, to undergo in-depth training in a requirements analysis methodology. I would expect that the next project any of these people work on would have a much better record (objectively measured) of matching the user's needs.
3. *Restructure the development group.* Get rid of the incentives and evaluation criteria that cause people to focus on meeting mechanical bureaucratic objectives; replace them with incentives to pay attention to the proper objectives of the group: helping the customers solve their problems. Organize around teams that are devoted to a particular customer (or class of customers) rather than around functional tasks (such as programming or testing). Appoint (and train) specific people on each team to coordinate (but not be totally responsible for) interactions with the customer. Meet with customers yourself and *listen*; have technical people, as well as managers, from the development group meet regularly with customers. And so on.

There are at least two major stumbling blocks to this: First, it is often very difficult to restructure an organization, especially with respect to incentives and evaluation criteria which are used by management for making personnel decisions. Just because it is impossible, however, does not mean that you should not try everything possible to bring it off; sometimes nothing short of the survival of the organization is the prize. Second, people will rightfully fear a new situation in which they are being asked to do something different and in which it is unclear how they will be judged.

Either, or both, of these problems can sink your whole effort if not approached properly. When I suggest they be top priority items, I am not suggesting they can be done completely in a short amount of time without all kinds of careful and subtle maneuvering to prevent upsets. I am suggesting that this kind of organizational restructuring is essential to turning around the kind of situation described.

4. *Change what managers do.* You have to do something to get the managers to manage the *right* system. Currently they are focusing on whether forms are filled out properly, meetings attended, budgets kept, reports filed, and so on; they are managing a paper system that is not getting the results desired (even though it was probably set up as a way of institutionalizing some behavior that is necessary to achieve the desired results). The system they should be managing is the SDS; the objectives, policies, people, procedures, tools, and information.

   The same caveats about the difficulty of changing people apply here, but with a difference. Managers (and good supervisors) are supposed to be able to manage anything and they are supposed to be used to following directions from above (note the use of "supposed"). That might lead you to believe that you can just order a change.

   In practice, it is never so simple. A mix of leadership from above, education, peer pressure, and incentives is needed. As the executive in charge of the operation, it is essential that you provide clear signals about what is important; for example, that the objectives that the group will be measured against are customer satisfaction, not the number of forms completed. You should use whatever organizational incentives you have to reinforce those signals.

   It doesn't do, however, to simply "order" that the managers and supervisors suddenly start doing things a different way; they couldn't (in most cases) if they wanted to, simply because they are probably unclear about what the important elements of an SDS are and how to control them. That is where education comes in. You must undertake a careful program of education that will provide managers with models of how to proceed and give them the personal confidence to deal with new technologies (for example, tools and methods for requirements analysis) with which they may be less familiar than their subordinates.

5. *Undertake to build the missing elements of the SDS.* The first step is to do a more thorough analysis of what is missing. Some one from outside who is familiar with other organizations and the state of the art can study your group and then recommend improvements. For example, if there is not an appropriate subsystem within the group for testing (policies, procedures, specialists, tools, reusable test sets, and so on), then that is an area in which you must plan to build over the longer term.

   There is always more to do than there are resources, so it is essential that you get some sense of the range of needs before plunging in to a long-range improvement project. After having an in-depth analysis performed, evaluate the payoffs and costs for different options for your organization. Then, begin the education, hiring, retraining, restructuring, and acquisition of tools that will be needed to reach the objectives for the improvements.

While this example does not cover everything that should be done in a situation such as this, it does illustrate the approach that is at the core of my message: View the development situation as a system, study it as a system, make changes to it as you would to any system, and expect it to perform like a system.

## 3.5 Some Essentials

Before we look at a second example, let's look at some of the essential aspects of a system that can be found in this example.

### Focus on Inputs and Outputs

If you want to know what a system really does, you must look at its inputs and outputs. This imposes a very existential viewpoint. We insist that a system be identified by its behavior. (There are similar viewpoints in some familiar aphorisms: "Don't judge a book by its cover" and "You are what you do.")

In the example, the title on the door indicated the group does software development, which is true; but in a larger context in which "software development" carries the connotation of "software development *to solve the user's problems,*" it is clear that a more accurate description of their function is "process development requests." When that function produces outputs that match those desired, there is no problem; but as the user's needs have diverged from traditional paths, the system's outputs (narrow responses to formal requests) have increasingly diverged from what is needed.

## Ends, Then Means

Using the systems approach leads you to consider the ends first and foremost, and only after you clearly understand the desired ends to consider the means for achieving them. Two immediate objections you may encounter are that "ends do not justify the means" and "ends must be modified to take into account the reality of limited means."

The first objection is usually just misplaced concern for humanity, typically revolving around the issue of not dehumanizing the programmer's job. That is never the objective and rarely a danger if a bit of common sense is applied to the choice and implementation of software technology. Indeed, if done properly, most of the worthwhile improvements in software development techniques have the effect of *humanizing* the jobs of those using them.

> *Carefully analyzing the relationship between desired outputs of the SDS and its inputs and internal resources can lead to insights and improvements.*

The second concern is valid, but not at all ignored by the systems approach. This is the same argument made against the use of "top-down" approaches—that you can't settle on the top (or the ends) until you've seen the bottom (or means). This is often true, of course, necessitating iterations between considering ends and means, iterations in which goals are set, means are explored, and goals readjusted on the basis of what you discover about available means. If one knows of certain limitations on critical resources (means) at the time you are setting the objective, then, of course, that information can and should be taken into account.

The critical issue, however, is to not focus on the means too soon. Sometimes what you think are critical resources turn out to be irrelevant when the goals are more carefully examined. At the risk of trivializing, I will observe that the systems approach in this regard is nothing more than the old adage of "Don't put the cart before the horse!"

In the case above, one problem with the SDS is that a lot of money and time had been invested in training (particular means) without examining carefully the objectives (in the system context) the training was supposed to achieve. In particular, the training had introduced the programmers to a number of new techniques, but had provided no guidance on putting the techniques into use; worse, most of the techniques simply reinforced their existing activities without helping them expand to serve the new needs of their users.

## Action at a Distance (Or, I Didn't Intend That!)

How many times have you issued a minor memo about office procedures, only to have a near-riot on your hands over some aspect of the procedures that you hadn't even perceived? Or had a minor part replaced on your car, only to have a major part break down two days later? Or made a minor change in a food recipe because you were short on an ingredient and found that the result was inedible?

In each of these situations—and countless more we all encounter daily—you were experiencing one of the essential, and maddening, aspects of systems: minor changes may result in unexpected major consequences. The reason?

It is often difficult to see or understand the connections between the parts of a system. For example, as supervisor of an office staff, you may not be aware of personal relationships that your new policy disturbs; you know that the water pump is part of the total power system of your car, but it would have been very difficult to know that a new pump increases pressure sufficiently to break through a weakened internal connection, mixing water with lubricants for the transmission, causing a poorly designed part to jam and destroy the entire transmission as you drive down the freeway; the chemical balance between ingredients in the cake batter is tolerant to most variations but not in the case of the ingredient you substituted.

Software-intensive systems are especially susceptible to the impact of unintended effects, at least partly because they are abstract constructs to which we cannot apply our normal senses of taste, smell, and sight. Similarly, the software development system not only must deal with software systems in which this action-at-a-distance property is rampant, but is itself susceptible to the malady. For example, in the case study above, the policy of enhancing the professional strength of the staff through training has had the unintended effect of hardening them into narrow technical specialities, which makes the overall SDS less rather than more responsive to the needs of users.

### Where To Draw The Line

Interfaces, by definition, are an essential aspect of any system since systems are made up of pieces that retain their identity but that work together. Interfaces in an SDS are of many sorts. In the example above, interfaces between individual departments in the SDS are apparently a problem because they force a specific class of information to be passed and restrict the flow of other, essential, information.

Interfaces between policies and people in the SDS are often a source of difficulty. In the case study, the interface between individual needs (for professional enhancement) and organizational needs is problematic.

An interface is simply the overt definition of boundaries between components of the system or between the system and external entities. Typically it defines the information that will flow between the components and the expectations one component has for the action of the other under well-defined situations (for example, if a particular request is passed from one department to another, what will happen?).

### The Whole Is Greater than the Sum Of Its Parts

It is sometimes observed that IBM equipment in any specific area is not the technological leader and that their software also may not be the most advanced. If that is true (and it certainly is *not* uniformly true), then the success of IBM can only be explained in terms of a system concept—that the whole (system) may be greater (and more important) than the total of the individual pieces. In the case of IBM, it is usually further noted that customers' great preference for IBM is due to the fact that they not only deliver hardware and software, but also training, service, supplementary products, assistance with adapting the systems to specific applications, and so on. In short, a system solution.

Most of us intuitively understand this aspect of systems. It is difficult to live and work in the modern world and not see it illustrated daily. Yet, of all the aspects of a system, this is the one that is most frequently ignored when dealing with software development systems.

In the case study, it seems clear that although many of the parts are good (personnel, stability, technical level), they are not working together as a system. The result is that the system is less than the sum of its parts.

With this added understanding of the nature of software development systems, let's look at a second example.

## 3.6 Doing It Right!

As a second case study, let's look at an SDS that seems to be doing it right.

Several years ago I was asked to study the development group of a small high-tech company, assess their situation relative to current software engineering knowledge and practice, and recommend how they should be preparing for the future; in particular, they were concerned that they should be actively preparing to begin using the new programming language Ada. Here is what a colleague and I found:

- The company's main product was design, but they were just preparing to enter the manufacturing aspect of the products.
- The company was under 10 years old and was still led by the original partners that had established it.
- Although small (fewer than 150 people), they were profitable, well established, and respected in their speciality. General expansion of their field, coupled with their entry into the manufacturing aspect, provided them with bright prospects for significant growth.
- The software development department was headed by a vice president who was one of the founders of the company and participated in general management. His professional training was in electrical engineering, but he had educated himself (through self-study and some formal courses) in programming and software engineering when he had taken over the development group several years prior.

Through a series of interviews with the development personnel, the manager, and selected users elsewhere in the organization, a clear picture of this SDS soon emerged:

***Objective*** Support the main business of the company. Measure success at reaching this objective in terms of the time it takes for design engineers to produce a typical product design and some specific quantitative measures of the quality of the design.

***Environment*** As a young and growing company, leanness was demanded. In particular, headcount was carefully controlled by general management. As leaders in a demanding field, the design engineers knew the state of the art in computer support for their work and would not accept anything less than the best.

***Resources*** The design engineers understood clearly the difference between tool building (the province of the software department) and their primary responsibility of product design. Yet they gave freely of their time and energy when appropriate to assist in the definition of new computer-based design systems. A second valuable resource was the detailed technical knowledge of the manager coupled with his native ability to look at things as a system. The spirit of excellence, smallness, and teamwork that permeated the entire company must also be counted as a valuable resource on which the SDS could draw.

***Components*** There were several specific elements the manager had taken great care to fashion; an interactive development tool base that was state of the art and that provided the infrastructure on which all organizational as well as technical communication and work took place; a set of policies that focused attention on the overall objectives and the quality of the software that was produced; a group of people chosen and advanced on the basis of their ability to contribute to the overall group objective.

***Management*** Minimal. Formal guidelines and policies existed, where needed, but were redundant since everyone except new hires had them fully internalized. The manager intervened in activities (technical or organizational) only when his greater experience was needed, or when it was clear that the development system needed adjustment to meet changed expectations of the environment.

In short, this was a system that worked.

*One can find examples of smoothly functioning SDSs that provide high-quality outputs.*

Everyone understood, accepted, and acted in accord with the objective of providing support. A specific question they had during the time of my study was whether they should be moving toward use of the Ada language (which was still several years away from completion at that point). One staff member, who was working on a master's in computer science, was interested in the language from that aspect but he and the rest of the staff framed the question of possible adoption of Ada entirely in terms of "Will it help us achieve our objective?" not in terms of "What can we find to do with this neat language I just found."

Looking at the inputs and outputs of the group confirmed to us that they lived up to their objective of providing support to the design engineers. Formally, there were very few inputs—really just a one-page project approval sheet, which also served as an in-process record of work on a specific project. Informally, there were a multitude of inputs—casual meetings in the lunchroom, directions from the department head to provide support to a special activity, verbal requests from a designer having difficulty.

Likewise, the outputs were not well defined in all cases. Formal development of new packages were well defined and properly entered into a standard configuration control system, as were changes to existing systems. But in some cases the "output" was a department member working directly with a designer for several weeks on a specific design project, which resulted in a better design but no new software.

The manager of the department was clearly a natural systems thinker, which certainly accounts for a large amount of the success of the group. He understood that he had built a development system consisting of attitudes, people, tools, and policies and he was loathe to tamper with it. He understood that resources, the environment, and objectives change over time, so that he was always sensitive and open to the need for change in the SDS. Yet we observed in several different kinds of situations (for example, the adoption of Ada) that he carefully weighed the impacts on his total development system of any change in an individual component.

This was especially noticeable in his management of the interfaces between components of the SDS. For example, an important part of their infrastructure was a program library system. The one they had used for several years was rather inadequate compared to some new database systems that had recently become available; it was clear they would have to replace the library system before long. There was considerable reason to do that in conjunction with their move to a new development machine; however, the change in the library would require considerable change in some of their other tools, as well as changes in their usage patterns. Because there were several critical projects underway in conjunction with their manufacturing startup, the manager decided to not change the library then in order to preserve the interfaces during a critical period.

The "whole greater than the sum of its parts" aspect of this SDS was amply illustrated in several ways. The delay in changing library procedures was one form of this. Another was clear in a personnel matter that came to a head during the study. A new second-line manager for the department had been hired six months previously. He brought considerably more experience and technical expertise to the group than any of the existing personnel (with the exception of the department head) could provide. He was productive in his own personal technical contributions and he got along well with the rest of the group at a personal level. But his style of management and his basic technical style of software development (he practiced a very mathematical approach) were sufficiently different from the rest of the group that it became clear that he was not a very effective member of the team; in effect, his presence subtracted, rather than added, capability. Once this became clear, the department manager had no reluctance in removing him.

It is important to keep this—and all such cases—in perspective. Nothing is perfect, conditions change, not everyone has the natural sense of a system that this manager had (or the opportunity to apply it). Yet I have seen similar settings (including one that is very close to being a direct competitor to this company) in which the system has not been so carefully constructed and managed and in which the results are quite different. I can only conclude that taking the systems view has some positive merit to it.

## 3.7 Making the Key Transferable

Case studies are useful in understanding a concept and developing some intuition in applying it. Ultimately, however, one must abstract the concept in order to apply it to a wide variety of situations.

The systems approach that I have outlined here is not a formal mathematical concept. Many complex systems can be analyzed, and later reorganized, on the basis of formal models that describe the components of a system, the relationships between them, and the performance measures that can be applied to their outputs. While such an approach could be applied to a software development system, it is very difficult to do so at this stage since we have very little understanding of what (or how) to measure in the software development setting.

To assist you in grasping the essentials of the systems approach to understanding and organizing software development, the next chapter presents a more abstract conceptualization of it.

CHAPTER

# 4

# The SDS Explained

CHAPTER

# 4

# The SDS Explained

*If it is true that every theory must be based upon observed facts, it is equally true that facts cannot be observed without the guidance of some theory.*

— *Auguste Comte The Positive Philosophy*

## 4.1 What's In The Box?

If you could go into a computer store and buy an SDS like a stereo, what would you find in the box when you got home and opened it up? The six parts of the SDS: objectives, policies, people, procedures, tools, and information.

You will want to use your SDS after you have assembled it; that will take place in some *environment.* Initially, assume that is a given that can't be changed. In the longer run, you may discover that a reasonable SDS cannot be operated in your environment, leading you to change it; further, operation of the SDS will eventually change the surrounding environment. But for a first approximation, let's assume your environment is fixed.

When you purchased your SDS, you probably had some alternative models from which to choose. When you brought it home, there were again some decisions that had to be made about which room (environment) to install it in. Once it is set up and running, it has to be operated and maintained. All of this can be rolled up into the topic of *management* of the SDS.

Thus to understand the SDS, we have to understand three aspects—parts, environment, and management, as depicted in Fig. 4.1. (By analogy, to understand fully the role of a stereo system in the home, you must understand the technology, the room in which it is installed, and the manner in which it is used.) In this chapter, we will describe each of these aspects and begin to look at how they interact to create a functioning system. Later we will look at each in more detail.

## 4.2 The Parts

There are many ways to skin a cat, as the old saying goes, and there are many ways to take apart a system. Let's begin by looking at the six types of "parts" in an SDS.

### Objectives

The objectives for an SDS are what you—and others—decide it should be doing. They may be very high-level ("Produce all the software needed by the company") or detailed ("Make any changes to version 17 systems that are approved on form 3B requests"). They may be appropriate ("Provide all needed software support to the engi-

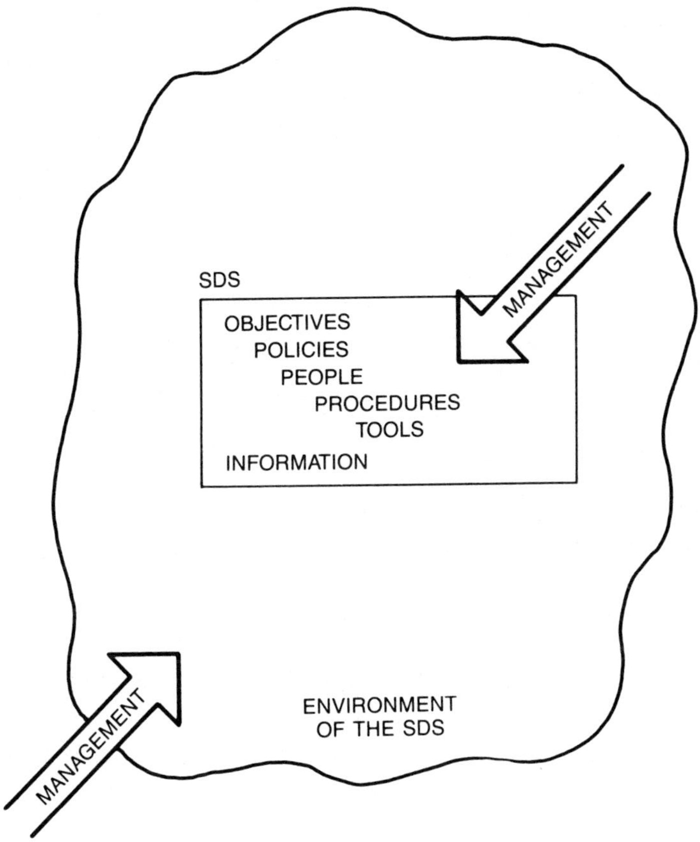


FIGURE 4.1 Aspects of the SDS

neering design department") or questionable ("Produce billable deliverables as quickly as possible in order to improve our receivables situation"). They may be feasible ("Provide as much maintenance support to operations as possible within your budget") or impossible ("Produce systems with no errors, on time, within budget, without additional staff").

In practice, objectives for an SDS are usually more carefully drawn than these examples (at least in a large organization) and are not so extreme. The basic problem then is how to recognize inappropriate, unrealistic, or unattainable goals that may be mixed in with others that are appropriate, realistic, and attainable. Further, only in the most highly structured organizations do you typically find objectives written down in much detail; rather, the objectives are in people's minds. Even when there is broad agreement among everyone concerned, it may be difficult to evaluate the objectives.

> *Clear objectives for an SDS can energize it more than any single thing.*

The value of clear, understandable objectives to systems work is clear. However, high-level goals such as "Reach the moon by the end of the decade" must be turned into understandable and detailed objectives that permit people to make day-to-day decisions.

Objectives may be established for the nature of the products produced by the SDS (e.g., "Delivered systems should not generate more than one level-0 problem report per 1000 lines of source code in their first year of use."), the use of resources (e.g., "No more than *X* dollars will be available for development"), the SDS's relationship to its environment (e.g., "Eighty-five percent of requests for development should be satisfied within six months"), or on other bases (e.g., "Profits, follow-on work generated, leadership for other units"). Whether they are formalized, written down, and published is usually a matter of organizational style, although from a systems perspective there is great value in being explicit about them.

Measurements are an integral aspect of objectives. Very simply, if you cannot measure it, you cannot tell if the objective has been reached. In systems work, this is known as making objectives "operational or measurable." For example, the goal of producing user-friendly software may have been reached in the opinion of a professional programmer and not have been reached in the opinion of a secretary using the software unless the objective has been made operational in terms of some measurements (e.g., the time it takes a novice to learn to use it and a checklist of user features it must have) that permit us to determine objectively whether or not it has been reached.

Identification of improper objectives is one of the hardest tasks for someone new to development. Because one of senior management's primary tasks should be to help formulate objectives and because they are often not personally knowledgeable in systems development, this is an area that is especially problematical in many organizations. There are no magic litmus tests to tell if an objective is proper (appropriate, feasible) but there are some guidelines[4.1]:

- *Is it achievable?* No characteristic has been more consistently ignored in setting objectives for software development groups than this one. Objectives are often set for individual projects that are completely unrealistic (because they have been set by people with no real understanding of the software development process or without even a modicum of systematic planning), leading to their being completely ignored by the technical staff. The result is that if realistic objectives ever are established, it is very difficult to get anyone to believe in them.

  Most often, if any objectives are set, they are strictly related to specific projects rather than being continuing, systematic goals that will apply to all the work that is done by the group. This means that the group feels it is being successful only on those rare occasions when the specific project goals (which are usually just time and budget figures) are met. Contrast this to a situation in which there are also system objectives, for example, relating to quality of the products produced; then the group can feel they are meeting some objectives even if some of the specific project targets are missed.

  And do I have to point out that you should not adopt goals to be achieved in a time frame in which it is impossible that you will have the expertise and resources necessary to accomplish them? I would hope not, but have certainly encountered groups that did!
- *Does it place emphasis on quality?* It is widely known, but often unheeded, that people attend to that which is stressed as being the most important objective in the environment. If your objective really isto have quality systems, then you must establish this objective and clearly communicate it in every way possible. When this is done, it seems to help materially, as discussed earlier.
- *Is it testable?* If the objective is to produce "quality" systems, but this is not defined in a way that permits its achievement to be tested objectively, then it will be of little use in comparing actual to desired performance of the SDS. Motherhood statements are rampant in the software field, so that like infeasible project goals, they tend to be ignored.

In most cases, being testable goes hand in hand with being decomposable. That is, a good objective is one that can be broken down into smaller objectives so that human-sized chunks of work or program can be compared against the objective to permit individuals to measure their progress.

This is one of those areas where your common sense will serve you well. Good objectives will be ones that you sense are achievable, general enough to last, specific enough to be measured, and, ultimately, important to everyone in the SDS.

- *Does it relate to the objectives of the surrounding environment?* In the case of elements of the SDS, this means, for example, that objectives for staff development should relate to the goals of the entire SDS by helping people obtain new skills which, when applied, will clearly help make progress toward the overall goals. In the case of the entire SDS, for example, if the parent organization's goals are to keep current costs at a minimum since it is in danger of bankruptcy, it would not be appropriate to invest in long-term acquisition of tools and new methods.
- *Is it clear and unique?* Central to the idea of a system is that it exists for some specific purpose. If you are not clear about what the SDS is supposed to produce, don't be surprised if it doesn't do it very well.

  It is especially difficult to obtain clear objectives in large organizations in which systems support many different people, are funded by a second large set of people, operated by a third large set, and created by yet a fourth mob!
- *Is it reasonable?* If typical productivity rates for application development groups are 1000 lines of delivered code per person per year, it is not reasonable (without some extraordinary changes) to set a goal for your group of 10,000 lines per person. If you don't know what is reasonable (which is precisely the problem for someone new), ask around—people in the organization, people in other organizations (both management and technical people), journals, consultants, books, etc.

  One problem with this approach is that if you take it too literally, you never improve. Obviously, there are times when one should establish objectives that are beyond the current average of the industry, but those times should be carefully chosen. Another problem is that because the software development industry is changing so rapidly (it's not fair to claim it's new when it is actually a quarter century old), few people have taken time to develop and record in any public way performance figures that would provide a baseline of expectations.[4.2]

- *Can you see a connection between the objective and the rest of the SDS?* This is often hard to determine, even if you are quite familiar with the technology and practice of development. The effort of analyzing an objective, however, can be quite beneficial to understanding needed changes in the rest of the SDS. Sometimes, however, a rather cursory analysis of an objective will permit you to decide if it is feasible or not. For example, if the objective of developing factory automation systems, including process control, is given to a group which has previously only been developing rather routine data processing applications, it should be clear that there are some areas of expertise necessary to the task that probably are not present in the group. More subtly, if a group that has been responsible for small-scale projects that involve only a few people over a few months is asked to undertake a major task that will involve many people over several years, it should occur to you that there may be a scaling problem and that the resources of the SDS may not be able to immediately tackle something that is qualitatively different.

Measurement does not always mean that one has a quantitative measure. It may be as simple as having a checklist of items or features that should be in any product or a set of milestones that must be reached during some phase of development. The critical issue is that there must be some explicit expectation before the fact, there must be some objective way of telling if the expectation is reached, and there must be the willingness to collect data ("measure") in an unbiased manner in order to determine if the goal is met.

So the first part of the SDS packed in the box has to be a set of objectives for its operation and a set of measurements that permit us to tell whether or not you are reaching them.

### Policies

Policies are often as intangible as objectives. Yet they are the instructions to the SDS machine; they are the rules that spell out how it should operate to achieve the desired objectives.

Policies determine the type of personnel we assign to the SDS. They control the investment of capital in tools and training. They specify the quality controls that are to be applied to development projects. They help us decide when to enhance a system once more and when to rebuild it. The range is great, and making sure your policies are neither too high-level nor too detailed is a critical factor as we will see later.

Some set of policies exists in every SDS. The issue is to fashion those policies so that they rationally work to guide the other parts of the system toward reaching the objectives.

## Information

Information is present to some degree in every situation, so it may seem odd to include it here. I have made it explicit in the SDS to emphasize its importance and to indicate that it can be managed for the betterment of the development system.

Specifically, there are three major kinds of information with which the SDS must be concerned: external technical information, measurements (internal and external), and the information that makes up the software being produced (e.g., documentation). Technical information is whatever is currently known about computers, software, and any other disciplines relevant to creating a specific piece of software (for example, the psychology of perception may be useful in designing better visual displays). The issue with respect to an SDS is to make sure that this information is available and used.

Measurements are essential to know whether or not we have reached the objectives that have been set for the SDS as discussed above. Measurements must be made on all parts of the SDS (including measurements themselves) where there is concern about their operation. This produces information; use of that information may be made in several ways.

The information that *is* the software (as discussed in Chapter 1) is the central focus of the entire SDS. It includes the specifications, designs, test plans, documentation of all kinds, previously built systems and pieces of systems to be reused, and all the other information that is essential to a complex task.

## People

Some analysts leave people out of systems, preferring to view them as the agents that operate whatever mechanistic system is being studied. Given the propensity of human beings to act independently (thank God!), there is a good argument for not including them in a system that we are trying to view in a systematic way. Excluding them from consideration in studying an SDS, however, will rapidly lead to a narrow, unrealistic view.

People are central to the SDS because so much of its operation is unformalized, requires judgment, problem-solving capability, and other features that only a person can provide. If we were to analyze the credit approval system in a large bank, for example, we would find that much of it could be automated in a rather straightforward way, because it does not require judgment, problem solving, or other informal processes.

This is not to say that there are not some significant gains to be made by automating some aspects of software development—because there certainly are. Much of the hour-to-hour work of the development professional is clerical and highly susceptible to automation. Likewise, some of the tasks which have required human problem solving in the past, such as routine coding, are now within the capability of automated techniques.

It also is important to realize that quite a lot of aid can be given the people in the SDS, even when they are still required. Methods that help people conceptualize complex relationships, analyze intricate conditions, determine useful abstractions for a design, or otherwise deal with the difficult and unstructured tasks of development, already exist in some respects and current research is aiming at improving these methods and implementing them with tools. Moreover, since we are not analyzing the SDS in a strict, mathematical way, we can tolerate quite a lot of variability in people's behavior and still understand (and to some extent predict) their role in relation to the other parts.

The people in the SDS are of many kinds: programmers, systems analysts, technicians, librarians, secretaries, supervisors, managers, customers, upper management, all are important to the overall success of the SDS. Understanding their roles, finding the right people, establishing effective relationships between them and the other parts of the SDS, all are challenging tasks on top of the traditional personnel management tasks.

In an objective sense, some truly remarkable software-intensive systems have been built in spite of the almost total absence of theory or tools. The systems that guide planes and spacecraft, manage large financial databases, control factories, or enable telecommunications are comparable in complexity to the most complex physical artifacts that we have built, yet they have been created with a fraction of the theoretical and pragmatic foundation that is involved in designing and building an airplane, for example.

The key has been the creativeness of people. In devising the functionality of such systems, complex and intricate problems have had to be solved. When people are encouraged, energized, and supported properly, they are able to build this complexity in spite of what seems to be insurmountable odds; when the SDS of which they are a part detracts from their efforts and makes the sum of their work less than it should be, disaster ensues. This is one of the primary challenges of working in and with an SDS: how to bring out this creativeness, support it, and expand it through appropriate policies, procedures, tools, information, and objectives.

> *Reports of the total replacement of people in the development process are premature.*

One of the constants in every conversation I have with seasoned software developers is the absolutely key role people play. The dominance of the human factor seems so great that many people are tempted to say that nothing much else matters. One of the important aspects of a system, however, is that all the parts have some effect on the overall operation (unless they are truly redundant or unused); further, one of the developments of recent years is that some of the other parts of the SDS (for example, tools) are becoming sufficiently capable that they can rival the people factor in some instances.

## Procedures

If policies are the "programs" for the SDS, then procedures are the "programs" for the people in the system. Procedures in an SDS may be formal work practices (e.g., design inspection techniques), or informal ways of doing things that everyone simply understands (e.g., procedures for creating and compiling source code).

Included in this category of system "parts" are the more well-defined methods for developing software that are becoming an increasingly important part of the SDS (e.g., structured design, stepwise refinement, Jackson System Design). In addition, the underlying problem solving and design processes used by people must be considered procedures. However, since they are generally something that we have little control over (once the person is hired) they will not be considered an explicit part of the SDS in the same way that a new design method is.

Procedures in an SDS permit us to spell out how policies are to be implemented. As such, they play a crucial role in the overall system. If we provide too much detail in the procedures (really try to "program" the behavior of the developers) then we quickly bog down in detail and stifle the all-important creativity of the developers. On the other hand, in many areas, if we do not indicate the preferred way in which policies are to be implemented, then their effect is dissipated by the plethora of implementations that spring up.

In the area of methods, there is the additional aspect of providing important intellectual aid to the people component of the SDS. The underlying purpose of development methods is to help people do their job better so that the choice of this variety of procedure can have an important impact on the overall functioning of the system.

### Tools

The last category of parts of the software development system consists of the various programs, forms, and devices that assist the developers in carrying out the procedures and policies of the SDS. "Tools" in most fields connotes physical tools, but in software development, "tools" usually connotes programs that in some way help the programmers, designers, and analysts do their job. (Although there are a few nonprogram tools, most are insignificant compared to program tools.)

Software tools come in many flavors. The assemblers, compilers, interpreters, loaders, and simple editors that we have had for years are still the most important tools because they are so essential. For many applications, simple text processors are an important tool. As the power of computers increases rapidly, especially in the area of graphics, we are starting to see some significant tools that help developers deal with representations of software other than just linear programming languages (e.g., design structure charts).

In Chapter 9 we will look at tools along two (of many possible) dimensions: One dimension characterizes tools in terms of how much they assist with the management aspects of development versus how much they assist with the technical aspects. The second dimension relates to whether the tool deals with static or dynamic properties of software. For example, a file system or text editor provides no help to the developer in working with the dynamic properties of software, while a simulator provides no help with the static properties of a piece of code.

Hardware tools are also important to software development. The strong influence of access to the computer on which the development is being done leads to the need for sufficient capacity, an ample number of terminals, special graphic display equipment and printers, and so on. Although this was one of the earliest studies of the important factors in development,[4.3] it is still quite often a major problem in an SDS.

In the last few years, there has been a rapid growth in the number and type of tools available for the software developer, especially workstations. There is considerable interest in tools, as there should be, since in many cases they can be an important element in the SDS. However, as is so often the case with tools in any area, there is a tendency to place more importance on tools than is realistic. Tools must support effective methods and help the people in the SDS do their jobs better and with greater productivity. A tool to support a design method that is not applicable to the type of application a particular SDS works with, for example, may be a great tool but useless or even counterproductive.

These are the parts you get out of the box. We will look at each in more detail in later chapters, but first let's look at the nature of the environment in which the SDS operates.

## 4.3 The Environment

No environment is ever static nor without some possibility of major change. Yet, on a day-to-day basis we have to make some assumptions about the things that are outside the SDS and which impact it, but over which it has little control (at least on a short-term basis). There are four major factors that are present in the environment of every significant SDS, as well as innumerable others that are sometimes present or that are not as major; in this section I will outline the nature of the four major ones.

### Financial

Myths about government spending notwithstanding, every software development system ultimately is controlled or constrained by the financial environment in which it exists. The impacts may not be felt by those buried deep in the organization in some cases; in others, an expanding and profitable market may release the constraints for a period of time. But eventually the cost of the SDS and the financial resources available come into conflict.

The SDS may be able to obtain more resources or produce new products that generate revenues or in some other way change this factor, but in the short term it appears more as a part of the environment (a given that can't be changed) than anything else. An analysis of the SDS will certainly be easier if you assume that finances are something that are a part of the environment.

This is clearly a simplifying assumption that doesn't capture reality very well. In most organizations, there is a continual interaction between the SDS and the environment over the issue of finances; indeed, many changes in the SDS come about solely for the purpose of obtaining more money from the environment. But once the financial parameters are set, it is usually easiest to take them as part of the environment.

> *Any SDS operates in a surrounding environment, over which it has little immediate control. Of the many factors present in most environments, four are usually dominant: finances, type of application, organizational culture, and technology.*

Two contrasting vignettes illustrate this control. In one organization, top management did not have a good understanding of the SDS (because the executives were not technically oriented, and had adopted a management style that made it difficult for them to dig into the nitty-gritty of the operations). Although quite a lot of resources were devoted over several years to a large project, it continued to encounter significant delays in completion. Ultimately, the top management was moved out by their management (the company was part of a larger group of companies), partly because of the lack of return on the resources expended on the large project. The new management demanded solid, cost-benefit justifications for the project and, when they were not forthcoming, quickly killed it. So, even though for some time it appeared that the SDS was independent of the financial constraints of its environment, eventually the environment imposed its control.

In a second case, the control was much more consistent and direct. Again, the top management was not technically oriented; in addition, because of the nature of the organization, they could not pay much attention to the SDS. However, they made sure that the expenditure of funds on the SDS resulted in some tangible benefits to the overall organization. For example, a request for funds to undertake an improvement of some of the software engineering methods and tools ultimately went to the chief executive. While he was already sold on the functional need, he demanded that people justify the expenditures in terms of what the overall organization would ultimately receive. The difference here was that the demand for a business justification worked to the advantage of the SDS (by pushing it to focus on what was most important) and the embedding organization (by providing the kind of directed results it needed for other purposes).

In the larger picture, the interplay between the SDS and the environment along the financial dimension (including the marketplace in which its outputs are sold) is extremely important and forms one of the most important interfaces in many systems in which an SDS is only one element. Analysis of this interface is the province of economics.[4.4]

### Type of Application

A second factor that exists in the environment once development begins, but which may be under the control of the SDS in the long run, is the type of system that is being produced. The nature of SDS will probably be quite different depending upon whethet you are building operating systems or financial applications for small business.

There are several reasons why the nature of the application effects the SDS:

- *Software structures needed.* A business application, for example, typically utilizes a database (i.e., a particular software structure); this requires a database management system to support application programming and procedures for creating and using test data sets. A process-control system for a rolling mill, on the other hand, may require the software to utilize a number of programs running in parallel (simultaneously); this software structure requires mathematically based procedures for organizing the parallelism and simulation tools for verifying desired properties of the software. In both cases, the background and training of the people in the SDS may be rather different.

- *Criticality of the application.* If you are building life-critical software, for example, to control surgical support systems, the amount of testing and analysis of the software that must be done before putting it into operation may be much greater than if you are building simple data-reporting applications for a business. This will affect the SDS in the policies and procedures that assure the quality of the product, and the tools that support those processes.
- *Size of the software.* Quantitative differences in system size lead to qualitative differences in the required SDS. If you are producing small systems, say a few thousand lines of code, formal policies, procedures, and tools for configuration management and documentation are not usually needed; a few simple procedures suffice. If you are producing systems that contain hundreds of thousands of lines of code, then without such elements in the SDS disaster will almost certainly ensue.
- *Lead times.* Although related partially to system size, the length of time that it takes to produce a system will affect the SDS in the structure of the development lifecycle it must follow (which, in turn, is manifested in policies and procedures). The length of time may be dictated by the customer's practices (e.g., military organizations typically have highly structured and lengthy development cycles), the complexity of the problem (e.g., a telecommunications system), or the degree of knowledge we have about the problem (e.g., weather forecasting).
- *Customer involvement.* A technology-driven development group, for example, one that produces software to control a medical electronics product, does not need the same type of requirements analysis procedures and support tools that a group does that is building applications for nontechnical functional groups in a large organization.

As with other environmental factors, the degree of success of an SDS is at least partly tied to its success in understanding the essential nature of the application—the required outputs of the SDS. The two case studies in Chapter 3 provide a good illustration of this. In the first, the SDS did not recognize that they were producing the wrong outputs; their focus was on an institutionalization of a previous application, not on the current application. In the second, the system was constantly attuned to the nature of the application that was being requested and was thus able to move easily from being a graphics support group to providing manufacturing support.

As with the financial dimension, understanding of the nature of this dimension of the environment and its impact on the SDS is not widely understood. Indeed, there are probably more myths than truths in this arena!

## Organizational Culture

Software development is a people-intensive activity. Further, its output—software—is primarily "consumed" by people, so it is not surprising that one of the ever-present elements of the environment of any SDS is the culture of the organization in which it exists. Even a single person developing software, if it is ever to be used by anyone else, must deal with those people, their styles, their wishes, their culture.

The culture in which an SDS exists has many impacts on it, both subtle and obvious. In the first case study above, the SDS did not accurately perceive the surrounding culture; the culture wanted flexibility and valued a problem-solving, results orientation while the development group did not. This divergence of culture had some obvious and predictable results. In the second case study, a more subtle impact of the culture was the set business and organizational attitudes (leanness, quality, results orientation) that greatly influenced the SDS even though most of them were not explicitly aware of the influence.

There are some other hidden factors, too. One is that it is necessary that people be permitted to fail and still be around to try again; most learning is the result of experience. Further, the culture must encourage and reward those that learn from experience, as demonstrated by their results. At the same time, it is important that the organization make sure that people have new experiences from which to learn, not just the same experiences over and over.

The impact of the culture can become the largest determiner of the success of the SDS, but it need not be. The connections between the SDS and the environment along this dimension are extremely important and must be managed carefully.

### Technology

The last element that is always present in the environment is, of course, the underlying technology. Although an individual group may produce a new piece of the technology which radically changes the general situation, in most cases the current state of the technology is a given that must be dealt with.

The underlying hardware technology is only the start of the technology dimension, and in some ways may not be the most important aspect for the detailed parts of software development. Available design representations and programming languages can be very important; algorithms for specific applications can make the difference between success and abysmal failure; techniques for organizing data can be critical. For example, sophisticated graphics systems were very difficult to construct before algorithms were developed to remove hidden lines from a display and do other basic operations; once that underlying technology was developed, construction of graphics applications took a quantum leap forward.

There is a developing technology of software engineering as well. Design and analysis methods, tools for generating test cases, procedures for checking a design for given quality criteria, means of quickly determining the suitability of a given set of requirements are all part of a "software technology" that forms the general environment in which a given SDS must exist. One of the key issues for any current SDS is the extent to which it stays abreast of new developments in software technology and puts it to use.

In several places above I have noted an issue that demands attention and direction, or an interface between parts of the SDS that must be carefully fashioned. This is where management comes in.

## 4.4 Fitting Them Together

The third, and critical, aspect of the SDS is management. Management assembles the parts, helps establish the connections to the environment, and sets the policies that guide the operation. Before you get a swollen head (if you are a manager), let me note that I am speaking of "management" in a broad sense to include technical as well as organizational direction.

A key aspect of a successful SDS is that it carefully integrates management and technical direction so that they work together. This is the first (and most important) thing to note about the management of an SDS. Management must be involved, for example, in defining the standard workproducts that will be produced and the development phases that will be used so that they will provide some of the structure management needs to guide projects; yet those workproduct and phase definitions are critical parameters for the technical work and so must be chosen with the full cooperation of the people who will be doing the technical work.

The parts of an SDS do not fit together automatically. Indeed, if they are just "purchased" and thrown together with little thought to making them work as a system, then the chances they will coalesce into a system are very small. All the usual factors found in organizations and human beings will come into play to insure that policies do not meet objectives, that the wrong people are in the wrong positions, and that people understand neither the policies nor the objectives.

You might think that at the level of procedures and tools—where we start to get down to tangible objects rather than intangible policies—it would be easier to put things together. Sadly, this does not seem to be the case. The factors that drive the acquisition of tools and procedures (at least the more formal ones such as design methods) are not particularly attuned to meeting objectives or implementing policies. For example, the choice of tools is normally driven by the technical perceptions and interests of technical people who may have little innate interest in the overall objectives of the organization.

The critical role of management should be clear. It must make sure that the various elements of the SDS are chosen to fit together and then work carefully with them to make sure that they do so in practice.

Similarly, the SDS does not just automatically fit into its environment. In addition to all the normal interorganizational conflicts, turf battles, and competition, the SDS often has special problems dealing with its environment. These stem from the fact that software (computers) is sometimes viewed with special suspicion or fear, on the one hand because of its capacity to cause change, and on the other hand, because it has become critical to the work of many other people and organizations and thus is viewed as a potential roadblock or critical factor in others' attempts to achieve objectives.

Again, management has a key role. In this case, the largely communicative and goal-setting aspect of the interfaces to the environment demand sensitive and active intervention in many cases by someone that has the scope and perspective to deal with them.

I have done little more than introduce the parts, environment, and management of the SDS so far. Before looking at them in more detail, however, it will be helpful to provide some additional overview of the SDS in general. To do that, I want to employ a very common approach in software development—modeling.

## 4.5 Modeling The SDS

Why bother?
What can we gain from it?
If we do, how?
What are the pitfalls?

Software development systems are complex artifacts and, like other complex subjects, can often be more easily understood if modeled. Modeling permits us to abstract reality and get rid of details of the situation which get in the way of understanding the essential nature of the subject. Models also can help us understand the big picture—the connections between major parts, the motivations, the connections to the rest of the world.

Software developers are discovering another reason for building models: sometimes a different representation of reality is easier to comprehend. Software—an abstract entity—is hard to grasp; a visual model of the software is generally easier to understand, especially if it helps us focus on those aspects in which we are most interested.

The value is more direct than improving our understanding, however. A good model of the SDS can be used as a guide in analyzing or constructing a specific one; it can serve as an organizer of questions, issues, concerns, and information; it can help us answer questions about possible changes at a fraction of the cost of making them in reality. In short, we are building a model of the SDS as a pragmatic aid to constructing and operating one, not as an intellectual exercise.

To model the general concept of an SDS introduced above, and to look at the interconnections among the elements, I will use SADT™[1] (Structured Analysis and Design Technique, one of the general-

[1]SADT™ is a registered trademark of SofTech, Inc., Waltham, MA.

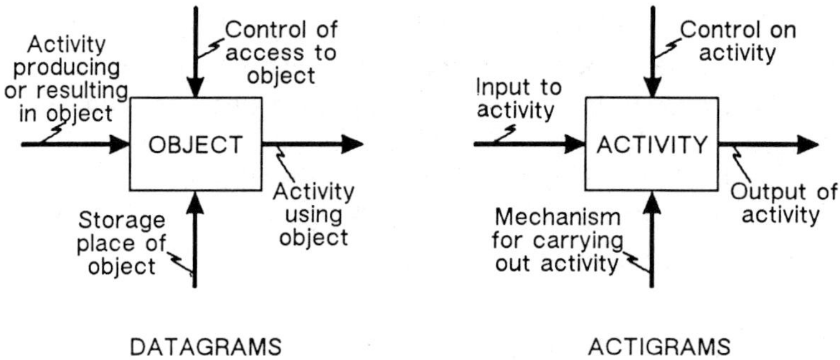


FIGURE 4.2 Nomenclature for SADT Models

purpose model building techniques used by software developers.[4,5] It is easy to understand models built in SADT; a few paragraphs of explanation will permit you to understand the small and simple models employed here.

Models in SADT are composed of a set of interconnected diagrams, and each diagram is contained on a single page (in fact, I will use only fragments of models here consisting of at most two or three diagrams). A diagram is composed of from three to six boxes and interconnecting arrows, all labeled with simple text.

Diagrams, and thus models, are either *datagrams* representing objects and their functional interconnections or *actigrams* representing functions and their data interconnections. The two types of models give different pictures of the same entity (the system being studied); for this reason, I will use both here.

Figure 4.2 gives the basic nomenclature for SADT models. In datagrams, we often do not show the storage place or access control (bottom and top arrows), but there should always be an activity that produces the object and one that uses it. In actigrams, we often do not show the mechanism that executes the activity and sometimes do not show the input, but there should always be an object controlling the activity and an output. The interpretation is that the activity converts inputs into outputs under the control of the objects represented by the arrow from the top.

An SADT model does not necessarily show everything; for example, we sometimes do not show inputs. Thus, for example, in the models below there is an activity that produces people! Now, I am certainly not modeling biological processes, but only a staffing process that provides people to the development group. There is a strong emphasis in SADT models on generalization; thus, a single term, for example, "tools," typically will represent an entire class of objects. However, it can also represent a particular tool or a subset of all possible tools; the meaning will either be clear in the context of the entire model (in which individual boxes are detailed in other diagrams) or unimportant for the purpose of the model.

SADT models are intended to be aids to communication between humans, not completely formal models that are precise in every detail. In reading one, first make sure you understand the syntax used. Then try to understand *factually* the message the author is trying to send. Only after you are sure you understand the message should you try to decide whether or not you *agree* with the message. (It puzzles me how often people make judgments without first seriously trying to understand the thing they are judging. In human affairs, such prejudice leads to inequities; in systems development it leads to disaster.)

SADT models are built using a consistent *purpose* and *viewpoint* chosen to model the position of the author. The purpose here is essentially the same throughout: to provide a concrete representation of the abstract concepts being discussed. (I could have had the purpose of illustrating a particular development environment which would have resulted in a rather different set of models. In fact, this is often done as a means of studying a specific SDS before understanding changes to it.) Unless otherwise stated, I will be taking the *viewpoint* of the manager responsible for making the SDS a business success by producing quality products on time and to budget.

As we start to use this technique, bear in mind that these are only *models* of reality. They won't contain everything that exists "out there." Different viewpoints may result in rather different models (compare your model of the SDS with that of a newly hired programmer), and there may be distortions due to the simple fact that I am not a perfect observer or reporter. Above all, bear in mind that these are general models that should be applicable to a wide range of specific situations.

Now, let's look at how the SDS fits together by modeling it.

## 4.6 A Rational View Of The Structure

I am assuming that you already understand reasonably well what a software development system is supposed to do—at least in general—let's look first at its structure. I have introduced the six major parts of he SDS and some environmental and management concerns, so let's look at some of the interconnections between them by building a simple model.

Rational is a loaded term that I hesitate to use, since we all think of ourselves as being rational! Here it is used to indicate that the model presents the situation as though the parts and connections were all explainable in scientific (rational) fashion (*A* does *X*, *B* does *Y*, if we put them together we get *X*+*Y*, etc.), i.e., that the world we are dealing with is a rational place. While that assumption may certainly not be entirely defensible in the larger picture, I have found it to be a productive approach for the purposes here.[4.6]

> *There are many ways of looking at reality. The rational view is only one, but it does provide a coherent way of understanding much of the behavior that one can observe in the SDS.*

Figure 4.3 presents a first approximation to a structural picture of a generalized SDS. (Keep in mind that this model is intended to help you understand the general concept of an SDS, and that it is built from the viewpoint of a person responsible for the overall direction of an SDS.)

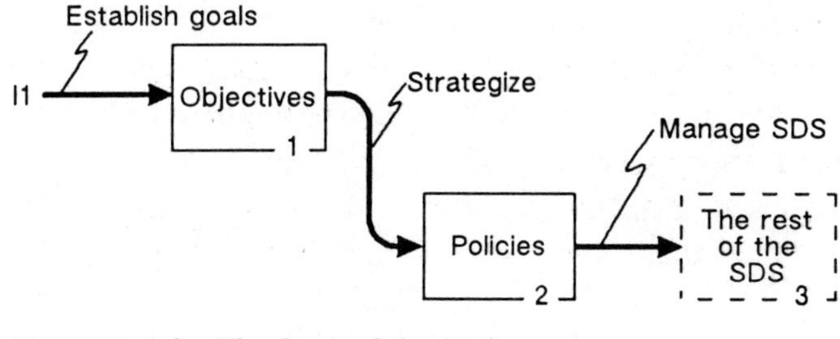


FIGURE 4.3 The Start of the SDS

It shows simply that the activity "Establish goals" (which uses something not shown in this model) results in "Objectives" and that to "Strategize" (about software development since that is the general context of this model) results in "Policies." Managing an SDS uses "Policies" (and obviously lots of other things) to produce the rest of the SDS. (Note that terms in this and the following diagrams appear within quotation marks when referred to in the text.)

Figure 4.4 adds three more components and indicates one way in which policies are used by the management activity. Note that in this model we are focusing mostly on the constructive aspect of management in building an SDS; we will look more at the connections relevant to operation of the SDS when we look at a functional model. (For example, policies are clearly used by management in directing the work of people in the system, but this is not explicitly represented in this diagram unless we interpret "Build staff" as an activity that includes changing someone's work by redirecting him or her to a new task.)

I have chosen the labels for the activity arrows carefully. Policies lead to the selection and professional development of specific people who will help carry out the stated policies. Procedures are the most systematic way of making sure that policies are implemented. For example, we may have a policy of shipping a system to the customer only when the error detection rate for the system during integration testing is below one error per 10,000 lines of code per test interval. We can implement this policy by establishing procedures for testing, measuring, and controlling actual shipment.

Tools exist for many purposes and come from a number of different activities: purchase from an outside supplier, adaptation of existing tools, creation by a programmer. Here I am primarily modeling their desired relation to policies, namely, that they should be the result of enforcing policies. For example, a policy on who can make changes to a system configuration may lead to particular configuration management tools; a policy on quality of specifications may lead to a particular class of specification tools.

The use of people, procedures, and tools in the activity of producing software is also multidimensional; I have emphasized what seems to be their prime roles in the SDS. The creative activity draws most heavily on people, while the activity of engineering systems—that is,

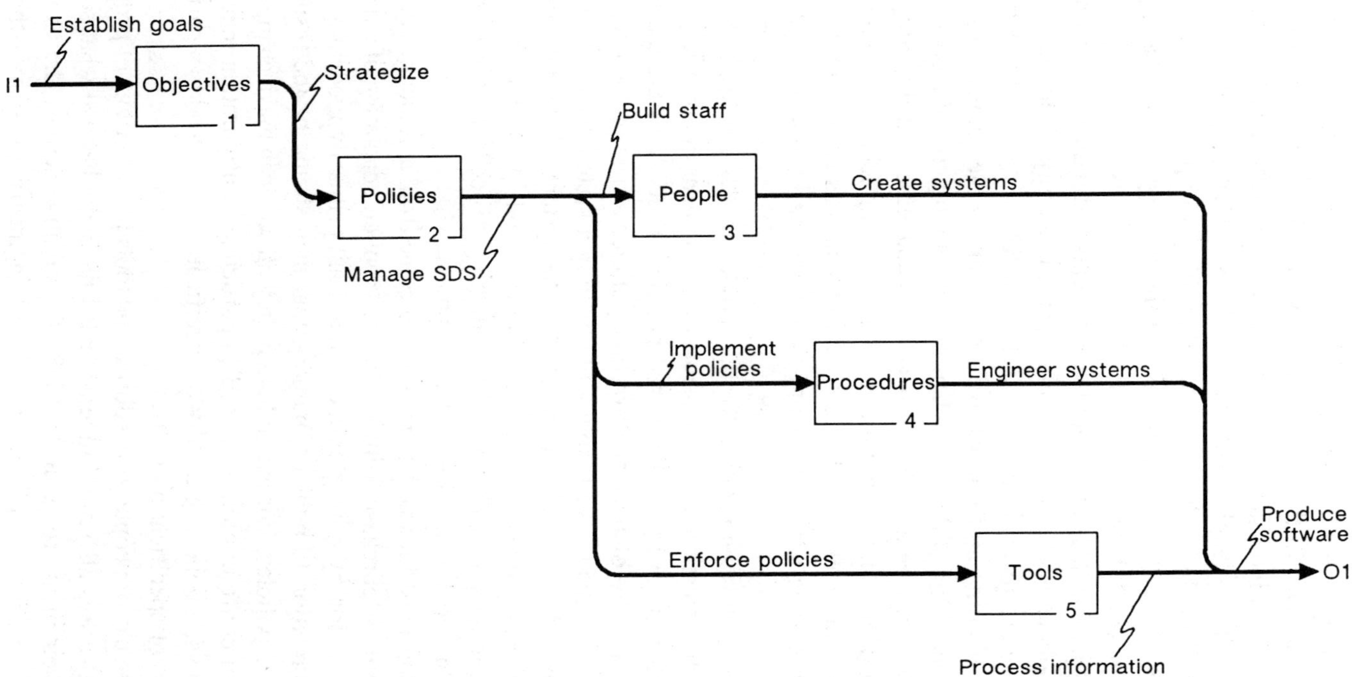


FIGURE 4.4 What Gets Managed?

taking a very systematic and rational approach, including teamwork and manufacturing considerations—draws most on procedures. In this context and given the present state of the art, tools are primarily used by the activity of processing the information with which the SDS must deal (e.g., libraries, specifications, trouble reports, configurations, etc.).

Figure 4.5 adds the final component of the SDS—"Information"—and indicates (as we would hope!) that it is used by the management activity. "Information" is produced by the activity of maintaining an SDS at the current state of the art—essentially by importing information from outside the SDS—and by the development activity itself ("Produce software"). Since I am trying to make the model as general as possible, I have shown that information is both produced by and used by the "Produce software" activity in accord with the view developed in Chapter 1. A specific example is reusability, in which during development information (e.g., a design) generated on a previous project may be reused and/or information generated is saved for future reuse.[4.7]

Additionally, some important connections between "People," "Procedures," and "Tools" are shown in this diagram. It is important to have procedures that support the creative work of the people in the system; this is indicated in the model by showing that the activity of "Support creative work" takes as input "People" (obviously, characteristics of people) and produces "Procedures" (which match the needs of the people). Likewise, the caveat that "Tools" should support "Procedures" is indicated by the activity shown connecting those two boxes.

So far so good; we have all the parts of the SDS shown and connected in a fashion that seems to make sense (remembering, once again, that we are not trying to show every detail). But wait! There is something very important to the systems way of thinking that is missing; do you see what it is?

Look carefully. I haven't shown any feedback! The whole system, so far, will be set up, run, and the objectives and policies will never change. That is clearly a distortion of reality and not in keeping with the systems approach at all.

Figure 4.6 closes the loop by adding the all-important activities of measuring the elements of the SDS and producing some additional

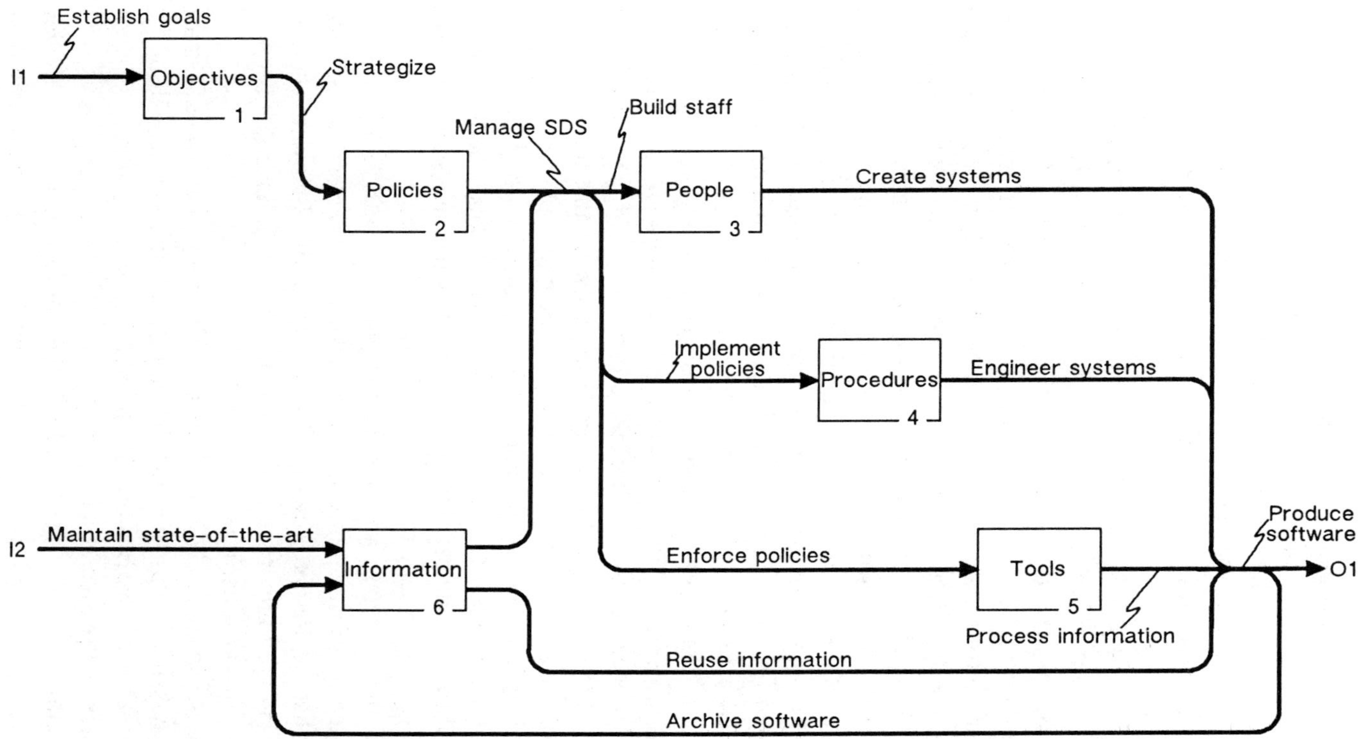


FIGURE 4.5 Information and Some Connections

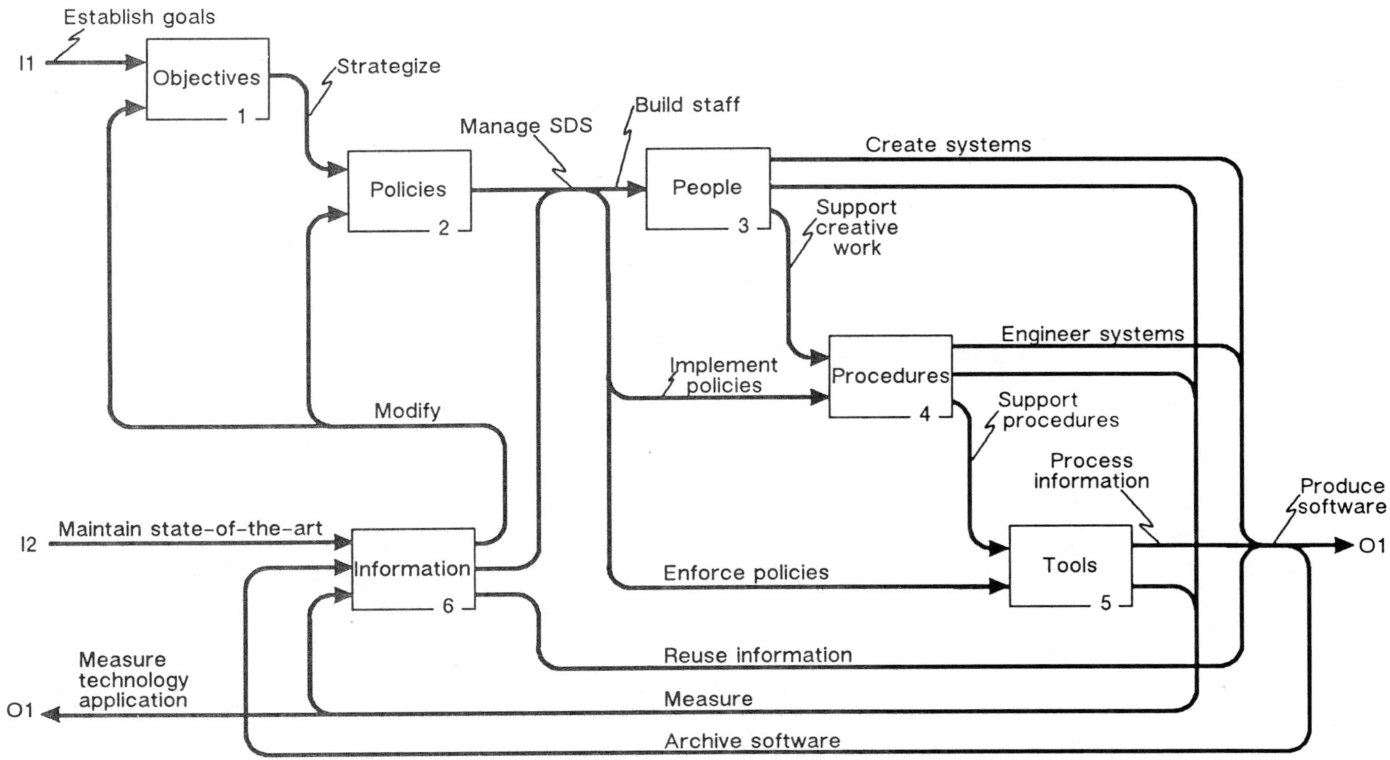


FIGURE 4.6 Closing the Loop!

"Information" (the data on the operation of the SDS) which is used by the activity of modifying the "Policies" and "Objectives" (on the basis of the measurements that have been taken). Both *process* measurements (how well does a tool or procedure work) and *product* measurements (how does its use effect quality measures of interest) must be taken.

We have about reached the limit of detail possible in a diagram such as this; if we start adding more, the result will be a loss of understanding rather than an increase. (This would be handled in a more complete model by producing additional diagrams that show the detail inside individual boxes and the fine structure of the connections between them.)

Figure 4.7 presents the structural model we have been building up and adds some of the elements (the dashed boxes) outside the SDS which are critical to it. Note in particular the addition of a line from "Software systems" indicating that the measuring activity also generates information from them; this is a critical class of information for control of the SDS.

There is a certain artificiality in modeling the software itself that is highlighted by this last addition. I have previously noted that the software was included in the class of objects labeled "Information"; now I have added a specific box, outside the boundary of the SDS, labeled "Software systems" which we want to be sure and measure. Where is the software?

In fact, it is in both places. For our purposes here, it suffices to think of the software as being in the "Information" box as long as it is under the control of the SDS and in the box labeled "Software systems" once it has been delivered to the customer. If the purpose of our model was different, for example, to study the proper structure for configuration management of software, then we would need a more accurate model of the different states of the software.

The proper way to show a system in its context is not to just keep adding boxes as I did in Fig. 4.7, but to encapsulate the entire diagram in a single box, carefully preserving the connections to the outside. Figure 4.8 does this for the SDS, placing it in a slightly larger context. Since you are now a proficient SADT diagram reader, I will not tire you with further explanation!

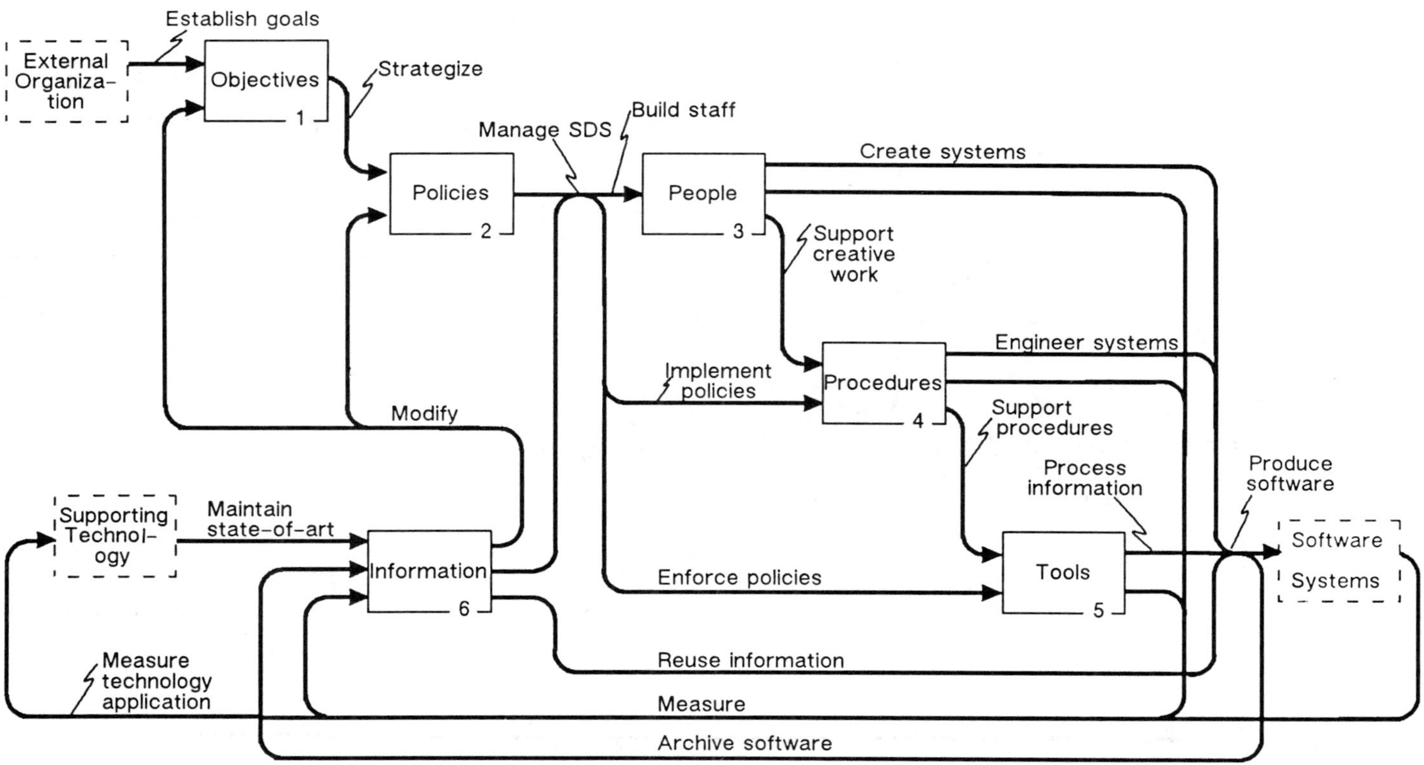


FIGURE 4.7 Structural Model of the SDS

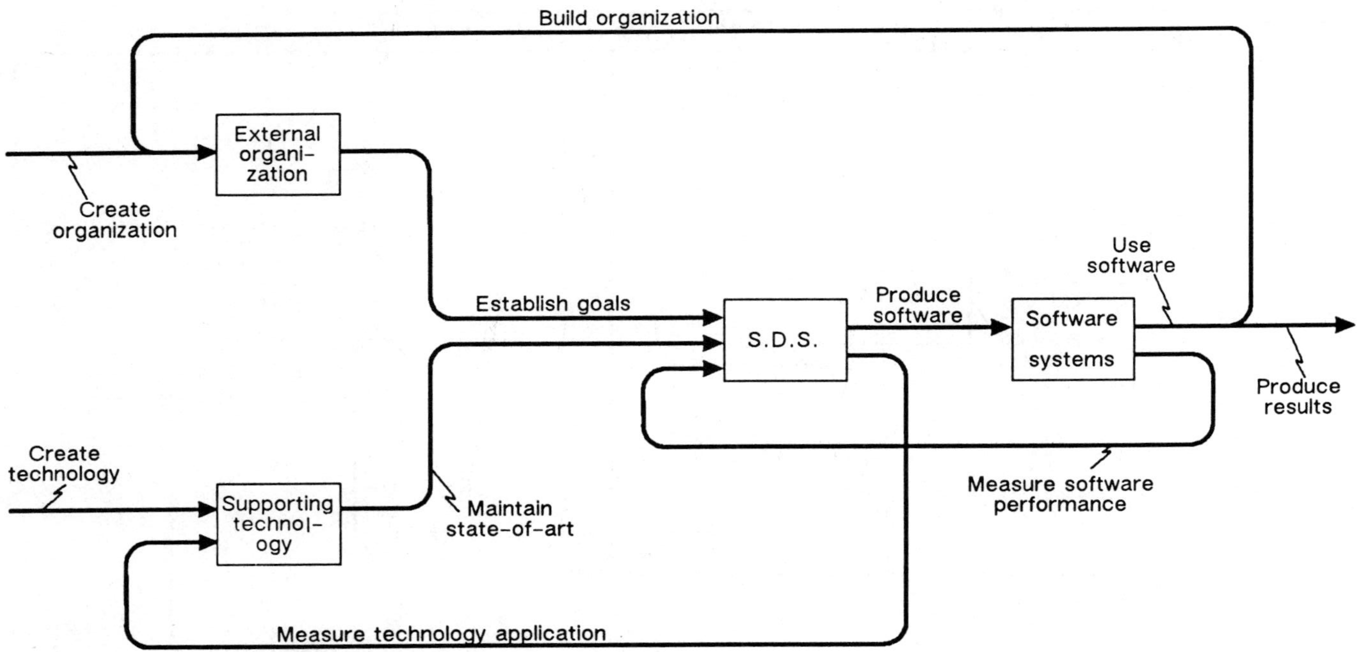


FIGURE 4.8 The SDS in Its Environment

## 4.7 The Larger Picture

Figure 4.7 presents a very simple model as seen by a manager taking a rational view of the SDS by itself. Models such as this are intended to capture some aspect of reality, not just provide an illustration of concepts, and, indeed, this one does.

I have laid out the diagram to emphasize what I have observed as some important realities about the elements of an SDS: "Objectives" and "Policies" have a close tie, and taken together are a prime input to the "Manage" function. "People," "Procedures," and "Tools" are connected, among other ways, in a very logical fashion by a natural ordering of support: "Procedures" result from a process which takes "People" as an input and effective "Tools" result from a process which takes "Procedures" as input. This models the reality of development: *People* do a procedure, not the other way around. Likewise, a *tool* can't be substituted for getting people commited to a procedure (such as carefully designing system interfaces); if you try, the technical process will ultimately fail (and the product with it). Tools (including some well-known ones) that are not tied to a well-thought-out procedure will probably never be successful.

These three elements of the SDS, then, taken as a group, are the prime input to the process "Develop software," which is our ultimate focus of interest. Underlying and tying it all together is "Information." Again, this mirrors reality in which people, procedures, and tools are the primary factors affecting the development process, and information is what all three operate on.

(If you are still not used to this somewhat mechanistic way of looking at a situation, let me provide a simple translation that may help you. In prose, I am simply saying that the management activity in this rational view of successful development is driven by policies and objectives and that tools should be chosen to support procedures, which in turn have been chosen to support the people in the group. I am further noting that the technical development work is done by the people, procedures, and tools, all of which are managed by a central management function.)

At this level, it should be easy to see that Fig. 4.7 can also represent a specific development project, as well as all possible software development systems as I have intended it here. Taking it in this way, if you are providing an SDS for a specific project, you must choose objectives and policies for the project, pick personnel, procedures, and tools that are appropriate, ensure that necessary information is available and handled properly, and develop the software.

As you start to use this highly simplified model, remember that many details have been left out to make it more understandable. Our purpose here is to illustrate, not perform a complete analysis. Further, remember that this is specifically a rational, "as it should be," view; reality in a particular situation may be quite different! One value of the model, however, is to provide a standard against which *your* reality can be measured.

> *Even a very simple model of a SDS can be useful in answering operational questions about it.*

Models are to be used and in spite of the simplifications, we can use this simple model to answer some questions. For example, imagine you are building your SDS from scratch and wonder what the consequences will be of buying a new development tool? The model tells us that if the tools are there first, then either we have thus also chosen a procedure (the one supported by the tool) or our procedures will not have tool support (assuming another tool cannot be purchased). (This relationship between procedures and tools is based on the fact that procedures, when carried out by humans, are active elements that require support by tools, not the other way around.)

Another way we can use the model is to ask how the SDS should interact with the environment. Figure 4.8 was based on the assumption that the SDS was embedded in an organization in which the task was to create software for existing machines. But suppose yours is an organization that produces products that are composed of special-purpose hardware plus software (a telecommunications device, for example). In this situation, it is likely that there will be a close tie between the hardware development and the software development.

Now what will the ties be between the SDS and the rest of the organization? You might choose to have analogous policies for managing both developments; what does this mean in terms of the information needed, types of measurements to make, activities to establish and modify policies? These kinds of questions can be investigated in terms of a model (especially if it is a bit more detailed and specific than the one presented here) both to see the result of proposed changes and to understand the requirements for doing things differently.

This structural model should be sufficient to give a little meaning to the concept of a software development system, at least in terms of its parts and roughly how they fit together. The fine structure of the connections is important, but studying it is well beyond the scope of this book.

Now that we have a picture of the parts, it is time to start considering how they should work together to achieve the results you want. Following the general systems approach, let's start that consideration by looking at objectives for the SDS.

CHAPTER

# 5

# The Development Process

CHAPTER

# 5

# The Development Process

*Get good counsel before you begin: and when you have decided, act promptly.*

— *Schiller Catilina*

5.1 Purpose (introduction)

5.2 The Basic Functions of Development (simple functional model)

5.3 Derivative Functions—That May Be More Important! (the bigger picture)

5.4 How to Do It (conclusion)

Photos Courtesy of Ford Motor Company

## 5.1 Purpose

That an SDS creates software, goes without saying.

Whether the SDS you are concerned with is simply the environment you are creating for yourself to develop some programs for your PC or for an entire company of several thousand people, it starts with some kind of request for software (it may be very vague, simply a statement of a problem needing some kind of solution) and then produces (in some way) the software (or an explanation of why it can't). This mainline function is clear.

It is all the surrounding possibilities for action that are confusing!

*Should the developers also operate the software?* Probably not, unless it is for a PC for themselves.

*Should they maintain the software or is that the responsibility of another group? If it is, what does that group do that is different?* There are strong arguments both ways.

*How do you tell the difference between maintenance of software and new development?* By relative amount of new software, percent change to existing software, objectives.

*If software is the organization's end product, does delivery and installation of the software belong with development?* Probably not, although there should be strong ties between the two organizations.

*If you are in an organization that develops integrated software and hardware systems (for example, process control systems for manufacturing), who does the overall systems engineering work?* The most important thing is to make sure they (whoever they are) have the proper skills for doing it.

The answer to each of these questions (which, of course, should be more refined) has an impact on the objectives for the SDS. So, even though you thought you knew what the SDS does, it may not be quite so easy to establish it in practice. Further, the characteristics of effective objectives are more subtle than those of a simple "Take the hill!" objective.

To help you answer questions of this type, let's begin by looking at the main-line functional aspects of the SDS. Before we do, I must warn my technical colleagues that Fig. 5.1 is *not* what you think it is; see the discussion under "A Simple Model," below.

## 5.2 The Basic Functions of Development

### Technical Processes

There is a heightened concern in the technical software engineering community about the *process* of software development: What are the appropriate activities and in what sequence should they be taken? This important concern, long overdue, and the improvements that should come from it do not change the underlying nature of the problem. No matter what policies, methods, and tools are applied, there are four fundamental things that must happen in development (as shown in Fig. 5.1):

1. *Analysis*: We must understand the problem to be solved. What are the constraints on possible solutions? What are the details of the objectives to be met? Does what the customer *really* need differ from what he *thinks* he wants? This must result in a clear specification of what is to be created (or an indication of why the problem is unsolvable as stated) and a clear indication of the conditions under which the customer will accept a solution.
2. *Design*: A feasible solution to the specification must be created. The parts must be chosen in order to meet the requirements and the constraints on the solutions. Technical problems must be solved. Blueprints for the construction phase, including testing plans, must be prepared.
3. *Construction*: The solution must be built, parts tested and integrated into larger assemblies, the entire system tested against the technical specifications, and, finally, tested by the customer or his representative for acceptance.
4. *Delivery*: Even in those cases where the developer is also the direct user, the system must be delivered. User documentation must be made to conform to the system as built. Maintenance documentation must be prepared that describes the system and its design so that it can be maintained in the future. Master copies of source code must be put into archival libraries.

These activities are implied by the nature of the task of taking a need and producing a software-intensive system that meets that need.

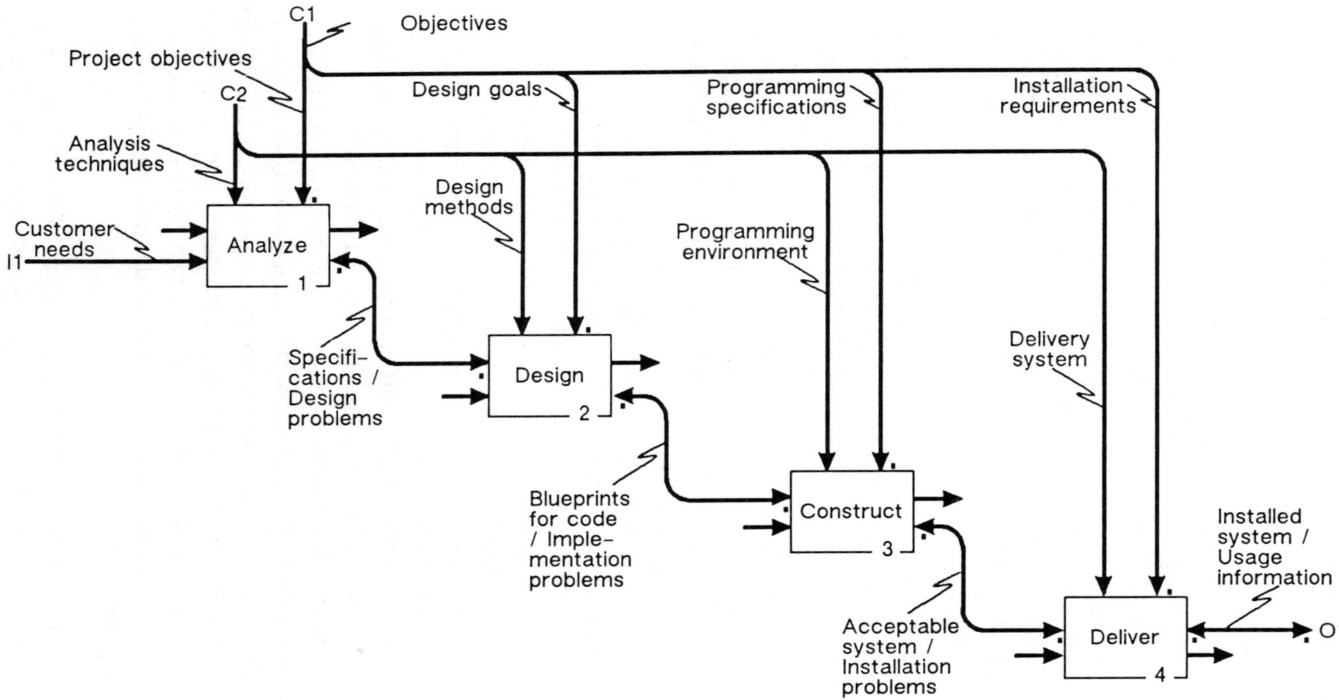


FIGURE 5.1 Basic Functions of Development

Even if you do not write a single line of program but merely buy the software in a standard package, you still go through some semblance of analyzing the problem, designing a solution (in this case, finding one in a catalog), constructing it (actual purchase), and delivery (installing it on your machine). The research, development, discussion, and arguments about various methods, tools, and processes for developing software may make some aspects of this basic process easier or less critical, but they will not change the need for understanding, planning, construction, and delivery.

## A Simple Model

Figure 5.1, an SADT actigram, appears to be the traditional "waterfall" lifecycle model (discussed in Appendix A). It is very important to understand that in spite of the visual simularity, this is *not* the case. The figure represents the fundamental activities that must take place in *any* engineering or design activity. The diagram appears to indicate a sequence of activities, but in the SADT notation the connections indicate constraints between activities which *may* be occurring at the same time. Thus, for example, the diagram indicates that construction cannot take place until design occurs, but it is not precluded that *some* construction may be taking place while the design of some *other* part is occurring simultaneously (i.e., prototyping).

There are additional differences. First, as an SADT diagram, each activity must have a control that indicates what constrains that particular function; that is typically missing in the lifecycle diagrams that currently spark so much argument. Second, an SADT actigram is a *data*-flow diagram, not a *control*-flow diagram (which is the popular interpretation of lifecycle diagrams).

The interpretation in a data-flow diagram is that an activity is considered to be operating when all its required inputs and controls are present. This means that it is possible for all the activities in the diagram to be operating simultaneously, or that they operate in some sequence other than left to right.

As with the structural models in the previous chapter, this model fragment is rather incomplete. To remind you of that, there are some unmarked arrows to indicate there is more to be included in the model. The adjective "required" used above in describing the activation rules, although vague in the context of a high-level model, is very important since it means that a particular function may be triggered even if all the inputs and controls shown are not present. (The conditions under which this could happen could be modeled precisely if we made the model more detailed by adding additional diagrams showing the expansion of the higher-level diagrams.)

> *The basic activities of development may take place at a number of different times, not just in a single, chronological sequence of activities.*

Let's look at a special case of some practical interest. It is common to find toward the end of a development that the system does not meet some part of the customer's acceptance criteria. This usually generates rework to bring those parts into line; meanwhile work on the other parts can proceed. Depending on the severity of the problem, some additional design work (not just "fixes" to the program code) may be called for, meaning that we would have construction and design work underway simultaneously. The model could represent this simply by the addition of an output from the "Construct" function that fed back to "Design" (either as a control or as an input) which would indicate under what conditions "Design" might be reinitiated.

Another critical thing to understand about the technical activities in software development is that they are not all performed in discrete time frames. The way we typically name the chronological phases of development work tends to indicate that all the analysis work is done during the "Analyze" phase or that all the design work is done during the "Design" phase. That isn't the way it happens.

We call the early chronological period "Analyze" because that is indeed the time when we are focusing on the analysis activity. However, we may also be doing some design to see if our understanding of the problem can be translated into a solution; we may actually do some construction if we build a quick prototype in order to study the desired characteristics of alternative solutions; we may be doing some testing to determine if the analysis results are what we intended. In short, there is an underlying set of development activities that may be employed in any of the chronological phases of development.

Current research and experimentation with different lifecycles basically comes down to finding for specific situations the most appropriate connections of the form discussed above: Should errors found in

"Construct" cause redesign, reanalysis, or both? Under what conditions? How do we control design so that some construction can begin before the design is completed? Appendix A discusses several different lifecycle paradigms. Models such as this are quite useful in providing a setting in which such questions can be discussed without ambiguity and in which at least some of the interconnections of the situation can be determined without finding them the hard way. The next time there is a discussion in your shop about alternative development paths, see if you can frame the questions in terms of a model such as this; you may be surprised at the results.

As you have probably noticed, Fig. 5.1 indicates no coordinated control between the various technical functions. While individual activities, such as design, can be fashioned to be self-operating, if we want this collection of functional elements to work together as a system, then the dynamic and variable nature of the system demands that we have some explicit management.

### Tying Management and Technical Activity Together

Figure 5.2 adds this dimension by wrapping a management activity around the four technical activities in a very specific way. On the one hand, management supplies resources (which it has obtained from outside the SDS) in the form of people and development resources used to carry out the technical functions; this is indicated by the mechanism arrows on each activity that are supplied by the "Manage" box.

The second, and most important, tie between management and the technical functions is modeled by the control lines on each box that are supplied by the management function. The individual technical functions are controlled to some extent by the technical aspects of the objectives imposed on the SDS by the external environment. Management, too, is controlled by these objectives, responding more to the resource and organizational aspects. One of the primary functions of the management of an SDS, however, is to help interpret these objectives for the technical functions and, where necessary, to establish priorities and to resolve conflicts.

### Feedback

Figure 5.2 models another critical aspect of a successful SDS: the feedback of information among individual technical functions as well as between them and the SDS management. This aspect could have

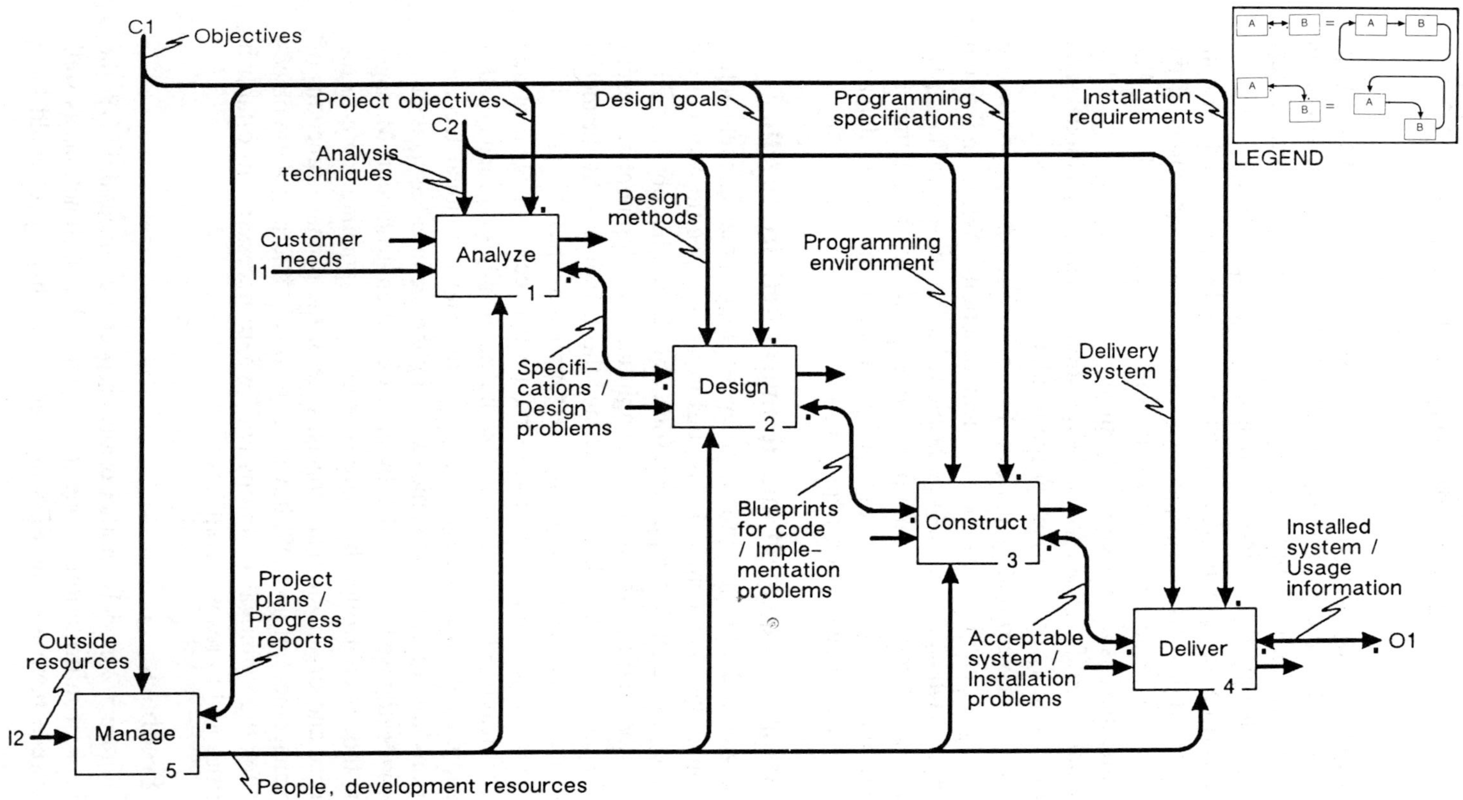


FIGURE 5.2 Technical Functions Coupled with Management

been shown as a specific feedback line output from each box and running to the other boxes; to keep the diagram visually manageable, I have used a short-hand notation of SADT intended for this kind of situation where two (or more) boxes are coupled in a feedback loop (the notation is shown in the legend of Fig. 5.2). In effect, this indicates that every function in the SDS has the potential of producing information that will affect the operation of another function, including management.

The dot by an arrowhead indicates this feedback situation; the label on the arrow shows the feedback object after the slash following the label on the forward-moving object. So, for example, "Manage" produces "Project plans" and receives back "Progress reports" (which include technical feedback as well as schedule and resource usage). The feedback between technical functions is labeled "problems," but this should be interpreted loosely; the flow of information between functions should be much broader than just problem reports.

As with the structural model, the technical accuracy of this model fragment (a complete model should contain several more levels of detail) breaks down if pushed too hard. Strictly speaking, the diagram does not indicate any feedback from "Construct" to "Analyze" except via "Design"; while that is the primary communication pair, there are often times when "Analyze" communicates directly with the "Construction" function. I will trust the reader's common sense to take the broader interpretation where appropriate since these are only illustrative models.

## Supporting the SDS

Figure 5.3 completes the functional model by adding the critical function of "Support." This support function provides the tools, methods, procedures, standards, development machines, and training that are an important constraint on the capabilities of the individual technical functions. ("Constraint" is used here in the sense that without them, those activities would be rather different.)

This is a relatively new function in many software development organizations, but is a standard component in many other situations. Hardware engineering organizations always have draftsmen and technicians; lumber mills have people whose only job is to keep the saws sharpened; hospitals have people to maintain the equipment used in the operating rooms; and so on. These other professions and activities

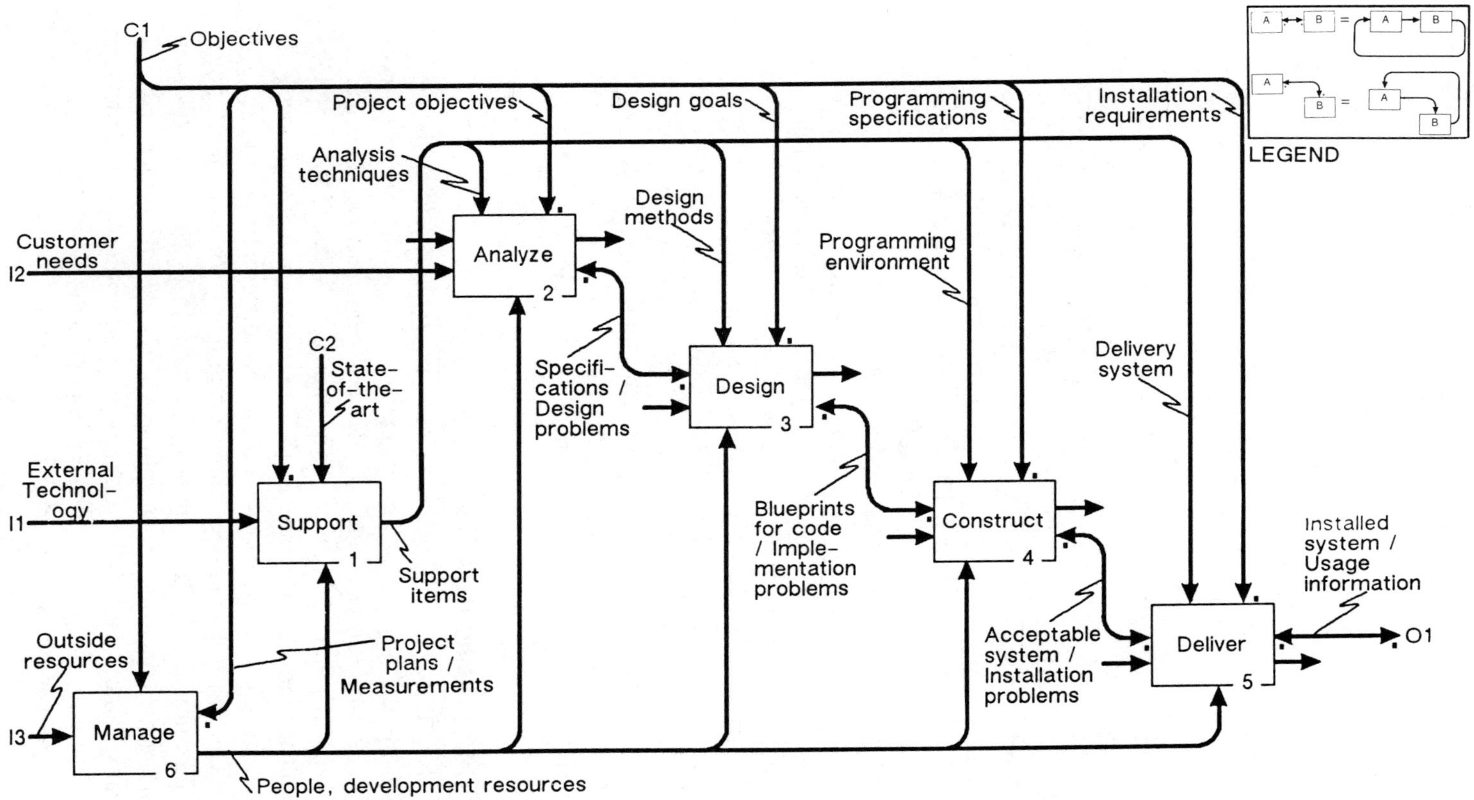


FIGURE 5.3 Functional Model of the SDS

have recognized and institutionalized the fact that their main function must be supported properly if it is to be productive and effective.

> *A formal support activity is an essential part of a modern SDS.*

Far from being a luxury, a proper support function is increasingly an essential component of any software development organization. The increasing complexity, depth, and professionalism of the software field is not unlike the development of medicine years ago. Whereas physicians once performed their own blood tests, sterilized their own implements, and made their own appointments, we recognize now that in most situations those support activities are probably better performed by someone else, permitting the medical doctor to concentrate on diagnosis and treatment. Further, in complex medical situations such as major surgery, there is a need for specialists such as anesthesiologists who can perform certain complex activities better than the primary physician because they have focused on them. Software development has entered that degree of complexity and has the same strong demands for productivity that make support activities of many kinds essential; to ignore it is to court disaster.

Five or six years ago an aerospace organization with which I am familiar had no formalized support group for their primary software development group. Then, as the criticality of software in their operations became apparent and they began looking for ways to improve the quality of their products, they undertook to improve the level of support for their software developers. Today, they have a group of approximately 120 persons whose primary task is to support the main development division of approximately 1200 professionals. They determine the needs for tools, training, and methods, build or buy them, and install them in their operational context. They teach courses, provide training on new languages and consultation on the intricacies of languages, operating systems, tools, and other support items. They develop standards in conjunction with the developers covering everything from stylistic guides for programming to protocols for intermachine data communication. In short, they do whatever they can to support the basic activities of development; this is an important factor in their reputation as a leading-edge development organization.

A second aerospace organization is just today starting to realize that the unsupported way in which they develop software is courting disaster—both financial and technical. Because of structural changes in the industry, they are now competing with organizations, such as the previous one, that are able to produce higher-quality software at a lower cost, even though they may have less expertise in other areas. Unfortunately, this organization still hasn't completely understood the critical need that is going unmet in their SDS. I suspect a real failure will be necessary to shock them into realization of the role of support in the SDS.

Devoting 10 percent of one's resources to a support activity is not uncommon today in sophisticated organizations that work on complex systems. Obviously, many organizations cannot devote that much to support—or think they can't. Before automatically rejecting the notion, however, take a careful look at what payoffs in improved quality and productivity could be purchased by providing more support to your development personnel.

The source for such support can vary widely. A large, sophisticated aerospace company will generally have to provide much of its own support internally because of the nature of their needs. However, a small, commercially oriented organization can probably buy most of the tools and training needed from outside sources on an as-needed basis. It is essential, though, that they have a clear understanding of what their SDS is like and what its support needs really are; if not, then random purchases of new methods or tools will change the SDS in ways that probably will not be beneficial in the long run.

## Don't Confuse Physical and Logical

One of the most common mistakes people make in trying to understand an organization or an activity is the confusion of logical function with physical entities. In Fig. 5.3, we might just as well have one person performing all six functions or one thousand performing each; the diagram tells us nothing about that since it is a logical diagram. My concern so far has been to make sure you understand what the underlying functions of development are. While I will address later some of the questions of how to staff such a functional organization and whether some functions should or should not be carried out by the same person, for the most part these are issues that can only be completely addressed in specific situations.

Now that we are clear on the mainline function of development, let's look at some of the other possibilities for activities for the group or person labeled the "software group."

## 5.3 Derivative Functions—That May Be More Important!

In the case studies in Chapter 3 one of the critical factors in each case was the group's understanding of what their function should be. In the first case, they failed to understand that in their organization people wanted solutions, not software; in the second case, they understood this. In the larger picture, that is a general truth. People want solutions to problems so that they can get on with *their* work, not software which may cause them more problems.

Yet that is an all-encompassing generality like "Reach the moon by the end of the decade." It does not necessarily help you make day-to-day decisions (although it certainly should help you formulate appropriate strategies). Let's take a look at some of the specific functions that the software group may have to take on. Note, by the way, that I am broadening the definition from just the "development" group, since in many situations anyone who deals with software in any way will automatically inherit everything dealing with software.

### Operations

Operating computers has very little to do with what goes on inside them. If you have a machine that must be "operated" (most today don't) in a large-scale operation of submitting data, mounting tapes, distributing paper output, and so on, don't expect the software people to do it, or vice versa. The type of work and the type of personality needed to do it successfully are quite different.

There are two situations in which the technical people also must deal with some operational tasks. Small shops that utilize modern equipment often will have only two or three persons in the computer group. Their primary responsibility will usually be development, but since the computers themselves are largely self-operating, they may have to double as operators in those infrequent instances when those tasks arise. That is fine as long as it is understood that those tasks are distracting from their primary work.

The second situation is harder to describe since the person involved is neither technical nor an operations specialist. In this situation a person (who may or may not have technical training in some other field) has a personal computer for which he or she is creating software. If he or she merely acquires standard commercial software and never builds up databases or produces output needed by someone else, then we can dismiss them from our concern.

Unfortunately, the latter set of conditions rarely exists. Especially in the area of databases and output data sets, organizations are finding that many problems of compatibility, proliferation of similar programs or data, quality, and so on are appearing. In this situation, even though the boundaries between operation, creation of the software (including data), and functional usage may be fuzzy, many of the concepts that might seem primarily applicable to larger organizations come into play.

## Purchase of Software

Increasingly, software is purchased in finished form from a vendor, installed on the customer's machine, and used without modification. Even in situations where standard packages can't be used, buying custom software from an outside vendor with none of the technical work done by your organization is common.

Some groups that are responsible for developing a system that includes special-purpose hardware and other gear will do the analysis and system design in-house and have the programming done outside; integration of the components of the total system is usually done in-house since it demands the overview of the whole systemthat comes from doing the analysis and design work in the first place. (Integration and installation also normally require a fair amount of understanding of the people and organization, which an outsider does not have.) An example of this type of situation is development of a process-control system for an industrial situation.

In all of these situations, these are entirely reasonable tasks for the software group to undertake; the decision is largely one of economics and effective use of resources. Remember that the basic functions we discussed above were framed in terms of understanding (analysis), solving a problem (design), building (construction), and installation (delivery); if some of these tasks can be carried out by buying the solution, fine. Indeed, purchase of software is often an excellent idea because it reduces risk. On the other hand, purchase of analysis and design services is much riskier because the outside people may have difficulty understanding all the factors in a complex organization which is new to them (although there are positive reasons such as a fresh viewpoint for using outsiders). The important thing to remember is that the basic tasks must be carried out somehow.

I would add that in some organizations, purchase of software for personal computers is now handled almost as one would handle the purchase of a typewriter or some routine piece of equipment or even a stock item like envelopes. That changes the nature of the acquisition process so that the cycle outlined above probably doesn't apply except in a very rudimentary form. That is OK as long as the customer is getting what he or she needs (not just what they think they need).

### Evolution (a.k.a. Maintenance)

Purchase and operation are straightforward tasks which generally cause no great difficulty in managing an SDS. Evolution (also known as maintenance) of software is another matter; it not only consumes a very large fraction of many software budgets (sometimes exceeding 90 percent), but it is often unclear to whom the task belongs: Should it be handled by the development group or placed in a separate organization?

Before we explore that question, let's look more closely at what we mean by "evolution." The common term for everything that happens to a piece of software after its initial development is "maintenance." That is rather confusing since the term also describes things like changing the oil on your car and putting a new roof on your house—activities that are aimed at keeping something in its current state or at replacing parts worn out by use.

Software neither wears out nor needs to have something added to it just to keep it doing what it now does. So what is it that we are doing in software maintenance? Three things, really: repair, adaptation, and enhancement. The term "evolution"[5.1] seems much better to describe this collection of activities since as we adapt and enhance software it changes, or evolves. Unfortunately, the entrenched usage of "maintenance" makes it doubtful we will soon get away from it.

There is no question that software is sometimes in need of repair. A parameter is wrong, a calculation is incorrect, a device is not initialized. In short, its behavior is clearly in disagreement with its intended behavior and it must be repaired. Unless there has been some actual change to the software through a mistake, it hasn't actually broken, but it is close enough to it that "maintenance" is a good descriptor. That is undoubtedly how the usage of the term came about.

Unfortunately, only a small part of what is called maintenance (sometimes as low as 10 percent) falls into this category.[5.2] The remainder changes the software from its original specifications through either adaptation or enhancement.

Adaptation occurs when we preserve the function of the software but must adapt it to a new set of operating conditions. Changing a system to work with a new and larger storage device or a new display terminal or a more efficient algorithm are all instances of adaptation. The main thrust is changing the implementation, not the functionality. This accounts for maybe another 30 percent of the maintenance activity (there are few studies that provide any accurate breakdowns; even the amount spent on evolution versus initial development is often unclear).

Enhancement seems to be the big consumer of evolution budgets. Tax laws change and we need to add a new function to the payroll program to indicate how much, for example, an employee can invest in a tax-free investment program; the inventory management program turns out to be a big hit with the operations staff and they suggest some additional functions they would like to add to the program; several machine centers on the factory floor are now computer controlled quite successfully and it is desired to hook them together—these are examples of enhancement in which we must add to or change in significant ways the functionality of a piece of software.

There is no question that evolution must take place. Software, especially large and complex systems, cannot be thrown away every time a change is needed. And changes will always be needed because software very rapidly becomes a part of the environment in which it operates and almost any environment changes over time.

Even though there is no question of the inevitability of evolution, there are plenty of questions on *how* evolution should take place. Essentially, adaptation and enhancement are the same as new development that is very tightly constrained with respect to the possible results of the development. Unfortunately, it is not often treated this way.

In many ways, evolution is the most demanding technical work in software development because of the constraints and the often poor state of design documentation. Yet it is common practice to put newhires, the least experienced people in the organization, on maintenance tasks as a way of breaking them in. (What usually gets broken is the software.)

> *Evolution of software is a demanding task that in some ways is the most challenging work in software. In effect, it is tightly constrained development.*

With this preamble out of the way, let's come back to the question of where evolution belongs.

In small shops, there is no question. Everyone does everything.

In larger groups, evolution certainly belongs in an SDS, that is, in a group that is organized systematically along the lines discussed above. So, it comes down to whether the same group should do initial development *and* evolution.

The repair portion of evolution clearly belongs to the people that built it in the first place. Professional responsibility alone would indicate that.

Adaptation and enhancement are harder to call. In some cases, an entire organization (SDS) is dedicated to a single system for many years at a time (a complex telecommunications system, for example); there is a mix of continuing development (new versions of the basic system) and more traditional evolution. In this case, clearly the base of knowledge about the system is so great that it would be senseless to differentiate in any strict way between new development and evolution.

In shops where the systems produced are not so mammoth (say, the DP department of a medium-sized corporation) and there is a continual flow of new development as well as evolution, this question is more sharply defined. While there is no completely obvious answer, in general, it seems better to mix the new development and the evolution for several reasons: much evolution work is essentially new development and should have the same controls and discipline applied to it; the knowledge of more experienced people (who may have helped build the system being enhanced) can be utilized; analysis of existing designs, which must take place during evolution, may lead to better designs next time, especially if the designers and enhancers are in close communication.

The issue of where to place evolution is largely one of management and job assignment since technically it is primarily a constrained form of development. In terms of management (and general organization of the SDS doing the evolution), it seems clear that the same structures and procedures are needed, with some additional controls (e.g., configuration or version management and regression testing) added to insure the integrity of the system being evolved. The job assignment question is one of specialization versus generality, as well as one of how to get good people to work on what is often viewed as an uninteresting job. We will consider that later.[5.3]

## System Engineering

As computers increasingly become a part of larger systems that encompass many kinds of equipment, the question naturally arises as to who should do the overall engineering for these systems. In many older manufacturing organizations, for example, engineering groups have been designing and building complex manufacturing systems for years. To some, the addition of the computer, and more especially, the software, is just another component to be handled in the same way as machine tools and power relays.

This doesn't work.

If the larger system is being built by people who understand the concept of a system and if they understand the special problems connected with integrating software into an overall system, then it may work for the overall system direction to be done by someone outside the computer area. Unfortunately, this is rare.

What it often comes down to is that computer systems, and in particular the software parts of them, are the most complex types of systems ever built. ("Complexity" can mean different things, but typically the number of parts, number of interconnections, and intricacy of operation are predominant factors; on all these, software systems are highly complex.) Add to that the fact that dealing with abstract entities like software systems requires a new set of tools and abilities to deal with conceptual products, and we have a situation in which quite often only the "computer people" have the skills and tools to fashion large and complex systems in which software is a critical component.

If I may be permitted a bit of prediction, I believe we will see the growth of a new systems engineering discipline in the next few years that will be oriented not toward closed, mathematically tractable systems (such as current systems engineering techniques are oriented toward) but toward the large, open systems that are characteristic of what we find when we use the computer to integrate a number of other smaller systems (for example, in factory automation). The people with the skills to do that are to be found for the most part in SDSs.

*The demands of software systems are leading to a new form of systems engineering.*

That does not mean that professionals in other disciplines do not have something to offer, of course. Rather, it means that the unique nature of software—being entirely abstract and having no basis in a physical science—is forcing us to develop new ways of dealing with complex systems in the software field that are extendible to other types of systems that are also largely abstract (or that can be represented abstractly).

The type of skills and knowledge necessary are not just what one gets when trained as a programmer (although that may be a start); indeed, some of us would argue that a much broader education is needed for computer scientists. However, increasingly in situations in which large complex systems must be designed and built, it is people with a background in software systems that seem to be able to best master the intellectual complexities of the situation. As we try to revitalize our industries, it is people able to deal with the essential characteristics of the underlying systems that may well be our best hope; certainly, it seems clear that almost total reliance on financial abstractions of industrial operations is not a productive path.

## 5.4 How To Do It

That is the subject of a fair number of textbooks, professional reference books, courses, and lectures.[5.4] For example, currently a topic of high interest is how to do a more effective job of determining the requirements for a complex system. There is no question that our practice of requirements analysis needs considerable improvement, both with respect to application of existing techniques as well as development of better methods and tools. Detailed consideration of the functions of development andd how to carry them out, however, is beyond the scope of this book.

My focus here is on how everything fits together to form an effective system for building the systems, so in the following chapters rather than focus on how to do *X*, I will describe the parts of the SDS in more detail. One of those parts—objectives—has already been discussed in some detail in Chapter 4 so we can proceed immediately to discussing the policies that drive the SDS. In passing so quickly over objectives, however, I don't want to leave the impression that they are unimportant or easy to determine. Quite the contrary. Beyond the discussion in Chapter 4, though, one is left in the realm of organizational dynamics and politics, human psychology, and general business philosophy.

CHAPTER
# 6
# Policies—The Software of the SDS

CHAPTER

# 6

# Policies—The Software of the SDS

*Laws too gentle are seldom obeyed; too severe, seldom executed.*

— *Benjamin Franklin Poor Richard's Almanac*



National Football League Properties, photo by David Boss

## 6.1 Where To Focus

Most of us are able to think of any number of interesting objectives. The thing that differentiates people—and development systems—is their ability to achieve those objectives.

I find it useful to think of the policies of an SDS as the programs that guide it. There are some important differences, however. The SDS cannot be so minutely programmed as can a computer—even if we knew what to tell it! Further, the most important element of the SDS, people, come with built-in programs and overriding policies (for example, professional and personal rules of conduct) that may make further policies redundant or ineffectual.

We rarely set up an SDS from scratch. That means that the policies a given SDS is following at any point in time are not only made up largely of those policies brought along by the people in the system, but by a large number of *de facto* policies that simply come about over time. While it is tempting to think in terms of establishing and following a policy, it may be just as accurate to think of a policy as an abstraction of the decisions and actions taken in an SDS.

The pragmatic issue, then, is which policies to focus on and explicitly shape in order to increase the chances of achieving the objectives established for your SDS. Specific policies will differ by type of software being built, the nature of the surrounding organization or market, and the maturity of the SDS and the people in it. In point of fact, one usually has control over only a small part of the total set of policies at any one time; further, only a few of those will have any dramatic impact on the operation of the SDS.

No one has perfect knowledge of which policies to give credit (or blame) to in any specific situation, let alone in general. The best that any of us can do is to provide some guidance as to those policies which seem to make a difference in real development situations. The purpose of this chapter is to focus on those few.

## 6.2 Integration of Technical and Organizational Policies

Ideally, every technical and organizational aspect of the SDS should work together toward a common goal—that is inherent in the definition of a system. While this ideal is never completely reached, it can be used as an organizing principle and applied:

- A technical method or tool should provide management with an enhanced ability to manage a project.
- A management structure or rule should provide the technical staff with enhanced ability to deal with the technical work of the project.

Every successful and exemplary instance of development systems that I know of has integrated technical and managerial structures and processes in ways that are productive for them. For example, a large government contractor has taken the rather extensive labor and schedule reporting requirements of government contracts and made them into a tool that helps the technical management keep track of what is happening on the project[6.1]; a small group supporting an engineering-design group with graphical design systems uses a system of on-line messages and weekly staff meetings to implement a low-key, but effective management system that keeps the group's output high and targeted on the main problems of their customers.

> *For every technical method or tool or procedure, there should be a management justification and for every management rule there should be a technical benefit.*

On the other hand, lack of integration invariably leads to problems: A process-control department responsible for building prototype systems was required to adhere to corporate financial reporting schedules that mandated lengthy, quarterly reviews; in spite of the large amount of time spent on them, the reviews were generally ineffective in assessing the status of the technical work since the mandated review dates rarely corresponded to any natural breakpoint in the software work. The result was development that was usually out of control.

Rationally, the strongest argument for integration is the added work caused by redundant organizational demands or the danger of out-of-control development if technical work is not tracked properly. The purpose of organizational structure is to track, guide, and report on the technical work; if it does not do double duty by providing something of use to the technical people, then it is simply overhead. Likewise, if technical work is performed that does not produce information useful for the organizational system, then that work is out of control (as far as the organization is concerned).

If we analyze the development system abstractly into two subsystems—one technical and one organizational—then simple systems reasoning implies that if the overall SDS is to work effectively, the two major subsystems must be properly integrated. It is preferable to look at it as a single system, however, in which individual policies have been formulated to integrate as much as possible the technical and organizational aspects of the specific situation with which the policy deals.

Some specific examples include:

- The critical position of first-level manager in the SDS *must* be filled by people who are both technically competent and managerially adept. These people are the primary interface between the technical and organizational subsystems; if they are not competent in both realms, the SDS will fail.
- Reviews should occur at points in time that correspond to logical divisions of the technical work. When reports must be generated at particular times of the year, they should build on existing technical reviews or made to augment the technical work in some way, not generate extra, nonproductive work.
- Technical methods should provide information that is useful to the organization for tracking and controlling the progress of the work. SADT, for example, clearly defines expected outputs, both in form and content, permitting easy management of its use by analysts.[6.2]
- Personnel policies should take into account the differing nature of skills needed in different technical positions. Performance reviews, for example, should measure how well the person contributes to the technical work, as well as more prosaic organizational measures such as promptness in submitting reports.
- Policies should exist which are effective in preventing high-level managers from making technical decisions in areas where they are not competent (for example, deciding which database system to use) and in preventing technical people from making organizational decisions when they are not competent in that area (for example, whether a particular feature will be offered to a customer or not).

For every technical aspect of the system, ask if it fits with the organizational system and supplies it some information or visibility of the technical work. For every organizational feature, ask if it fits with the technical process and in some way contributes to it.

Another way of looking at the principle of integration is to note that every new component of the SDS (technical or organizational) must fit into its local context. Integration then means that we must make sure that the new element either contributes to the interface between the management and technical subsystems or, at least, does not degrade it.

When the managerial and technical aspects work together, 2 + 2 = 5 (i.e., we get synergy); when they don't, 2 + 2 = 3 (i.e., conflict).

## 6.3 Some Basic Policies

Let's look at five classes of policies that are basic to the proper operation of the SDS, specifically those governing:

1. Work flow
2. Personnel roles
3. Quality standards and mechanisms
4. Methods and tools
5. Product integrity

There are no universal truths that I can magically provide for these policies. Ultimately, you must invest the hard work necessary to fashion them to the objectives and individual characteristics of your situation. Nonetheless, there are some features of each that appear again and again in successful environments (and that seem to be ignored in less successful ones).

### Work Flow

Development of software has a natural rhythm to it just as much as does a chemical reaction, the growth of a baby chick, or the course of diplomatic negotiations. Ignore it and you run the very real danger of destroying the process altogether or badly damaging the outcome. Learn to understand the sometimes subtle variations on the underlying process and you will be rewarded with enhanced control of the process and its outcomes.

That basic philosophy does not mean, as some would like to believe, that programmers should be left alone to "do their own thing." Indeed, there are a number of good arguments that the process should be more highly structured and systematic than the informal approach that is often followed: to focus attention on critical areas such as design, to prevent careless mistakes, to make it easier to identify technical problems, to make it easier to schedule work and budget resources, and so on.

The central policies of an SDS must structure the work flow in a way that is sensitive to the underlying nature of the technical tasks and responsive to the needs for visibility and control. This is typically done by establishing a lifecycle of steps or phases that a software development project must pass through and by defining a set of explicit workproducts that should be produced by the activity of each phase.

Lifecycles are currently one of the more hotly debated topics among software professionals because they are the visible embodiment of the software process. They are important because they incorporate critical policy decisions. It is important to remember, however, that lifecycles are really only *models* of reality, to concentrate on what that reality should be, and to be aware that there are many ways of shaping it.

Any development will go through stages of analysis, design, and construction. The issue is what emphasis to place on each phase and how to break each phase up into smaller and more manageable segments.

In general, it is wise to concentrate time and resources on the analysis and design activities, since a dollar spent there will often be worth ten or a hundred dollars spent later. The reason for that has been presented repeatedly in the literature and comes down to the simple fact that as in most things, understanding a problem and planning a solution, if done carefully, will help prevent mistakes during construction or operation that are very difficult and costly to fix. Additionally, there are critical properties of software, such as reliability, that cannot be added on to a system during construction; they must be *designed* in.

Programming is often viewed as problem solving; for example, many introductory computer science courses include "problem solving" in their titles. A well-understood principle of any problem-solving process is that you must understand the characteristics of the problem before you can rationally formulate a solution. In programming this corresponds to understanding the requirements for a program (or a software system) before starting the design or implementation of it.

What happens when this "natural" order is violated? Programs are written that do not provide what the customer needs, systems must be changed in major ways when it is discovered they violate the basic constraints of the situation they must deal with, and frustration follows delay follows confusion!

Consider another example. In their rush to deliver a piece of software, some try to cut corners by integrating all of the pieces of the system without adequately testing the individual pieces. One might think this would be OK since if the system doesn't work you can always find the malfunctioning parts.

Unfortunately, this is often not so easy since there is a natural order of making sure parts work before you integrate them into larger assemblies. The reasons behind this order are not terribly difficult to understand. A part buried inside a system, whether it be a fuel pump in a rocket or a subroutine in a system, is harder to fix than when it is sitting by itself; worse, it may be difficult to pinpoint exactly which component is giving rise to the observed erroneous behavior. And this doesn't even consider the fact that very often unacceptable system behavior is due to intercomponent interactions rather than individual components by themselves. The result: greatly complicated testing problems because the natural order of putting complex systems together has been violated.

> *Every software process has a natural order to it dictated by the nature of the technical work it is intended to accomplish. Make sure the policies you employ fit well with this natural order.*

## Personnel Roles

Systems development work is a new activity in many organizations, without much tradition or built-up culture. In that situation, a few explicit policies governing expected roles and responsibilities can be quite helpful.

The roles that different people in the organization are expected to play should be as clearly defined as possible. This provides a guide for the newcomer and serves as a reminder for those that have been with the group for a time. While there are far too many alternatives to cover properly here, there are a few personnel policies that stand out.

Having one person ultimately responsible for the technical work associated with a particular system, including the schedule and use of resources, is generally desirable. Of course, that person must have the authority and resources necessary to fulfill those responsibilities, an implication that is sometimes forgotten! Whether you organize along the lines of a chief-programmer team, an airplane crew, or a traditional project organization may depend on your particular environment.[6.3] The policy should be clear, however; one person is responsible for making sure that the end result is what is desired technically. (Obviously, for very large systems, this principle may be extended to provide for one person per subsystem, with one person having overall responsibility for the subsystems.)

This is a policy which may well be at variance with established practice in many organizations where the norm is that managers manage and technical people do the technical work. That attitude would lead to surgeons being directed in their operations by hospital administrators, professors in their research by deans, or musicians in their performances by their agents. In all these cases, there must be a productive cooperation between the manager and the professional. What seems clear to some of us, including some rather successful organizations, is that the technical work must drive the development and that there must be a clearly discernible focus for the responsibility.

The person in this position of responsibility must clearly accept the objectives of the SDS, as instantiated in the product being produced. He or she must be trained to think in terms of, and *report* objectively, what they are *accomplishing*, not just what they are doing.

This is also a policy that is at variance with current practice in many large engineering organizations. The day of the single technical genius who single-handedly drives a large development project seems to be gone in many cases; instead, we have teams of teams, each comprising many committees, and so on, with little direct individual responsibility. There are many problems with such an approach, perhaps best summed up in the aphorism that "a committee never designed anything."

In software development, this is an especially critical problem because we often do not have the representations and processes necessary to permit us reliably to break up a complex task into many pieces to be worked on by teams of people. The other side of this issue, however, is equally dangerous because it may be used to argue that development should be done by a single person, unencumbered by any requirements to produce a coherent, written design.

What I am urging here is a policy that places the responsibility for the overall technical quality of a project on the shoulders of a single individual so that organizationally things can be directed from a single place and so that technically there will be some hope of achieving coherence among the various parts of the system. This must be supported, however, by methods and tools, as well as organizational structures, that permit this single person to deal at an appropriate level of abstraction, both technically and organizationally.

Defining the composition of the standard development team can be helpful, especially in large organizations. A general rule is to make sure that every group that is impacted by a system development, or who can generally be expected to contribute to the development, is included. For example, representatives of the customer (whoever is paying for the system), the actual users, and the operations staff should all be included in some way in the development team. By defining the composition of the team (or the expected information inputs) in advance for all projects, an expectation of cooperation will be created and no one need feel left out.[6.4]

Teamwork is an essential aspect of almost all systems development. One cannot legislate teamwork any more than you can legislate morals, but policies can help. In addition to defining team composition, policies that mandate open reviews of technical work and reward teamwork can help foster a willingness to cooperate in individual development personnel.

A final and very important part of the personnel policies that surround successful SDSs is the existence of two or more advancement tracks. While the details must depend on your organization, the concept of permitting and encouraging people to continue in basically technical work while still advancing within the organization in terms of financial rewards and status is very important—and successful.

### Quality Standards and Mechanisms

The most important policy with respect to quality is one which effectively promotes paying attention to it, for example, by tying bonuses and promotions, at least in part, to measures of product quality. The second most important quality policy is one which establishes objective, measurable standards for quality. If there is the incentive to use them and agreed upon standards, they will be used.

> *The best policies regarding quality are those that motivate people to pay attention to quality.*

For example, one can implement an objective measure of the thoroughness of testing in terms of the percentage of paths through the software that have been tested; this is one aspect of testing quality. Likewise, the quality of a software design at the architectural (structural) level can be measured in terms of the number and strength of connections between its component parts.

It is only common sense that people will pay attention to something if properly motivated. In most organizational settings, if quality is preached, but rewards are unconnected to quality, little real attention will be paid to it. For example, several years ago an organization became concerned with quality and set up a new organization and set of procedures for checking the quality of all software developed. The development workproducts were carefully checked by an independent group at several stages (preliminary design, detailed design, etc.); however, the approval to proceed to the next stage of development was independent of the quality checks, at least partly because the manager's bonus was tied to schedule, not quality. Several times, a system was found to be below desired quality standards, but rather than delay development until it passed the standards, work proceeded while a half-hearted attempt to fix the problems was undertaken in parallel! I will leave it to you to imagine the results.

In establishing policies for quality, it is important to keep in mind the difference between quality *control* and quality *assurance.* Although often confused, they have rather different meanings. As discussed in Chapter 2, quality assurance provides the methods, tools, information, and management needed to assure that quality software is produced. Quality control checks that a given product has the required level of quality. Policies can be easily established for quality control, but not for quality assurance. For example, we can state that every design must score above a certain level on a set of established tests. Quality assurance, on the other hand, is something that must permeate the entire SDS so that the policies that we need to establish for quality assurance are, at one level, simply the policies we must establish for the entire environment. There should be, however, policies mandating responsibility and general levels of effort for overall quality assurance efforts in the organization.

A final point about quality policies is that the people and functions of quality control should be separate from the development functions themselves. At the low end of the development lifecycle, it is well known that programmers tend to overlook mistakes in their own programs; the same is true in design and analysis as well.

### Tools and Methods

It is difficult to establish effective policies governing the methods and tools in the SDS.

On the one hand, you should attempt to establish policies that can cover a broad range of situations over significant periods of time; that objective is best served by policies that specify desired results of using tools and methods but leave open for implementation the choice of particular ones. On the other hand, because we are still in the infancy of systems development as a discipline and because firm guidance is usually needed, policies must often be established that specify the use of particular methods and tools. I will discuss the comparison of specific methods and tools later; here I am concerned only with the types of policies that will aid us in building and running an SDS.

There is a growth curve of software technology maturity, as shown in Fig. 6.1, that seems to apply to many organizations. Initially, most groups are rather unsophisticated in their understanding of the SDS; for these, it is probably best to mandate that specific methods and tools be used (subject to certain caveats) and that experienced people be assigned to guide them and to approve any exceptions to the standards.

As a group, and the individuals in it, become more sophisticated and mature in their use of software technology, these policies can be relaxed and focused more on the desired results. (In a mature organization, we typically investigate poor results after the fact, and, if caused by failure to follow appropriate procedures, those responsible are disciplined for unprofessional conduct.) This is like teaching a child to cross the street; initially you demand they take your hand every time, but as they learn the importance of the rules of crossing a street you can gradually trust them to apply the procedures that at first you had to mandate.

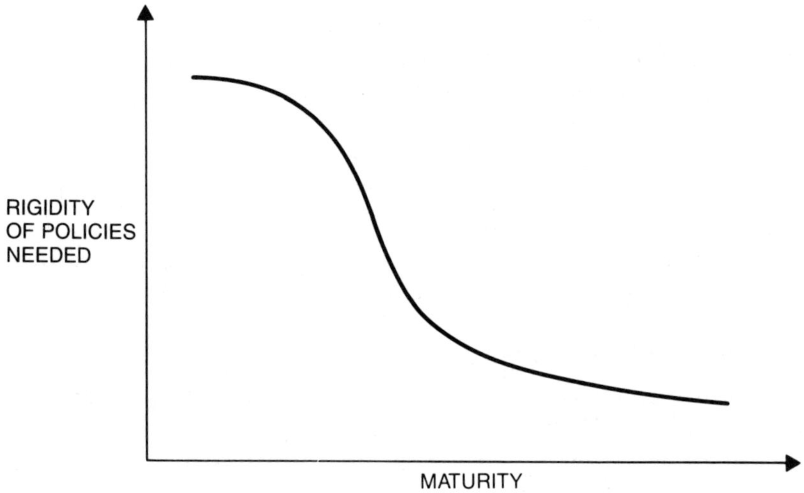


FIGURE 6.1 Maturity in Use of Software Technology

This effect seems to stem from two things—motivation and experience. At first, many people are not truly motivated to use a new method or tool; indeed, there may be definite disincentives (such as the difficulty of learning how to use them) weighing against their use. If good methods and tools are chosen, then as people learn their value they will be motivated to apply them on their own.

Experience not only motivates but provides the developers with a refined sense of what is needed to achieve the desired results. They will then have more understanding of the development situation they are working with than any policy writer can have and should be permitted to choose their own tools and methods to the extent feasible. Again by analogy, this is similar to a novice photographer who at first is instructed precisely what kind of film, shutter settings, and so on to use, but who later will be better able to choose these himself based on the photo opportunity at hand.

There are several caveats that must be observed with respect to policies for methods and tools. Even if selection is permitted on an individual basis, there will often be valid reasons to make sure that everyone on a given project or in a specific group use the same methods and tools. This is usually necessary just to make sure that everyone can readily communicate (both physically and logically).

When establishing policies in this area, bear in mind that different tools and methods may be called for depending on the type of application, size of project, number of people working on it, and objectives. Thus small enhancement projects on a large system written in COBOL should not have to use the same methods mandated for development of the real-time control software for an industrial process. Documentation requirements will be quite different if there are 500 people on the project instead of five. Software to guide a missile, which must be guaranteed safe, will not require the same methods and tools as the development of a piece of code to provide a rough simulation of a new financial decision process.

These considerations are often handled by having several methods and tools specified, along with the conditions under which they should be used. Another way is to define a standard, along with a description of the situation for which it is intended, and provide for ways of allowing variations from the standard under special circumstances.

Policies can be key to insuring that tools or methods match the standards established for the lifecycle and the workproducts produced as a development travels through it. For example, if the lifecycle defines an architectural design workproduct that clearly shows interfaces and module definitions, then a policy should guide the developer in choosing methods and tools to help produce the desired workproducts. Looking at it from the negative side, if you do not restrict choice of methods to those that produce this type of workproduct, then someone will use some other technique and simply translate the results into the desired form, thus losing some of the value in producing the mandated workproduct. (This used to be very common in situations in which flow charts were required documentation; the system would be built and then the flow charts would be produced as a side product rather than serving as an intermediate step between concept and code.)

Another dimension to the policies governing methods and tools is that they should ensure that they fit each other. While it is good to let the professional and mature developer choose their own methods, this must be kept in balance with the need to create a true SDS. One of the aspects of a system, by definition, is that the parts must work together; policies regarding tools and methods are a key way of causing this to happen.

I saw a good negative example of this some years ago. An organization mandated the use of a particular detailed design method and provided all their personnel in-depth training in it. The method lived up to its claims and helped them more easily produce high-quality programs. However, no policy was established over the methods to be employed in changing the software produced using the method; the result was that within a few weeks of completing a system, the original detailed design documents were obsolete and useless since the programmers continued to modify systems directly in the code rather than going back to the design documentation produced by the method. Eventually, they gave up using the method, essentially because their various policies did not match each other.

## Product Integrity

Integrity, as I use the term here, connotes completeness, soundness, or unity. This is a quality that most of us can recognize when we see it in a system, but that is difficult to create. Indeed, the best system designers are typically those with a natural talent for bringing integrity out of the chaos that often seems to surround a complex development task. There are, however, some specific things that one can do to help create integrity in a system.

The first aspect of integrity that can be consciously shaped is to make sure that the system matches the *true* requirements for it. If the fit of the system to the complex of needs, desires, and expectations for it is rough, then it will usually be perceived as incomplete, unsound, or otherwise lacking integrity, no matter what its actual state may be. Policies should be formulated for your SDS that do whatever is possible to ensure the creation of an optimal fit between requirements and actual system.

In general, getting an accurate determination of requirements that will still be valid when the development is finished is very difficult; the fact that development may take years whereas requirements may change in a matter of months is certainly one of the contributing factors. However, policies which call for a careful study of requirements, appropriate approvals by the customer, periodic checks during development, prototypes that give early experience with the system in an actual setting, and a design that provides the flexibility to permit modifications can all help create a better fit between the system and the requirements for it.

Determining requirements varies considerably between different organizations so that I cannot provide a complete list of policies here without writing an entire text on the subject. What must be done in a situation in which contracts are written with external clients for custom development of a system will be quite different from what must be done in a situation in which the functional specifications are completely established by an external group and passed to the SDS for technical development.

This example points up a key problem in development, however. The development of a system includes determination of the requirements for it. If the requirements analysis activity is not part of the organization that has the responsibility for creating the system, then we have a situation in which the SDS (which by definition includes the requirements analysis activity) is split between two or more organizations. While that may be appropriate for some purposes, it imposes an additional requirement for communication and coordination between the groups.

A second aspect of integrity in systems work stems from the quality of the design itself. If the design (either the external functional design or the internal technical design) is incomplete, uses different approaches in different areas for similar purposes, is more complicated than it needs to be, or does not meet reasonable requirements, then the product overall will lack integrity.

One of the purposes of using good design methods is to help ensure design integrity. Policies can guide that behavior along effective paths. Careful reviews of the design by the customer (or his surrogate), by other designers who are knowledgeable but not involved in the specific development, and by the implementors who will have to build it can all help bring about design integrity; policies can set expectations for these measures.

> *Product integrity is one of the most important characteristics. Policies should be carefully formulated to help achieve it.*

A third aspect of product integrity, and the one that should be the easiest to deal with, is simply making sure that all the pieces of the system are in place at the proper time, with the correct version. To the neophyte, this may seem obvious and straightforward; unfortunately, it is often neither to undisciplined development groups.

It is not straightforward because a large software system may consist of thousands of individual programs, each of which may have gone through multiple versions. The system itself typically goes through multiple historical versions which differ from each other by using different versions of some modules; then there may be different versions of the same system at any point in time by the inclusion or exclusion of certain pieces (for example, a reduced version that leaves out some functions); finally, different configurations may be created for different customers depending on the characteristics of the environment in which the system is to be used.

Why it is not obvious to everyone that this situation calls for carefully formulated policies that will help maintain the integrity of the physical system, I cannot say. Fortunately, of the three aspects of integrity I have been discussing, this one is the easiest to do something about.

Technically, the issue is one of configuration management.[6.5] Policies must be carefully formulated that will ensure that the different versions, releases, and forms of the system can be easily and reliably referred to, delivered, or worked upon. There is no reason that such policies cannot be established and followed so that this form of integrity, at least, is not a problem.

## 6.4 Useful Metapolicies

*A few strong instincts, and a few plain rules.*

— *William Wordsworth "Alas! What Boots the Long Laborious Quest?"*

A favorite prefix with computer scientists is "meta-" meaning above or beyond. (For example, a metalanguage is a language for describing languages.) I cannot legislate policies for writing policies for your SDS, but I can identify some metapolicies that will enhance their chance of being effective in practice.

### Make Them General and Simple

Easy to state; hard to achieve.

As in design, the best policies are those that are simple; that makes them easier to understand and follow and harder to misinterpret. If the policy you are trying to state is complicated, has multiple cases, and a plethora of conditions, then it is time to step back and find a simpler formulation. Any policy that takes more than a few paragraphs to state in its entirety is probably not simple.

Sometimes simplicity can be found by generalizing the policy. Whenever possible, replace two specific policies with one more general policy that covers all the same situations. The biggest obstacle to this is the need to keep the policies operational (testable) and unambiguous; the general policy "Do the right thing" is not much good for guiding individual actions!

A specific policy would mandate a particular language to be used for each stage of development; a general policy would describe the characteristics of a desired language for each stage, perhaps giving a particular language as an example. A specific policy would mandate that the requirements definition must always be signed off by the the customer and the Account Representative (a specific job title); a general policy would require that it be approved in writing by the customer and the person within the organization directly responsible for continuing contact with the client.

### Make Them Flexible

Another reason to strive for general policies is that they will normally include more possibilities and thus be more flexible. Even if all possible cases can't be covered in a policy, there must be provisions for the odd case that isn't strictly permitted by the policy, but nonetheless should be permitted. The phrase "spirit of the law, not the letter of the law" captures exactly the meaning of flexibility that we want to instill in the policies for our SDS.

Another dimension of flexibility is the ability to change. No policy is going to work forever, so it must be capable of being changed without completely upsetting all the other policies that are guiding your SDS. This is a matter of how it relates to those other policies and how general it is; think of the policies as a jigsaw puzzle where the relationships between policies are represented by the boundaries between pieces. If the boundaries are very jagged, weaving in and out of one another's domains, then removing one (or changing it) will disturb the other pieces.

The need for flexibility comes about not only because the policies must change over time, but also because we are dealing with a system in which people are the primary component. We can't program people precisely (even if we wanted to) and must allow them to adapt and complete policies as appropriate for their own situations within.

### Only Bound Results, Don't Prescribe Them

A good rule to follow is that a policy should place bounds on the set of acceptable behaviors or results that you are willing to accept. This is just another way of looking at one dimension of flexibility.

For example, you may want to ensure that every program specification undergoes a thorough quality check before programming begins; a policy that states that and defines what is meant by "quality check" in terms of the information about the specification that is to be produced will bound the results satisfactorily without writing into policy exactly how that information is to be produced.

### Policies Should Be Useful

For the most part, policies are not something in which most people, especially creative software types, are very interested. A surefire way of making a set of policies unpopular is to include in it a number that are redundant, meaningless, impossible, or otherwise unuseful. I have two good tests for a policy: (1) Does it help people do their work better? (2) Can we tell when it is being followed?

There are many useful policies that may make life more difficult for some of the people in the system, but which taken overall improve things. For example, in order to have appropriate data for resource planning, estimating, purchase of resources, and so on, it may be necessary to have weekly time reports from each member of the technical staff that are broken down on a detailed form. Filling out such reports will probably not directly help the technical staff but in the larger picture, if it serves a legitimate management need and results in better resource allocation and overall operation of the SDS, then it should be tolerated.

## 6.5 What Is a Policy Without a Procedure?

Nothing.

Policies and actions must mirror each other for a successful SDS. If the policies are just written reflections of behavior that is already well established, we don't need to worry about formal procedures. On the other hand, if the policies come first, then we must pay attention to procedures for translating the policies into action. So don't think that once you have chosen a good set of policies you are through. Of course, if you don't implement the policies with a good set of procedures, you probably won't see much action in any event and be relieved of the burden of knowing if the policies are in fact good!

# CHAPTER 7

# People: The Indispensable Element

PROSPECT
PARK
DOC
Playboy

CHAPTER

# 7

# People: The Indispensable Element

*The new age, the new empire, is the empire of the mind, not the body.*

— Robert E. Kelley *The Gold Collar Worker*

## 7.1 Without Them You Have Nothing

In spite of the highly technical and formal nature of software, creating it remains a very people-intensive activity. Although a good bit of current software engineering research is aimed at removing as much of the inefficiency and error-proneness as possible (which is generally ascribed to the large people-component in the process), there are reasons to believe it will remain a people-intensive activity for some time to come. It is interesting to note that Boehm[7.1] identifies personnel as the most important factor, by far, in software productivity.

It should be obvious, then, why I subtitled this chapter as I did. People are truly the indispensable element in the software environment as we know it today, and it is thus imperative that we know how to deal with them properly.

I intend to lecture here neither on basic management nor on psychology. What I can offer, however, are some insights gathered over the years by myself and others which will help to explain some of the people and behaviors that are encountered in systems development.

## 7.2 A Rose Is *Not* a Rose Is *Not* a Rose!

*Underneath all, individuals, I swear nothing is good to me now that ignores individuals.*

— *Walt Whitman, By Blue Ontario's Shore*

In fact, some roses are thorny weeds! But they have their use as well. The trick is knowing how to sort out the weeds from the roses from the sunflowers and knowing where to plant them so that they will grow best.

Have I suddenly switched to gardening? No, unless you like to think in terms of gardening when considering how best to develop your personnel. The point that is often overlooked by many is that there are some strong differences in personality types that have direct and important bearing on people's performance in software tasks, and on how they fit into the SDS.

That there are different personality types is certainly not a startling revelation; common sense would suggest that different types can be found among software personnel as well as in the general population. Unfortunately, some people, especially those new to dealing with software personnel, overlook this elementary reality, and believe there is a single "software type."

There are, of course, hundreds of studies and books on personality and industrial psychology. Some of these undoubtedly have some words of wisdom for dealing with "software people"; indeed, you could probably find the basis for everything I have to say on this subject in such books. My purpose here is not to summarize them nor indicate which (if any) are appropriate to help deal with software people; that is better left to your human relations department or other professionals of that ilk.

On the other hand, one does not need to be a psychologist in order to understand and communicate with a variety of people. The trick is to understand enough of the way someone's mind works to be able to communicate with him or her on matters of common interest (for example, what the objectives are for the next phase of a project), guide or place the person in work positions where the demands on his or her talents will be well matched to capabilities, and thus be able to help this person with problems.

While I believe strongly in individuality, one of the realities of the world is that we can often place people in broad categories. I find that about 90 percent of the time, once I recognize that a person is of a particular type, I can then accurately ascribe a set of characteristics to this person that guide me in interacting with him or her in ways effective for both of us.

I don't have a nicely worked out set of personality types to give you; indeed, I'm not sure there is such a set. As with Walter Lowen's theory of the mind,[7.2] I often use a set of dichotomies to explain people's behavior. Figure 7.1 lists four contrasts, with examples, that explain a lot of what I encounter in software people; more importantly, they help me work with development people smoothly.

These dichotomies are not absolutes; someone may be somewhere between a detail and a structure person, for example. Further, some lucky people are able to deal well with either extreme and, of course, hardly anyone is totally at one end of the spectrum. Even

| | | |
|---|---|---|
| detail (programmer) | vs. | structure (designer) |
| particulars (operating system specialist) | vs. | abstractions (external designer) |
| technology (hacker) | vs. | application (business specialist) |
| worker bee (beginning programmer) | vs. | manager (project leader) |
| dedicated (loves the work) | vs. | just a job (9 to 5) |

FIGURE 7.1 Personality Types

someone who prefers to deal with generalities can force him- or herself to deal with particulars.

The difference between the left- and right-sided capabilities of the brain are of this type. Wonder and Donovan in their book *Whole-Brain Thinking*[7.3] describe quite well how people may favor activities that seem to be clustered on one side, but are able to deal with those on the other side as well.

Let's look more closely at these dichotomies.

Perhaps most people currently working directly with software are very comfortable working with details. The programmer that is presented with a list of requirements for a new program and who immediately begins to focus on the details of the individual commands for the program is a classic example of a detail person.

The computer is legendary for its insistence on attention to detail, so it is not surprising to find that many of the people working with software pay great attention to details; if they didn't, they would soon lose their jobs! When one must deal with detail, which is almost always when actually writing programs or testing them or figuring out precise algorithms or defining interfaces, this is a most important characteristic.

In some situations, however, detail is not the most important thing to focus on. The programmer presented with the list of requirements, in fact, must be able to also look at structure; for example, to see if the required functions form a complete set and have consistent connections when they must interact.

Most of the "front-end" activities of software development—requirements analysis, specification, preliminary or architectural design, external design—require one to be able to deal well with structure. A system architect is the typical structure-oriented software person. He or she is concerned with the pieces of the system and how they fit together, the definition of the interfaces, the nature of the data in the system and its relation to the processes. Sometimes this person must deal with detail, such as the precise nature of the interfaces, but the person who can only deal with details, or who prefers to deal with details, will not do well at design.

People who deal well with structure are aware of patterns and aggregations; they are able to see easily how parts fit together to form assemblies. They see the framework or outline or classes in a situation first and the details later. These are the people who gravitate toward system design jobs, for example.

Detail-oriented people jump first to the details of a situation and keep trying to return there. They are uncomfortable dealing with structure, just as structure-oriented people are uncomfortable dealing with details; in extreme cases, people of one type are not able at all to cross over and deal with the other.

Programming, detailed design, specification writing, and unit testing are all activities that demand great attention to detail. Architectural design, integration testing, requirements analysis, and external design, on the other hand, are all activities that demand a greater strength in and sensitivity to structure.

It is important to recognize, however, that in some situations either the detail or the structure approach may work equally well; the difference is only in the way the individual works. In finding a problem in a system, some people start by focusing on the details of the situation—the contents of particular variables when the problem occurred, the precise command being executed, and so on—whereas others start with the structure of the situation—the last several commands executed, time of day, whether the program had been run before on this data set. We have all encountered medical doctors with similar, or with widely disparate but equally effective, approaches to diagnosis.

One must be very sensitive to the proclivities of the people asked to do specific jobs. They may be able to expand their capabilities, or they may not. Specific jobs may require attention to detail or structure, or they may not. In this context, building the SDS means analyzing each job and each person to determine if they are made for each other.

The dichotomy between detail and structure is not unlike the one between particulars and abstractions, but there is a difference. It is the difference between focusing on individual tasks in an organization (or system) and focusing on the relationships between different tasks (or parts of a system). The difference between particulars and abstractions is the difference between considering specific individuals (or functions in a system) and job types in the organization (or classes of functions in a system).

The particulars-oriented person likes to deal only with specific cases. The operating systems specialist in many shops may seem to be of this type, dealing only with specific commands or characteristics of the system. Sometimes the programming language specialist behaves this way, always answering your queries with specifics. (There is a chicken and egg problem here. Are these people of this "type" or does the task demand they do this because of the large number of special cases with which they must deal?)

The power of this characteristic is that you are always dealing with concrete situations, so confusion may be reduced. On the other hand, you may have to deal with a larger number of cases if each is to be treated individually. In contrast is the abstractionist.

Some people seem to prefer to always deal with the general case rather than specifics. The mathematician who answers a specific question ("Can I find the roots of this equation?") with an abstraction ("A second-degree equation in one variable with real coefficients is always solvable") is an example familiar to many of us in computing. The person doing the first, broad-brush external design of a system often deals in generalities ("The system should have data-entry, editing, and report-generating functions as part of the user-interface package").

A third dichotomy that I find well represented among software people is between those that are technology-driven and those that are application-driven. The proverbial hacker (one who enjoys to an excess seeing what he can get the machine to do) is an excellent example of someone who is technology-driven. His whole orientation is to the machine and what it can do, sometimes all but ignoring what effect the operation of the machine has on people or organizations or specific tasks. At the other end of this spectrum is the applications specialist who is focused on some task (e.g., registering guests at a hotel, managing the inventory of a store, or controlling a rolling mill) and is interested in the computer only for what it can contribute to this applications task.

As with the other dichotomies, one who is completely stuck at one end of this spectrum will be dysfunctional in all but a very small number of positions in an SDS. Indeed, one of the most valuable people in the software world is someone who can focus very clearly on the applications objective and who can also deal with the technology in an innovative way.

The next dichotomy—worker bee versus manager—is not peculiar to computing, but I include it because so many seem to ignore it when dealing with software people. There are some special cases in the software world in which progression beyond a worker-bee category is ill-advised. Sometimes this stems from organizational issues—lack of proper advancement paths for good technical people who wish to continue to contribute technically even as they move up in the ranks. But more often it seems to be a natural outcome of the way people's minds work. Recognizing one's proclivities—whether to be simply a good worker on tasks set by someone else or to be largely self-directing—is as important in the software world as in any other, and may well have some special forms in software.

A dichotomy that is relatively new to computing is the one between people who are in a software job because they love the work and those that view it simply as a job. Most people who have the nine-to-five viewpoint do quite acceptable work and fulfill useful roles. In many situations (customer relations, field service, routine maintenance, to name a few) this may actually be preferred because you want to make sure that the job is done in a consistent, routine manner; the person who views his work as something less than his entire life will not become easily bored in these positions because he doesn't expect too much out of the job in the first place.

Many (if not most) development projects, however, still require the extra push that can only come from someone who loves the work and is prepared to make personal sacrifices for the sake of the job. Some would say that this is exploitation, but the fact remains that many of us still derive great personal satisfaction out of diving into a task that demands so much that you can stand it only if you really love the work. That is true of accomplishment-oriented people in many fields, of course; initially, almost everyone in computing had this orientation. Now, as the field expands, there are many who do not take this viewpoint, so that one must assess carefully whether the task at hand requires complete dedication or not.

*There is no single "software type"; rather there is a range of people found in the SDS. All have useful roles to play—if allowed and encouraged to do so. Just be careful not to miscast the players on the one hand nor typecast them on the other!*

My own experience is that the leadership positions in most advanced development situations (and "advanced" may mean heavy schedule pressures just as much as technically advanced) demand dedicated, self-motivated people and that you are almost always going to get superior performance from such people (other things being equal) *except* in routine jobs such as trivial maintenance (where they rapidly become bored).

So what should you take from this brief discussion into personality types? The most important thing is to remember is that in this people-intensive business of software, it is very important to understand the different types of people that you may run into.

## 7.3 You Are Where You Were Planted

There is a marked difference in the behavior of people in an SDS, which can be traced in some respects to their intellectual backgrounds (which in turn may be linked to their inherent personalities). People with a scientific (or mathematics) background sometimes are more focused on finding the TRUTH than on finding a workable solution. This may lead to too much emphasis being placed on optimal solutions on the one hand, or on simply proving intellectually that something can be done without worrying about feasibility, on the other.

In contrast, the person trained as an engineer is more accustomed to driving for a workable solution that will satisfy most of the constraints of the situation, but is willing to accept something less than perfection. This person also may be more attuned to making sure that the total solution works in reality, not just in the confines of the laboratory.

One can differentiate between those with a largely mathematics background and those with a scientific training that includes experimentation. In this case, the mathematics orientation tends to lead to elegant, but perhaps impractical solutions; the scientist, on the other hand, is more attuned to building something to see if it works (experimentation, but still different from the engineer).

Computer science majors may come from a variety of backgrounds. Indeed, computer science departments reside within schools of engineering, science, and business, to name a few. Nonetheless, there is a strong tendency among many computer-science-trained people to tend toward the mathematics orientation because of the nature of computer science as it is typically taught at the undergraduate level. This orientation may or may not be ameliorated by one's work experience. (A current trend in academic computer science departments is to increase the emphasis on experimentation, both in research and the classroom.)

Yet another distinction can be drawn between those with any sort of science-based education (math, science, engineering, computer science) and those from the humanities. The lack of axiomatic discipline and rigor of thinking that is heavily drilled into the science majors often shows up in the form of an underlying lack of rigor in systems work by those without the benefit of this type of training. I would hasten to point out that this is certainly not uniformly true (any more than it is true that all science majors are careful and precise) and that sometimes those from nonscience backgrounds bring a freshness and creativity to systems work that may be missing from the science-trained person.

Finally, people from business, psychology, and other soft sciences (and also from biology in some cases) do not fit neatly into any of these categories. For people with these backgrounds, it depends heavily on the type of training they have had. Certainly some business curricula provide a rigorous and disciplined training that may be as quantitative and rationally based as many undergraduate science programs, yet other business programs may be so qualitatively oriented as to leave the student with an intellectual orientation that may be inappropriate for systems work.

The question is: What difference does all this make? Basically, systems work in most of its aspects demands rigor, preciseness, and the ability to deal with highly complex situations. For this type of work, the intellectual preparation of most science-based backgrounds is best. When dealing with the overall problem of creating large and complex systems THAT WORK, many compromises must be made and attention paid to issues that are not strictly (or even remotely, sometimes) concerned with the underlying technology; for this level of activity, the engineering mindset may often be best. Finally, the creativity and ability to communicate that is necessary at the outer edges of a project may often come from a variety of backgrounds.[7.4]

## 7.4 The Peter Principle Is Not Limited to Managers

The Peter Principle is familiar to most: People tend to rise to their level of incompetence.[7.5] The examples given in discussing this phenomenon (which is disturbingly common) are typically of people in the management ranks who are promoted to a new position in which they are incompetent. This might give the impression that managers have a monoply on the Peter Principle; much as technical people would like to believe this, nothing could be further from the truth.

Indeed, software development personnel suffer from several variants of the Peter Principle that to an outsider seem indistinguishable, but that are in fact quite different. Understanding those differences—and applying the consequent insights—can be quite important.

In addition to the traditional situation in which the step taken seems normal (for example, from district manager of sales to regional manager of sales), a very common situation is one in which the excellent technical person is promoted to a position involving supervision of other's technical work, or of leading a technical group in some task. There are cases where this works beautifully; but there are uncounted thousands of others in which it does not work at all, no matter how hard everyone involved tries.

It is not that the technical person is incompetent in the technical job, of course; it is simply that he or she does not have the skills for the supervisory job. *They are incompetent for that job.* The critical thing to recognize is that most technical work requires a set of skills that are quite different—even opposed to—the skill set required for successful supervision of others' work. Some technical people have both sets of skills and some don't. The obvious point is to look carefully before pushing the technical person into a supervisory position.

Management skills, distinct from supervisory skills, share the same problem. The good technical performer may not be able to perform well in a management role and thus seem to be incompetent. There are several common traps that organizations and the people that run them seem to fall into. One is to assume that technical people can never be trusted in supervisory or management roles; another is to assume that only "management" people can oversee the work of technical people. It is extremely important to remember that *some* technical people make excellent supervisors or managers (and that many more can do a satisfactory job at these tasks) and that a "manager" who has only management and no technical skills will have great difficulty "managing" technical work.

There is an even more subtle Peter Principle problem with software personnel, however, that to the outsider may not be very noticeable, but which can cause great difficulties. Further, it is magnified by the common career path in software work.

Most big organizations have multiple classifications for personnel. Software people typically start out as programmers (in the days before the great shortages, they started out as coders or operators or programmer helpers!), proceed through several levels until they are made system designers, and if they are really good, eventually are promoted to be system analysts. (Smaller organizations may not have the classification levels, but the progression of responsibilities is often similar; likewise, shortages may reduce the time in each position, but the concept is the same.)

To the person unfamiliar with the details of software work, this may seem quite logical: As the person gains experience and knowledge, he or she is placed in a more responsible position. Obviously, a programmer will work on only a small part of a system while the designer (like the building architect) influences all of it, and the system analyst, who sets the specifications for the system, may ultimately have the most impact *vis-à-vis* the overall organization. All quite true!

Only it overlooks the Peter Principle: The person who is able to perform capably in one technical job may not be able to perform well in another job, and thus will seem incompetent. Only a person with NO understanding of computing technology would take a hardware engineer and put her into a purely software job; yet managers all the time move programmers into designer's positions or system analysts' positions, thinking that they are all just "software jobs."

> *The Peter Principle is not monopolized by managers. Indeed, there are some subtle forms of it that are especially prevalent in some of the technical positions in the SDS.*

They are not and the results of such promotions are predictable and, unfortunately, widespread. Why? Don't system designers just do more of what programmers do? Or at a higher level?

Not really. Programming is focused on the machine. It is concerned with preparing sets of instructions that will cause a machine to carry out a desired set of computations on some specific collections of data. The demands on it to be precise and detailed are extreme and unforgiving.

Design, on the other hand, is concerned with structure. What are the parts of the system? How should they fit together? Does the structure of the system correspond in an appropriate way to the structure of the requirements? Design is concerned with translating requirements into systems, with making global decisions that can be implemented by the programmers to achieve the desired system.[7.6]

It does not take a genius to understand that the person who is good at figuring out detailed wiring plans for a large building may not be very skillful at conceptualizing the overall arrangement of the building—not because of lack of experience but because of the different skills required. Likewise for programmers and system designers.

But, again, CAUTION! The system designer must have the underlying technical knowledge of the programmer in order to tie his grand designs to reality. Typically, the best way to get this intuition is by working as a programmer, so the traditional path is not inappropriate—just fraught with a Peter Principle danger when the particular person does not have the generalization skills necessary for competence in design.

What about the transition from design to analysis? Why is that a potential Peter Principle trap? Actually, that is less subtle than the programming-to-design move. Nonetheless, it seems to be as frequently a trap.

The basic difference in required skills is that the analyst or person responsible for setting the requirements or specifications for the system must have considerable communication as well as generalization skills. Indeed, the communication skills may well predominate in the successful analyst. Since some programmers and designers of software are poor communicators (verbally or in writing), the potential for an inappropriate promotion here should be quite evident.

As always, caution must be applied. The analyst without a firm understanding of the underlying technology is a dangerous person, and is thus incompetent in other ways!

The basic lesson, which applies in all areas of human endeavor, is twofold. First, most tasks require a certain set of skills that differentiate them from other, seemingly similar, tasks. Although programmers and designers both deal with software, one must be strong on detail work and one must have good generalization skills; although both designers and system analysts must have good generalization skills, one must be able to communicate clearly with noncomputer specialists and the other must be able to communicate clearly with computer specialists.

Second, while we can—must, for organizational efficiency—establish standard patterns of career progression, we must not assume that a particular individual can automatically make each transition without falling into the Peter Principle trap. Perhaps the single most important organizational structure in this regard is dual career paths. This permits capable technical people to achieve the status and rewards of promotion without being forced out of technical work.

The implications for choice and promotion of personnel should be obvious (if not, perhaps the Peter Principle has caught up with *you*!).

## 7.5 Nits and Nitpickers

Systems, especially software-intensive systems, are full of nits. In the vernacular, one might say: "That comes with the territory."

Indeed, in some situations in systems development (for example, detailed design and implementation of programs) it is exceedingly important to pay attention to nits. Fortunately, this is something that good programmers are usually quite adept at doing.

Unfortunately, that focus on detail is often exactly the wrong focus to have in other situations in development. The important thing is to be able to recognize and place in perspective nits and nitpickers. For example, it is certainly true that a precise interface specification between a new program and an existing one must be established during detailed design; the programmer will properly pick nits if it is not. However, if one is trying to understand the proper logical relationship between the two programs during architectural design, then minor inconsistencies in the interface specification may not be so critical, and focusing on them may prevent the developer from properly understanding the logical relationship.

Historically, the supreme importance of picking all the nits out of a program sometimes gave the nitpicker an aura of authority that extended beyond the logical boundaries of his relevance. The results of letting a nitpicker dominate considerations of broader significance are all too familiar. Thus one of the most important factors in creating a quality SDS is to understand the scope of relevance of the individuals involved and to make decisions on the basis of that understanding.

## 7.6 Fifty Percent Is Wasted

Some researchers estimate that as much as 50 percent of the mental capacity of the typical person is wasted simply due to not effectively using both sides of the brain. For a culture that prides itself on efficient use of resources, that is a shocking figure. What am I talking about here? Does it apply to systems development? What can we do about it?

Regardless of our cultural and educational backgrounds, most of us from Western cultures have at least an intuitive understanding that some people are more scientific, logical, and orderly in their thought processes whereas others are more artistic, intuitive, and spontaneous. Medical research since World War II, some of it rather recent, has strongly suggested that the physical halves of the brain (the left and right hemispheres) are in most people the site of these different types of thought processes, leading to the terms "left-brain" or "right-brain" thinking. In short, we may someday be able to explain different modes of thinking scientifically.

In many organizational settings, the difference between the left-brainer and the right-brainer is seen as the difference between technical people and managers. The technical person is viewed as focusing on details, being very logical in reaching conclusions, not having the big picture, being somewhat introverted, and often placing too much reliance on cold facts. The manager is viewed as focusing only on the big picture, reaching conclusions by intuition rather than logic, dealing in generalities, being outgoing, and often not utilizing facts that are obvious. These characterizations, which in many cases are actually caricatures, do, in fact, describe the end points on a spectrum of types ranging from "pure" left-brain thinkers to "pure" right-brain thinkers.

In reality, however, no one (except for a very small number of medical cases) is "pure" in either hemisphere. Most of us are a mixture of left-brain and right-brain characteristics. To confuse the issue further , some people are bimodal, sometimes behaving like a person with dominant right-brain abilities and sometimes behaving like someone in whom the left brain is dominant. Even though we do not completely understand the physiological mechanisms, it is relatively easy to identify tendencies of one sort or the other. People who are quite good at programming typically have strong left-brain tendencies (attention to detail, strong logical reasoning ability) while a good systems analyst usually has stronger right-brain tendencies (ability to generalize, to come up with creative solutions to seemingly insoluble problems); successful project managers often have an intuitive knowledge of people (right brain) while a good systems architect is able to develop logical and complete pictures of a complicated technical situation (left brain).

Coupled with the physiological research is the attempt to understand the cultural and social causes and impacts of the fact that different brains work in different ways. Several conclusions are emerging:

Although everyone has capability on both sides, most people seem to favor one side or the other

Traditional Western education, almost by definition, works on building up left-sided capabilities and all but totally neglects right-sided capabilities

Human performance in almost every situation can be improved by using the capabilities of both sides of the brain in an integrated fashion. (It appears that the two sides of the brain can function largely in parallel, so that the trick is to integrate their operations—just as with parallel computers!)

In spite of years of neglect, people can often train the side of their brain that they normally neglect to work effectively with the other side.

Even though there is a lot we do not understand yet and a lot that we do not have hard evidence for, there seem to be some important implications for systems work in all this (definitely a right-brain conclusion!).

I suspect that you, like me, have noticed that the most successful development manager is one who can integrate solid technical understanding and ability with an intuitive understanding of people and the ability to make complex judgments; that the best system architects combine the ability to deal with a large amount of technical detail while at the same time developing a superior view of the overall system; that the successful business systems analyst can communicate equally well with end-users and technical implementors. The concepts of how the halves of the brain work help us to understand why this is so and what we can do to improve the situation.

> *There are some important applications of new understandings of brain function and personality to SDS personnel.*

The manager of systems development is faced with a double task that demands both sides of the brain. On the one hand, the technology must be managed: assessing capability of specific items, deciding what to use when, determining if development progress (or lack thereof) is due to technical problems or something else, allocating resources to competing technologies, watching for places where new technology can be applied effectively. All of these require deep understanding of the technology itself.

On the other hand, people and budgets and organizations must be managed. While these activities may require some detailed knowledge, they tend more toward the right-sided activities of seeing the big picture, tuning into the feelings and unspoken agendas of people, relating seemingly unrelated facts, and making decisions when quite often there are not sufficient data to come to a completely logical conclusion. The work on whole-brain thinking (in which the strengths of each side are combined) is applicable to the performance of almost any individual task; the management of systems work requires another kind of integration due to the need to manage technology and people together in a single functioning system.

The system architect is another player in the development drama who must not only have superior performance on individual tasks but, like the development manager, integrate essentially left- and right-brain functions. The architect is primarily concerned with structure: What are the parts? How do they fit together? Can we find another arrangement that will satisfy our design goals better? What impact will a small change in one area of the system have on the overall system?

Can we find a simpler structure that will do the same job? These demand an ability to see the big picture, relate individual pieces to an overall structure, to create new structures. Yet, the architect must understand the inner workings of any of the pieces if their complete impact is to be understood; his special ability is to be able to turn off or abstract this detailed understanding while working at the structural level. This has always seemed to me to require a very special blend of what we call left- and right-brain skills; the natural architect is able to do this.

The systems analyst (broadly defined) also has a dual task: he or she must be a communicator who can understand and respond to what is found in observing and talking with those who are commissioning a new system or who will be the end-users of it; above all the systems analyst must be able to perceive correctly what is needed. Yet at the same time, he or she must know the technology, be able to prepare detailed specifications and models of the new system, analyze in detail the data collected, and arrive at logical conclusions. This job, too, can be described as requiring a higher-level integration of the left and the right brains.

We can all benefit from learning how to integrate better the two parallel computers with which we are endowed. In the systems development arena, the frequent need to make complex judgments, find connections between seemingly unrelated facts, communicate with a wide range of people on a variety of subjects, and handle rather different types of tasks at the same time demands that the system professional, especially, must make full use of his or her brain system.

Although there are only a few books or references on this subject,[7.7] there are several practical things that one can do immediately. The first is to recognize that there are different types of minds and different types of tasks and that one of the primary leverage points one has is to make as good a match as possible between tasks and people. A person who is truly left-brain-dominant is not going to do well as a system architect (who must not only understand details, but create a big picture in which they all fit); a truly right-brain-dominant person is not going to excel at programming.

Next, recognize that every approach or style has limits. There are places where the highly rational, logical approach to situations is essential, but eventually it will reach its limits of applicability since the world is not always rational. Likewise, there are many situations where an intuitive, generalist approach is necessary; many situations in management are of this type where one must make decisions and set directions without having all the data. Yet this approach will eventually reach its limits because in most situations, especially technical ones, we must eventually have hard data on which to base further intuitive decisions.

Finally, be aware that some relatively simple training can often be very effective in helping the individual learn to integrate the two equally powerful halves of the brain. Some of what is written or presented in seminars is undoubtedly trivial, but if carefully selected, a small investment in the personal mental development of your system development personnel will have a large payoff in their ability to deal with the complexities of systems.

A final note: You will rarely have a problem getting systems personnel to work on improving the integration of their two mental computers once they understand the possible results. As illustrated above, systems work has a special affinity to whole-brain thinking since it requires so much of it. Systems people are generally highly motivated and challenged by precisely this unique blend of left- and right-brain skills. Given the chance to improve their ability to tackle the systems problems that excite them, they will jump at it.

## 7.7 But Aren't Specialists Needed?

Most definitely.

My comments in the previous section might be construed as saying that everyone working on systems must be a generalist able to paint beautiful pictures, program intricate algorithms, and leap tall listings in a single bound. Indeed, systems work, especially its technical and organizational management, does require more generalists than some other activities (for example, financial management).

One of the trends in systems work, however, is toward specialization. This should be strongly encouraged, within limits. In the early days of building complex software systems, one person was expected to do everything. He talked to the customers and end-users, designed and programmed the system, performed the integration testing, installed the system and trained the users, and maintained it for the rest of his life.

While not necessarily based on the brain research concepts discussed above, system developers have recognized for some time now that building complex systems involves many different tasks for which different skills (and thus different people) are required. This means that in most cases, systems are built by a team of specialists.[7,8]

Language specialists that know all the intricacies of the programming language being used and its compilers are common and valuable members of many teams. Data communication experts that understand the hardware and software protocols necessary to permit communication between the system and outside entities are often needed. Data base specialists that are able to advise other team members on how best to organize and utilize the data base system being used are increasingly common. In addition to these specialists in various aspects of computer technology, experts in human factors, process control, numerical analysis, or any number of other disciplines that support or enable or augment the development team may be necessary.

This type of specialist is characterized by having an in-depth knowledge of some subject (e.g., data communications, psychology, numerical analysis) that would be impossible for everyone to have. Their utilization and integration into the fabric of the development team is one of the primary challenges for everyone involved. They are, in effect, an added resource for the SDS to draw upon.

There is another type of expert that is sometimes seen in the development environment—the process specialist. Since the late 1970s, many organizations have realized that the process of developing complex software-intensive systems can be studied and supported in the same way that manufacturing processes or technological processes can be studied and supported. Increasingly, organizations try to make sure that there are software engineering specialists available to support the systems development personnel through specialized knowledge of the SDS.

> *Teams of specialists are a favorite way of bringing maximum expertise to bear on a development task.*

Thus specialization should be encouraged in order to add more knowledge and expertise to the SDS. No one individual can know everything to the same level of depth, so that only by having specialists can we hope to have a group (the SDS) that is equally expert in all the needed disciplines. That is the essence of the systems approach.

On the other hand, overspecialization hinders communication. There must be a common core of knowledge and a common language to facilitate communication. One of the present obstacles to good systems work in the software area is the lack of any universal language for communication of technical design concepts above the programming language level; another hindrance is the lack of any accepted common educational background. In other disciplines, such as electrical or chemical engineering, these problems either do not appear or are less inhibiting due to their relatively greater maturity. While some of us feel we understand what a core set of knowledge for the systems professional consists of, and have at least a start on higher-level design communication concepts, software development is still at a rudimentary level in these respects.[7.9]

If we look at the specialization-versus-generalization issue in terms of the SDS models presented in Chapters 4 and 5, several things can be said. Information is often embodied in individuals so that to build that part of the system as shown in Fig. 4.7 means in some cases that we must include people with certain information in the SDS. Figure 5.3 shows clearly the different functions of development which demand different skills. Thus the resources (people) supplied by management to support development may differ from the resources supplied to carry out the analysis activity, and so on.

In the past, there probably has not been enough specialization in most development situations so that more specialization is generally needed. On the other hand, integration of different specialists is often not done well so that one must proceed carefully to guard against the dangers of overspecialization. This issue is sometimes labeled "team building" and is a critical aspect of the systems development scene. In fact, it is more than simply building a team of people (although they are the central component) since it must be a part of building the overall SDS.

## 7.8 An Emerging Profession

Whatever their individual capabilities and whatever blend of specialist and generalist is right for a specific SDS, it is clear that a profession (actually several) centered around the development of complex software-intensive systems is emerging. A profession is usually defined by a set of knowledge and techniques that requires advanced education and is characterized by some common ways of doing things and a set of ethical or behavioral standards.

The medical profession, for example, requires advanced study in biology, chemistry, and various other scientific disciplines. In medical school, students learn a number of techniques for applying the scientific knowledge they are acquiring. A practicing physician, presented with a specific medical situation, will generally proceed in some standard patterns that differentiate him from a witch doctor or faith healer. And physicians clearly have a code of ethics and standards of behavior to which almost all adhere.

The profession of software specialist may never be so clearly defined, although we have a pretty good idea of what knowledge the novice should start with in several specific areas of software systems: business applications, scientific/engineering applications, and basic systems software. Further, there is a significant body of commonality between these three areas so that at least some of us believe that a single basic education will prepare one for specialization beyond that base.

The techniques that software development personnel use—software engineering in a word—are only starting to be clearly understood so that there is much less agreement as to how much should be taught in formal instruction and how much should be learned on the job. Again, I am optimistic that we are moving toward a more rigorous definition and transfer of this knowledge as well.[7.10]

The third area of a profession, ethical and behavioral standards, is the least well developed in the case of software professionals. There are some ethical standards[7.11] and the growth in professional societies in computing would indicate that many people are interested in communicating with their professional peers across organizational boundaries. The issue of ethics is not a major one in spite of a few, well-publicized instances of crooked programmers. Most software people are not (yet!) faced with the kinds of ethical questions that physicians must face daily.

> *While only beginning to emerge, the most advanced SDS personnel will eventually form a professional core as strong as that now found in other disciplines.*

A word of caution is in order, however. The present educational level of the vast majority of people in systems development work is well below what it *could* be, let alone what it should be in a few years. Until we take seriously the need for rigorous education and training of systems professionals, we will not realize the true potential of the computer.

It is in the area of standards of work that we are the weakest. To simplify the issue, it comes down to using a sensible pattern of development (lifecycle). Most experienced personnel understand through hard lessons that complex systems must be developed in a careful manner, giving sufficient time and resources to the various phases of development. Yet organizations and individual managers very often do not understand this and insist on shortened development cycles (or other abbreviations) that ultimately lead to ulcers for all concerned.

Managers do not deserve all the blame, however. Technical personnel must have the strength of conviction to insist on proper development; that is their professional responsibility. A medical doctor would never rush a surgery just because the hospital administration insisted on it, yet software personnel permit themselves to be rushed in some critical aspects of development.

There are any number of reasons why this is so. Most software personnel have not had formal training in their profession. While membership in professional societies is rising, local activities that would put younger members in touch with more experienced people are generally very weak. Most organizations have only recently begun to treat software personnel in a respected, professional way. The image of the barefoot programmer dies slowly!

My interest is not in placing blame, but in encouraging the growth of a true profession. Managers must encourage professional societies and other activities that serve to define a profession that has wider validity than a single company can provide. Management must understand (and behave accordingly) that software personnel deserve to be treated in the same way that other technical professionals are treated. Individuals must have the sense and bravery to stand up and insist on appropriate standards of development.

All must study and continually learn more about the knowledge and techniques and standards of which this emerging profession is comprised.

## 7.9 Creating a Structure

If policies are the software of the SDS and people the essential element, then procedures are the framework or structure within which people can work to implement the policies. Even the best professional needs some structure and guidance in doing his or her job; indeed, good professionals very often depend heavily on standard ways of doing things and respond well to objectives that are stated clearly and implemented effectively through procedures.

Methods and techniques are needed to help structure the technical aspect of systems work as well. The unaided human mind can no longer keep all the parts and relationships of a software system clearly in view nor draw all the inferences that must be made. In this area, too, the procedures of the SDS are a key element.

That is my next subject.

CHAPTER

# 8

# Do Procedures Make Any Difference?

NO
HUNTING
OR
TREASPASSING
PUBLIC
HUNTING
GROUNDS

CHAPTER

# 8

# Do Procedures Make Any Difference?

*You know my methods, Watson.*

— *Sir Arthur Conan Doyle "The Crooked Man." In The Memoirs of Sherlock Holmes*

8.1 You Bet They Do! (introduction)

8.2 Who's In and Who's Out? (detailed example of procedures)

8.3 All Procedures Are Not Created Equal (types of procedures)

8.4 How To Recognize a Good One (or a Bad One) (characteristics)

8.5 Choice and Evaluation (how to go about it)

8.6 What Else? (two other issues)

## 8.1 You Bet They Do!

The procedures component of the SDS is often the hardest part to build.

As the basic model of the SDS presented in Chapter 4 indicates, procedures result from our implementing policies and trying to support the creative work of the people in the SDS. Neither is easy. It is one thing to set a policy, for example, that all development projects should use the same lifecycle; it is quite another to turn that policy into a procedure that will effectively implement it—in this case, a development road map of specific tasks and deliverables that will work for your particular environment.

Supporting intellectual work is even more difficult. Much of the work in development is creative and not well understood. Further, we do not have the base of scientific/theoretical knowledge yet on which to base software engineering as we do in the case of more traditional engineering disciplines. Indeed, there may be fundamental differences that demand an entirely new intellectual basis for software engineering.[8.1]

To add to the confusion, there are today many different procedures that are touted as *the* answer to all your software development problems. Given this state of affairs, it is not surprising that many people ask, out of desperation and the hope that the answer is yes, if procedures really make any difference.

The answer is yes.

Let me illustrate: Several years ago a small computer company was having great difficulty deciding what features the next version of their operating system should have. It was the usual story—engineering had one set of very firmly held ideas, field service had a second set, and marketing a third. No matter what they did, corporate management could not get the three groups to agree on a common specification.

A group of professional analysts were called in to try to make some sense out of the situation. Somewhat out of the ordinary (at least at that time), they were not operating system specialists promising a common solution by imposition of their "superior" wisdom. Rather, they had a procedure: a requirements-modeling technique. One of the features of this method is that it emphasizes that a model must be built initially from a single viewpoint; if there are multiple viewpoints, as in this situation, separate models are built to serve as the basis for rational negotiation on what should be in a combined model.

Guess what? When this procedure was carefully applied, the warring parties found that in fact (as shown by the models that represented each viewpoint), there was a large degree of commonality among their different viewpoints. Further, by making their desired requirements explicit and tangible, a development sequence strategy that would ultimately accommodate almost all their combined requirements was fairly easily found.

The outside analysts did not bring a solution; they brought a method which permitted the company to arrive at an acceptable solution to their problem (which, by the way, is a good example of a combined technical and managerial problem). In short, the method of tackling the problem did make a difference.

The answer, also, is that procedures need not be such a confusing issue. Indeed, establishing appropriate procedures for your SDS can often be your best opportunity for making it work in reality the way you planned it in the abstract. Establishing procedures for a group should really be considered an opportunity.

It is especially important to note that procedures are not created in a top-down manner. Indeed, if you try to do things that way, you will most certainly fail. It is essential that as many participants as possible be involved in devising procedures that will effectively implement the agreed-upon policies. For example, an organization should generally have established procedures for reviewing and approving work-products, such as specifications, designs, and code. The procedures may best be worked out by the technical people who will actually be doing the reviews, with the cooperation of the supervisors and managers who must track the results; this will permit the technical people to choose or develop techniques that will best suit the technical specifics of their situation.

In many places in this book, including this chapter, phrases like "establishing appropriate procedures for your SDS" could be interpreted as suggesting that a single individual builds the SDS and that everyone else just follows along. That doesn't work. The language I'm using is oriented toward those of you in leadership positions who may take the initiative, set goals, worry about the overall health of the SDS, and so on. But if you fall into the trap of believing that *only* you can build it, then you will fail.

An SDS is a system of many, independent processors called people. They are intelligent and have no end of good ideas, if properly challenged and coordinated. Thus as you read on about procedures and, later, tools, bear in mind that building an SDS must be a cooperative effort of all of the people in it (and a lot more, too).

> *Procedures are implementations of policies, and provide one of the best ways of shaping your SDS.*

Much of my research and lecturing over the years has been oriented toward methods (one form of procedure), but I don't intend to repeat here what you can just as well find elsewhere.[8.2] What I will do is to provide some perspective on the different types of procedures that are important to the SDS, what some of their important characteristics are, and suggest some ways of choosing and evaluating them. Before doing that, I want to discuss one particular type of procedure in enough detail that you will be convinced that procedures *do* make a difference.

## 8.2 Who's In and Who's Out?

Clubs such as Kiwanis, organizations such as the Boy Scouts, and companies such as IBM, carefully distinguish between those that belong to them and those that don't. Further, they may have several categories of members, such as newhire, probationary employee, temporary employee, contractor, or retiree. Although they may permit visitors (another category), they are careful (for reasons both good and otherwise) to control membership in the organization.

Manufacturers of complex engineered products (for example, refineries, computer systems, airplanes, and machine tools), especially when the products are made up of a number of pieces of equipment, or are one (or few) of a kind, have learned that they must carefully control and keep track of the elements of the product. These procedures, often called *configuration management* (CM), have simple and compelling justifications.

The specifications may call for particular versions of some elements of the product, for example, a central processor with an attached array processor in a computer system. For quality-control purposes, it is important to be able to easily check that the final configuration has the proper elements. Once the product is shipped, the manufacturer normally has certain maintenance responsibilities; again, knowing precisely what pieces of equipment a particular customer has will be quite important. (This is especially critical with computers or other equipment in which a large number of modifications may later be made in the field or in which it is important to locate specific pieces of equipment in which a problem has been detected, as in the case of aircraft.)

In some situations, the complexity of the product may be such that control over the developing configuration is necessary during the time it is being built to insure that processes are applied in the right order, equipment assembled properly, and the correct model of each item installed (as opposed to the later and similar need to quality-check the final assembly). This in-process configuration control can be just as important as knowing precisely what equipment has been shipped to a customer.

(I have heard the story of an aircraft manufacturer who had a program to keep track of the wiring configuration in aircraft during manufacture—which wires had been installed, where they were in the fuselage, and so on. Unfortunately, the program destroyed its data base for several partially built planes; it was impossible to proceed with construction without the data and to recreate it was essentially impossible. The result was that many millions of dollars worth of partially finished planes had to be scrapped for lack of an accurate configuration description.)

As you might suspect, all this has something to do with software! In the early days of computing, there was a one-job, one-programmer, one-program rule. As the size of jobs and programs grew and the nature of software development matured, the rule became one job, hundreds of programmers, thousands of programs. Further, software became a product to be built, shipped out, and maintained, not something that was the personal possession of the programmer. The situation then was essentially identical to the manufacture of a refinery or an airplane—large configurations in which it may be critical to keep a precise description of the product both during and after development.

Common sense might lead you to believe that configuration management procedures, long used for physical equipment, would be immediately applied to software. Unfortunately, that is not the case.

The specific problems posed by the fact that software can be readily altered by a single individual, that it is invisible so that changes can go long undetected, and that programmers, being the ultimate optimists, are prone to believe they have just found the last bug and rush into the machine room at 2 A.M. on the night before the acceptance test to patch in the fix, are legion. Classic are the situations in which an incorrect library routine is included in the system; a new and correct version of a program is used for testing, but an older (and incorrect) version is used to generate the version of the system shipped to the customer, or one module is not included even though it has been written but this is not discovered until 3 days into a stress test. I could go on, but suspect that you can supply your own horror stories.

The point is that configuration management of software is fundamental and essential if you are building software. Further, it applies just as much to the individual building end-user applications using a fourth-generation language in a sales department as it does to IBM building megasoftware to control a nuclear submarine. The potential for losing track of what you have, of using the wrong version of something, or of someone making unauthorized changes is just as great and (relatively) just as disastrous.

Configuration management, in a form appropriate to the product and the organization, should be a matter of policy in every SDS. There is ample material available on software configuration management procedures and an increasing number of software support systems (tools) that include at least some facilities for controlling software configurations.[8.3] So that you can understand that there is nothing mystical or even very difficult about the subject, let me briefly outline what configuration management procedures are all about.

From the discussion above, you could probably guess what is required. One must have a way of naming configurations, defining what is in a particular one, and controlling additions and deletions. So far, very simple; a card file box and a simple naming scheme works very nicely for small sets of physical equipment and even some software situations.

That works fine until we consider additions and deletions, since now we are considering the actual elements of the configuration, not just a written list *describing* a configuration. (There is always a problem of ensuring consistency between the actual configuration and the representation of it that is written down somewhere.)

For physical equipment, this control can sometimes be quite rudimentary but effective. Once the product is placed under configuration control it is physically locked in a cage or room and placed under the guard of someone not involved in the manufacturing process; any changes to what is in the cage must then be approved by a person with the authority to do so and the independent guard has the responsibility of making sure that any changes in the physical equipment are properly recorded in the configuration control lists.

The access control problem is a bit more subtle for software, however, since we cannot just lock it away in a cage. (I heard that procedure proposed in all seriousness once by an industrial configuration control specialist who was used to dealing with configurations of military communications equipment and thought he could just lock up the disk packs containing the software; beware of senior specialists who may not understand that although the form is the same, the substance is different.)

Software is very easy to control since we store it on files and must access it with automated tools which can be set to disallow unauthorized changes. On the other hand, many systems do not normally contain these controls (most of which are simply a matter of someone deciding administratively that controls should be applied) so that then the ease of reaching into a system library and changing code becomes a problem.

The problem of ensuring that the list of names that represents the configuration corresponds to the actual programs making up the configuration is also quite easy to deal with—if it is done. Indeed, it can be done automatically, or at least semiautomatically.

Military contractors have long had to deal with configuration management and were among the first to try to cope with software CM. Unfortunately, many of the military standards for CM are overly restrictive during development so that an organization will do whatever it can to delay putting the software "under CM." This is understandable, but unfortunate, since there are some very real benefits to the development manager from using appropriate CM procedures. (It only takes one disastrous loss of a partially completed system because of unauthorized changes in the current configuration to convince one that some controls on the developing software are called for.) The obvious solution is to have in-process CM procedures that are geared to the need for flexibility during development, but that still provide protection against loss of efforts due to unauthorized changes in a configuration.

In short, software configuration management should not be a problem. It is one of those elementary aspects of software development of any type (from megateams of thousands to the individual working in an applications department) for which procedures can be appropriately defined that make it an effective part of the SDS.

Two further things are worth noting here. First, CM is very much a systems concept and part and parcel of the idea of an SDS. A configuration of anything, especially software, can usually be viewed as a system. It is elementary that to have a system we must make sure that it is properly defined and contains exactly the elements we intend for it to have. If we don't, then we really don't have a system. In that context, CM can be seen as simply the mechanism that ensures that the basic objects the SDS deals with are well defined.

I think it is also instructive to ask why CM is not more carefully practiced. The answer is that we are all at fault. Software development people historically have had backgrounds in math, science, or business, with only a few having engineering backgrounds. Those fields are generally not concerned with configuration management at all and even most engineering disciplines are design-oriented rather than production-oriented. So, the technical people are simply not used to focusing on such issues.

Management, too, is at fault for not helping structure effective and productive CM rules (after all, what is the second word in CM?). Further, at least until recently, management woefully underinvested in tools for software development. Providing effective tools for CM is not difficult technically, but may require the purchase of new library mechanisms and even new compilers and operating systems that can support the desired controls.

Will things get better? Probably. Will it happen by evolution? Probably not. Configuration management, a basic tenet of software or system engineering, will only come about through the application of combined management and technical leadership aimed at making it happen. It is essential that procedures for CM be established to fit the specific SDS in which they are being used.

## 8.3 All Procedures Are Not Created Equal

It should be clear that I am using "procedure" in its informal meaning of a rule for doing something, not in its software meaning of a self-contained program for performing a calculation.

In the case of configuration management, the procedures generally consist of administrative rules, protocols for entering programs into a controlled library, and perhaps technical processes for creating new configurations automatically. As you might expect, these procedures differ, ranging from guidelines written in an office procedures manual to programs that create configurations on the basis of a set of parameters.

Further, their purpose differs as well. A configuration generator exists to produce a technical product; a protocol for entering a program into a configuration (and the tools that enforce it) exists primarily to make sure that the quality of the configuration (i.e., its definition) conforms to desired standards; the administrative rules may be oriented to making sure that project records are kept up to date for scheduling and contractual reasons.

There are lots of ways to differentiate among procedures in the SDS. Figure 8.1 presents a set of procedure definitions organized along two dimensions: What does the procedure do? and How does it do it? I won't make any claim that these are eternal dimensions—only that they provide a coherent way of thinking about and sorting out the procedures in an SDS.

In some cases, of course, a particular procedure may well fit in more than one category; for example, SADT has elements that are oriented toward all three points on the "WHAT" dimension. That simply means that you must be a bit more precise in referring to it by indicating which part of it you are considering.

> *Development procedures range from highly specific methods (for example, for project scheduling) to heuristics (for example, suggestions for design structuring).*

There are other dimensions that one can consider, as well. An important factor in many cases is how the procedure is implemented: Is it a set of rules in an office manual, a verbal procedure passed from

HOW the Procedure Works

Method — a mostly complete set of rules for arriving at a desired result; in extreme cases, it may be an algorithm.

Technique — a rule or pattern of behavior which if followed will often produce a desired result; it generally requires that more judgment be applied than a method needs.

Guideline — a loose rule which if followed may result in the desired result; often, guidelines are in the form of boundaries or constraints on behavior.

Heuristic — a rule of thumb, which if followed may result in the desired result, but may just as well not.

WHAT the Procedure Does

Technical — the primary result of the procedure is intended to be a technical workproduct such as a design or a program.

Quality Assessment — the primary result is information about the quality of a technical workproduct.

Management — the primary result is the scheduling, allocation, monitoring, or control of the resources of the SDS.

FIGURE 8.1 Procedure Characteristics

team member to team member, a program that admits only desired behavior? Another dimension that may be of interest is the basis of the procedure: Is it based on a complete and consistent body of scientific knowledge, a hunch, corporate history, the best collected wisdom of the field?

Without worrying about whether I am employing a complete procedure for discussing procedures, let me explain Fig. 8.1.

The most common way of differentiating among procedures in the SDS is on the basis of how they do their job. As the definitions indicate, there is a rough hierarchy: methods are more definite than techniques, which in turn are more definite than guidelines (in the sense of defining what one should do); heuristics are a bit different in that they may be very precise in defining what is to be done, but they are not guaranteed to work.

Figure 8.2 presents a number of examples of procedures found in an SDS, organized by these dimensions. Let's look at the first column,

| HOW \ WHAT | Technical | Quality Assessment | Managerial |
|---|---|---|---|
| Method | Jackson Structured Programming | Path Testing | Critical Path Scheduling |
| Technique | Top-Down Programming | Inspections | Management by Exception |
| Guideline | Structured Programming | Thread Testing | Use of Rolling Estimates |
| Heuristic | Critical Component Design | Test Error Code Only for Fatal Errors | Concentration on Largest Modules |

FIGURE 8.2 Examples of Procedures[8.7]

which presents four different procedures whose purpose is to help produce a technical workproduct. In my judgment, Jackson Structured Programming[8.4] is a method in the sense I have defined since it leaves little room for independent judgment as one follows it (which is precisely the intention its inventor had for it). Top-down programming,[8.5] a common and favorite procedure in many shops, is not a method in this sense, but rather a technique since it spells out a pattern of behavior for the programmer to follow but leaves a lot of behavior unspecified. Structured programming[8.6] in its pure form is no more than a set of guidelines that specify boundaries on what one should do in creating a program.

An example of a technical heuristic is the design approach that suggests that one design around the most critical component in the system; in some cases, this will work beautifully while in others it will lead to disaster. This is a very vague heuristic; a more precise one can be found within the context of structured design in which suggestions are given for finding what is called the central transform.

This points up an important thing about procedures: Rarely will they be all of one kind. Jackson Structured Programming has some heuristic elements; a guideline may specify a precise way of doing a part of a task and leave the rest of it unspecified (e.g., structured walkthroughs); a technique may be very close to a method (e.g., top-down programming), perhaps differing only in our knowledge of how complete it is.

Looking at the "WHAT" dimension in Fig. 8.2, you should see overlap in several ways. Sometimes a procedure will have several purposes; sometimes it will produce a single result which can be viewed in more than one way. For example, while workproduct inspections are a quality assessment procedure, they obviously result in technical products when they are coupled with the change procedure necessary to fix problems found by the inspections; further, they produce invaluable management information concerning the number of errors per unit. Nonetheless, one can ask what the primary purpose of a procedure is.

Remember, these are not perfect dimensions; if you find a set that works better for you, great! The important thing to bear in mind is that procedures are not all the same and that one must have some way of comparing, evaluating, and choosing among them.

## 8.4 How to Recognize a Good One (Or a Bad One)

There are some characteristics that seem to be associated with good procedures (or bad ones) that can be used to guide their choice and use. These are not the result of careful scientific investigation; even if we could run controlled experiments on an SDS (and we generally cannot), it is still much too soon to expect such statistically significant results. So use them as they are intended—as guidelines.

### Some Good Features of Procedures

There are five positive characteristics to look for in a procedure for an SDS: guidance, intellectual aid, visibility, control, and integration.

***Guidance*** Does it provide guidance for the people in the SDS, showing them how to proceed in particular cases in which they need it? Look again at the model in Fig. 4.7: The primary source of procedures should be the activity of supporting creative work.

We don't need to establish procedures that simply record what people do (except for continuity and training). A procedure that laboriously explains how to turn on a computer terminal is a total waste in an

SDS populated by professional software people. On the other hand, a configuration management (CM) procedure that helps a programmer decide when a piece of code should first be placed under CM will help him or her to make a difficult decision.

Many of the standards and procedures manuals that one finds in development shops are full of the trivial kind of procedures that simply record what everyone knows how to do. Not only are there not enough manuals that provide substantive guidance in situations in which it is needed, but the trivial ones repel most people so that even if there are some that provide guidance they will probably be missed.

***Intellectual Aid*** A more advanced form of guidance is intellectual aid. Many of the procedures in an SDS will primarily show you how to proceed in relatively routine situations, such as entering an object into CM or defining the proper procedure for changing a delivered system. Some, however, should go further and help with the harder problems encountered in development.

A friend of mine, who is a highly experienced development manager, described to me what I call the "fog factor" of large projects. He finds that the intellectual complexity of large projects makes it difficult for him to keep his bearing during the middle stages of development. He notes that from the outside (for example, as a reviewer) it may be possible to see and hold in one's mind the big picture of a project—where it is headed, what the right course technically is, and so on. Often, however, he finds that when he enters the project (for example, as a team member or as project manager) the big picture is often lost—"We lose our way."

> *Good representations and procedures are essential to cut through the "fog" of big projects.*

The reasons for this are not well understood. Probably it has to do with the amount of detail that one must deal with when actually working on a project, as opposed to when one is an outsider or a consultant. This, in turn, is a reflection of the fact that we often do not have representations that are really sufficient for all of the information that is generated in a large project. The result is that one is swamped by the detail.

Another, similar, effect is that the creativity of the project leaders sometimes goes down in the middle of a project; they have difficulty generating creative solutions to the technical problems that arise on the project, compared to routine or older solutions. (Of course, new solutions are not always desired, but if it is felt that the old solutions are lacking in some respect, then this can be a serious problem.)

Again, the probable cause is the fact that one is inundated with thousands of technical and organizational details that capture one's attention. These details are typically focused on existing ways of doing things, rather than presenting an opportunity for creative thinking. In addition, most "creative" solutions are fundamentally large-scale or structural solutions rather than ones that are focused on a specific detail. One thing that distinguishes the innovative technical person, especially the person working at an architectural level, is the ability to get above the details and see patterns.

The purpose of procedures, especially technical methods, is to help deal with the "fog factor." No design methods at this time will totally automate the creation of a design for a program or a system of any significant size. Thus, any design method must ultimately be an aid to a human designer in doing what he or she normally does.

Structured design,[8.8] for example, provides a set of steps for helping the designer derive a starting structure for a design; this can clearly be an aid to a rather difficult intellectual task. It goes on to provide specific ways of judging and improving the quality of a design; again, these are aids to the intellectual tasks with which the person is faced. Finding an initial structure and making quality judgments are something the designer would be doing anyway, however.

Sometimes a technical method (or other form of procedure) will create new problems to be solved in the course of helping with the main problem. Structured design focuses on the problem of helping the designer determine good structure for a system. It does this by setting up a number of smaller problems to be solved (relating to the evaluation of technical properties of individual modules such as coupling and cohesion). Sometimes these problems are indeed easier to solve but for some people or in some situations these derived problems may be equally difficult so that in those cases this method does not really provide an intellectual aid.

An attendee at a training course in a specific method observed to me during a break that he really liked the method being presented because it would permit him to think less at work and thus he would be able to concentrate more on his stock market investments! This isn't exactly what I mean, but it does illustrate that methods can be intellectual aids. Clearly, wherever possible, one wants procedures that help us with the tough intellectual problems of development.

***Visibility*** One of the primary difficulties for those dealing with software has always been that it is an invisible product. You can't feel it, taste it, kick it, or visually determine its status as you can with more traditional engineered products. That should not be used as an excuse (as it often is) for not controlling it, however. The key is to make sure that the system has as much visibility as possible at each stage of development. That is the role of the representations and documentation that are, in fact, the product up to the point that we have executable code.

But there is another form of visibility that is essential as well: visibility of the process by which the software is being produced. This visibility is intricately linked to the product visibility but has additional importance as well. At this stage of immaturity of many individuals and organizations in the practice of system development, a relatively large amount of explicitness (visibility) about the procedures being used is necessary in order to facilitate their improvement.

Thus in choosing procedures for the SDS, whether we are looking at methods, techniques, guidelines, or heuristics, it is important to make sure that they provide an appropriate amount of visibility of the process they are specifying. In addition, in those cases where the procedure produces a product, it is important that it utilize representations that will give the product visibility.

I emphasize "appropriate" here because we do not need to make explicit absolutely every detail of every procedure. The trick is to capture enough of the process so that it will be visible to those that are to use it and those that are to manage it. The amount of visibility they require will vary according to their familiarity with the procedure and their needs.

The lack of visibility inherent in software development has led, for example, to some of the "development methodology guides" that can be purchased off the shelf. One of the characteristics of these guides is that they specify a form to be filled out for every conceivable task (leading one wag to label them "development by the numbers" approaches). This leads to mountains of paper, but not necessarily better systems.

Simply recording everything that is generated is not the kind of visibility we need, because among other reasons, we often don't generate what we should. For example, most software development does not create a sufficiently complete architectural design to permit a thorough quality determination to be made at that stage.

***Control*** There are two aspects to control in the SDS. On the one hand, we desire to control the technical work, to make sure it reaches desired objectives within budgeted resources and to ensure its quality. On the other, we must control the flow of work, schedules, and use of resources. A good method will help us increase our control of the SDS in at least one and preferably both of these ways.

It is important to understand that "control" is used here in the systems sense. That is, if we have control, then we are able to detect differences between a desired state (for example, the quality of a product) and an actual state and cause a change in the operation of the system which (at least in theory) will bring the values of the two states into line. This is a form of control that is essential to the operation of any type of system if we are to be able to direct its operation toward desired ends.

A good example of a very useful control procedure is one that determines when to make a formal release of a system. One can establish levels of expected error detection and correction in the modules of a large system and then use observations on what is actually happening to determine when (or if) to make a release.[8,9]

Unfortunately, the word "control" sometimes has a connotation that repels people. I once encountered a former student who had been working for several years for a large systems development organization. When I asked him how he liked it, he replied that he was planning to change companies as soon as possible because where he was at the time was "like a factory" in which everything he did was heavily controlled, making him feel like a cog in a large machine. Apparently the management of that particular organization had applied the concept of control to their SDS in a manner that was rather inappropriate.

We want procedures to help us direct the SDS toward desired ends within the constraints of the resources available. The most critical of those resources is almost always people, and any sensitive manager understands that you cannot control people in the performance of creative tasks such as system development in the same way that you control the actions of assembly line workers in a traditional factory (which has its own problems of excessive control).

In order for a procedure to help us enhance control, it must be able to do two things. First, it must help us detect differences between actual and desired situations. Sometimes this is a part of the procedure (such as in structured design) and sometimes the procedure depends on another procedure to produce the information (as is the case with many programming techniques which depend on testing procedures to determine if the goal has been achieved).

Second, it must be able to bring about changes which reduce the detected differences, preferably to zero. For example, in structured design, there is a part of the method which guides the designer in reducing the coupling between modules when that is found to be excessive. Most programming techniques, on the other hand, do not guide the programmer in how to make the program correct when it is found to contain errors.

> *A good procedure enhances control of development by detecting differences between actual and desired conditions, and by helping us reduce those differences.*

***Integration*** The need for two types of control in the SDS—technical and managerial—highlights another property that good methods should have: integration of their technical and managerial aspects. A critical factor in successful SDSs is the successful integration of these two primary aspects. Procedures are the primary place where this integration can be brought about.

Ideal is the situation in which a single method integrates technical and primarily managerial considerations. A good example is SADT[8.10] which has explicit methods for controlling the flow of work, reviewing the results, coordinating work among several people, and so on. Likewise, some of the "methodology packages," which are often largely a set of phase and workproduct definitions, include specific technical procedures that have been chosen to match the management/organizational parts of the package.

More commonly, specific procedures are either primarily technical or primarily managerial; quality assurance techniques, however, are quite often a rich mixture of both. The issue then is to make sure that a procedure provides needed information and is formulated in a way that permits it to be integrated with other procedures that deal with the complementary issues.

To assist with integration, a programming procedure must provide information that can be used for determining progress or be stated in a way that will permit division of labor under appropriate circumstances. Likewise, a management procedure must be formulated to include technical information as input in those places where it should be used.

These seem to be very basic properties, as indeed they are, and you may be surprised that they are not always present. The problem is primarily one of focus. The technical person is focused on the solution of a technical problem; he is very happy when he can come up with a procedure for solving the problem and often does not take the time (or even see the need) to make sure that the procedure also provides information for management and is of a nature that will permit it to be integrated with other procedures. In a similar fashion, the person focused on organizational/managerial issues will not naturally spend much time on refining technical inputs and making sure that the management procedures that are defined will fit well with the technical procedures.

A group I am familiar with defined a development procedure for the overall flow of project work. They carefully tuned the steps to the nature of their applications and work style; for example, one of the features of the procedure was carefully placed technical reviews that also provided progress and resource usage information for management that would be based on accurate technical assessments. When they tried to implement the procedure, however, they were forced by Corporate Engineering (of which they were a part) to insert additional, one-week project reviews once per quarter to fit with the standard organizational review cycle. These extra reviews added nothing to technical progress (actually, they detracted from it) and did not provide management with accurate assessments since they did not fall at appropriate times in the development lifecycle (except by chance). Sometimes the best laid integration plans come to naught because in the larger system to which an SDS belongs other things (such as uniformity of practice, as in this case) are considered more important!

Integration, then, is one of the properties that we want a procedure either to possess within itself or be capable of entering into. As with most properties, however, it is neither absolute nor easily obtainable.

### A Few Bad Ones

As with the features that we always want to have characterizing the procedures in an SDS, there are several that you want to avoid:

***Lack of Net Results*** No one would consciously choose to use a procedure that did not produce results that were important to the SDS. Unfortunately, this is too often defined in a very narrow way, resulting in the rejection of procedures that would be very useful in a larger context. Many managers unfamiliar with software technology demand that a given procedure (for example, a new cost estimation method) must do the specific job in shorter time or at lower cost, without looking at the fact that use of the procedure may result in much greater savings at some other point in the development cycle or in the SDS.

The important thing then is to make sure that the procedure will result in some net positive results taken in the largest possible context within the SDS. If this does not happen (typically we cannot completely predict the results so that some experimentation is called for), then the procedure should be replaced.

***Overkill*** There is no reason to shoot mosquitos with elephant guns or to use a procedure that is stronger than is needed. This is really just a refined version of the previous characteristic, but it comes in several flavors.

Sometimes a procedure is simply more powerful than is needed for the case at hand. Structured design, which helps impose structure on large bodies of code, is overkill for a situation in which only small, stand-alone pieces of code are produced.

Other times a procedure is too involved. A *full-scale* configuration management procedure is not needed for a three-person development group responsible for developing small programs to support the work of a group of scientists, although some form of configuration management is essential for even one-person projects. Insistence on using a full-scale CM procedure would be overkill.

In some cases, the overkill is due not to the procedure or the particular setting, but to the specific people using it. One might produce rather elaborate descriptions of how to do management by exception in a specific company for use by first-line managers; such detailed descriptions would be overkill, however, when used by first-line managers who already had experience with the technique because of their work in another part of the organization.

> *Choose procedures carefully so that they are in balance with the needs of the particular situation, being guilty neither of overkill or underkill.*

***Infeasible*** Again, it would seem merely to be good common sense not to adopt a procedure that really can't be carried out, either because of its complexity, demand on resources, or inexperience of the people who must use it. On the management side of an SDS, this is usually not too great a problem (although reporting procedures that demand too much time sometimes approach the threshold).

The danger more often than not comes from technical procedures that someone is convinced are really great (which they usually are in some situations), but which will not work in the SDS at hand. This may be due to the reasons noted above or others, such as the level of basic education needed (e.g., a method may require considerable mathematical sophistication which a particular group's people may not have).

***Untried*** I have frequently lectured publicly on a wide variety of technical methods for software development. In the course of those lectures, people have often remarked: "I'm not going to use any method that hasn't been thoroughly tried out by someone else!" Such a cautious attitude is certainly understandable and probably appropriate in many situations. Yet, invariably, these same people proceed to describe to me their SDS, which is an attempt to develop a large and complex system essentially by the seat of their pants—what I would consider a very risky undertaking indeed.

This attitude is foolish, if not outright irresponsible professionally, when carried to the extreme. Someone must be the first to try and as members of a profession, we all have a shared responsibility to help further it. On the other hand, there is a kernel of good sense buried in such remarks. What must be done is to apply it sensibly.

The developers of procedures, especially technical methods, have a responsibility to package and try out their procedure so that it can then be applied with a minimum of difficulty. In that sense, you must be careful not to try to apply a completely untried procedure in a production environment unless you are aware that you are essentially participating in a research endeavor. The need for new procedures is often so great that people are tempted to pick up a new idea and immediately try to apply it; that often leads to severe disappointment.

On the other hand, ultimately any procedure must be tried out for the first time by production-oriented people in a production environment. So to guard against undue aggravation, make sure that the procedures that you adopt have been tried at least minimally in practice. If this is not possible, then be aware that you are dealing with untried technology that must be handled differently.

One can, and should, develop more comprehensive sets of factors to look for or avoid in the procedures used in an SDS. That generally must be done in the context of a particular organization or a specific type of procedure. The factors outlined here, however, should provide a start.

## 8.5 Choice and Evaluation

As much as you might like me to, I cannot give you a formula for choosing and evaluating procedures, either before or after their use. Because of the role they play in the SDS, that is essentially the subject of this book.

There are some serious studies of the impact of various kinds of procedures on the SDS that one can consult both for results of evaluations and for evaluation procedures.[8.11] The greatly increased use of explicit methods in the SDS in the past few years means there are now numerous people whose task is the choice and evaluation of procedures; as their efforts are reported we can expect a richer literature on which to draw.

The previous section discussed factors that I look for when trying to evaluate or choose procedures. Obviously, asking if a procedure has these characteristics or not is a place to start. What else can be said at a conceptual level?

***Be Clear About Your Objectives*** Elementary, but still the most important single factor in choosing and evaluating procedures. You must know what you want a procedure to do for your SDS before you can pick one. Then, before you can evaluate it you must have some basis for comparison with a situation in which the procedure is not used.

Numerous times in my role as one knowledgeable about a range of technical methods, I have been asked to help choose or evaluate methods. Typically, the organization does not know what it wants the methods to do for the SDS. Further, as I start to dig into the SDS to help establish some criteria for choosing the procedures, I discover that it is not at all clear what the objectives for the overall SDS are either. I often find that in order to solve the more narrow problem of choosing technical methods I have to first help solve the broader problem of organizing the overall SDS in a sensible manner.

***Be Systematic*** There usually are a large number of features on which a given procedure should be evaluated. As in any complex situation, you must do this in a systematic manner when developing the data on each feature. Feature comparison matrices are often a good way of organizing the information that you are deriving about the candidates. This then permits you to establish an evaluation formula that assigns weights (chosen by you) to the different dimensions in order to come up with a single overall rating for each candidate.

I am not suggesting, however, that you must use such a technique absolutely in making the decision. The point is to be systematic in collecting and recording information about candidates. This will usually permit you to reduce the choices to two or three; at that point, a purely numerical evaluation may not be the best since your intuition about the importance of various features may outweigh any formal evaluation procedure.

Again and again I see people trying to choose procedures by what appears to be randomly asking questions. They seem not to realize the degree of complexity involved and the amount of information that can be collected on possibilities. On the other hand, I find some people who think they can choose a procedure through a completely defined evaluation procedure that assigns a number to possibilities; they seem to not realize that the degree of complexity demands in many cases that the final selection be made on the basis of a combination of facts (as far as they will support a decision) and intuition (to help integrate the disparate facts into a comprehensive framework).

***Empirical Evaluation*** Wherever possible you should collect some empirical information about procedures. Unfortunately, in most cases such empirical information is very costly and difficult to obtain. Aside from finding some data in the literature that exactly meets your situation, the best way to obtain some empirical evaluation of a procedure is to measure some parameters of interest (time, cost, number of errors detected) before you start using the procedure and again afterward. The problems with doing this in a way that results in any valid information are well known. Other factors may change as well, the measurements on the parameters may be highly suspect, and accurate "before" data is hard to obtain, yet if you don't attempt any measurements then you certainly won't have any empirical basis for later decisions. And in many cases the data collected in this way will, in fact, be useful even if it is flawed in a purely statistical respect.

> *Ultimately, procedures can only be evaluated in the context of their usage in a specific SDS.*

A most useful variant of this rather straightforward approach is to try out a proposed procedure in a pilot study or test case. This permits you to obtain actual experience with it in your SDS, collect data in a relatively controlled situation, and have an accessible showcase project to use in later refinement of the procedure and installation of it in a wider context within the SDS.

If this discussion is dissatisfying to you, don't worry—it is to me, too! I think that is because when we try to discuss choice of procedures in a narrow context, there is not much that we can say. That is not because we don't know much about it, but because it is a subject that really can only be dealt with properly in a broader context that includes information about the specific SDS in which the procedures will be used. Local optimization of the procedures in an SDS—that is, choosing the best available, without considering the broader context in which they must work—will usually be counterproductive.

## 8.6 What Else?

There are two other things about methods that are important to address: tools and standards.

As the model in Chapter 4 shows, there should be a very direct connection between procedures and tools since wherever possible we want to have tools to support our procedures. The next chapter looks at tools in the SDS directly and in this context we will look more closely at this topic.

The issue of standardization of procedures occurs at two levels: on the level of the entire field and within a specific SDS. There is no reason to restrict the development of new procedures and variations on existing ones that make them useful in particular settings; thus, I am not in favor of restrictive standards. However, it is very useful to have standard definitions of particular procedures to foster better communication and education; in that sense, I am very much in favor of having definitions of procedures that are widely understood.

The same reasons for having common understandings of what is meant by particular procedures (such as structured design or design inspection or rolling estimates) apply to an individual SDS. If there are standard procedures, then there is less ambiguity for people to deal with, a smaller number of things for a manager or supervisor to deal with, and greater flexibility possible in assigning people.

The tradeoff is sometimes less flexibility in tackling a problem. In most environments the advantages of having a known way far outweighs the disadvantage of sometimes having a suboptimal approach. Further, a well-constructed SDS will have alternatives, optional procedures, ways of obtaining exceptions, and other ways of reducing rigidity. Thus, when applied in a reasonable manner, I favor the adoption of standard procedures in an SDS.

Now, let's look at the role of tools in the SDS.

CHAPTER

# 9

# The Shoemaker's Children

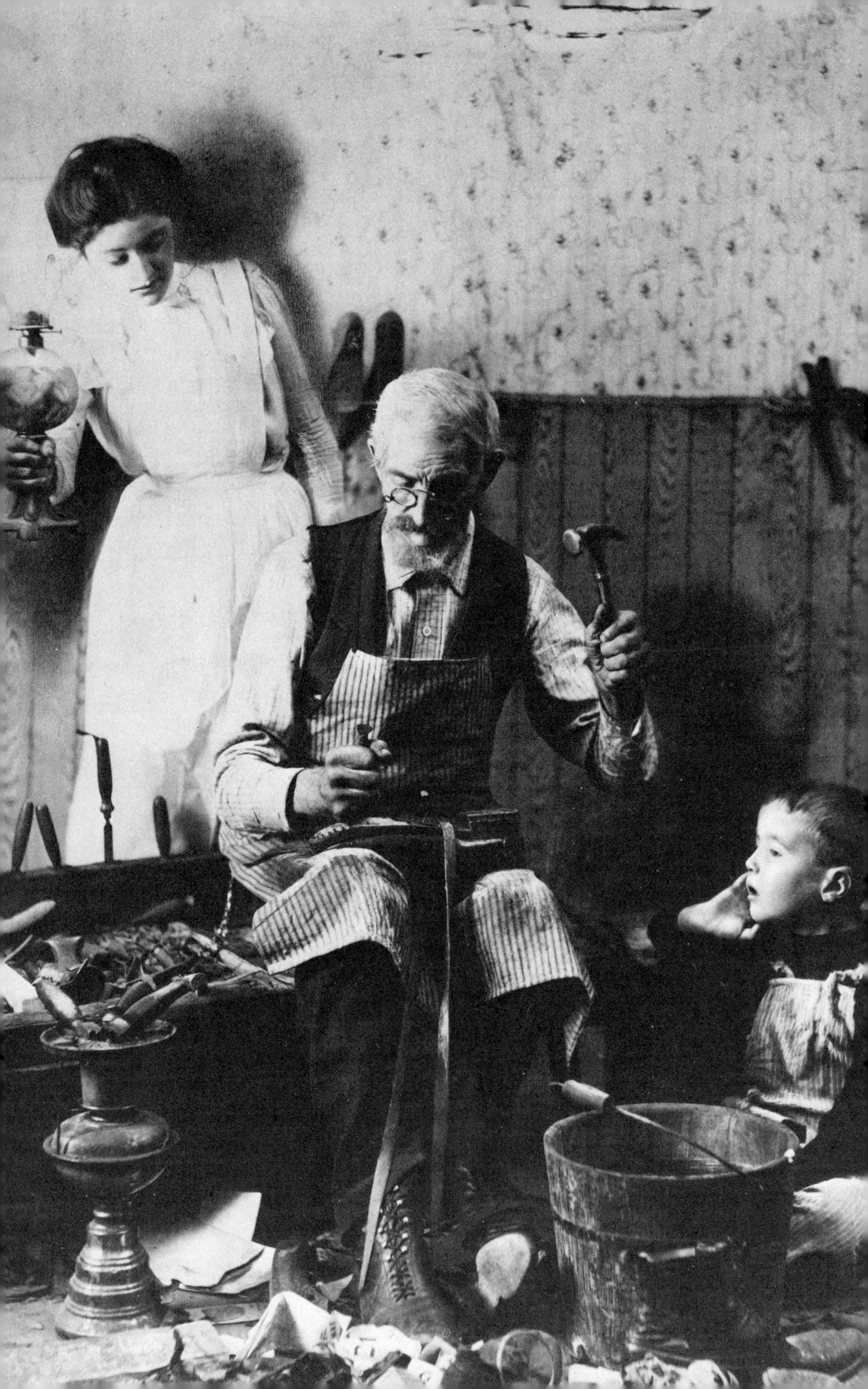

CHAPTER

# 9

# The Shoemaker's Children

*Him that makes shoes go barefoot himself.*

— Robert Burton *The Anatomy of Melancholy*

9.1 Who Are They? (introduction)

9.2 What Type of Shoes Are Available? (taxonomy and definitions)

9.3 Put Your Socks On First! (process understanding necessary)

9.4 Who Makes the Choice? (evaluation)

9.5 Invest in the Future (need for capital investment)

The Bettmann Archive

## 9.1 Who Are They?

The computer is one of the most pervasive and influential tools ever developed by man. To say that it is revolutionizing the way that many tasks, indeed entire processes, are carried out is a gross understatement.

Yet until recently, the impact of the computer on the task of preparing programs for computers has been rather minimal. Some would say this is an instance of the old proverb that holds that the shoemaker's children are always the last to get new shoes. It seems that we have been too busy solving other people's problems to pay much attention to our own.[9.1]

Several things have caused us to recognize that more tools are needed in the SDS:

- *The demand for higher quality.* The connection between quality and tools is straightforward. Many of the tasks of systems development—for example, checking for name conflicts of a new data item or generating test cases to force execution of every path in a system—either involve so much detail or are so prone to errors when done by hand that if the task can be done (or aided) by a tool, then a significant increase in the quality of the task (and hence the resulting system) can be achieved.
- *The huge increase in the size of systems.* Systems of a million lines of source code are not uncommon; if good design practice is followed, then modules will be around 100 lines of code each, meaning there may be 10,000 modules in the system. Simply keeping track of 10,000 parts of a system is essentially impossible by hand.
- *The demand for timely development schedules.* Computing has become a strategic tool for many advanced organizations (e.g., airline reservations, financial management, industrial process control.) If an organization is forced to wait two years for new functionality, it may be out of business. Increased productivity of the SDS is essential, and this often comes down to magnifying the capabilities of individuals.
- *The complexity of systems.* Even in moderate-sized systems, determining the impact of a change or locating all the places that must be changed to adapt the system to a new environment may

be a task that is beyond the reliable capabilities of most people. Tools to help deal with complexity are becoming essential.

- *The need for more control of the development process.* One of the lessons that most people have learned is that a reasonable amount of control and systematic behavior is necessary in order to develop complex, large systems. Tools often are the primary way of enforcing desired systematic behavior.

From these general objectives, the tool builder or purchaser must develop a set of requirements that will permit him to obtain tools that are effective. The exact form of these requirements will depend on the nature of your SDS, but may include:

1. Providing visibility into the development process
2. Providing visibility into the product
3. Enhancing communication among different audiences
4. Leveraging the efforts of individuals
5. Facilitating teamwork
6. Providing economic savings
7. Supporting multiple development procedures[9.2]

There are several perspectives that one can take with regard to the tools in the SDS. On the one hand, one can take a *toolbox* view. There are a set of tools available and the people in the SDS simply choose whatever they want. No encouragement or enforcement of particular tools is involved.

At the opposite end of the spectrum is the *fixed environment* view. In this viewpoint, all interactions with tools are carried out in a prescribed and fixed format, and it is assumed that all systems development is done with the aid of those tools. For example, an applications generator package that makes no allowance for other tools or procedures would be of this type.

The viewpoint that most people take, however, and that certainly is consistent with the SDS framework, is that of an *integrated tool set.* The essence of this viewpoint is identical with the SDS concept—that the tools should work together and with the procedures and people involved in development in order to provide maximum support toward reaching the common objectives.

Who, then, are the shoemaker's children? Are they only programmers?

If you look at the tools presently on the market, you might come to that conclusion, but that is only a result of the very early stage of development in which we find ourselves at present. In fact, tools are needed to support every activity in the SDS. The analyst needs ways to mock up a proposed system rapidly and determine if it will meet the customer's needs; the designer needs ways of assessing the quality of a design and of determining the ramifications of alternative choices; the maintenance engineer needs ways of assessing the impact of proposed changes on a system; the development manager needs to be alerted to potentially troublesome trends; the system manager needs to track the multiple configurations of a system. And, of course, the programmer needs assistance doing detailed design, coding, and testing.

> *Tools are needed in all aspects of systems development. Restricting tools consideration to only the programming effort is very short-sighted.*

In short, tools are needed throughout the SDS.

While the realization that tools are essential to an SDS is not new, organized activity to create and install them is still in its infancy. What that means is that this aspect of an SDS is typically very chaotic due to the rapid changes that are taking place at present. This chapter is meant to provide some perspective on what is happening in the tools area.

## 9.2 What Type of Shoes Are Available?

Before we consider answers to this question, let's make sure we are thinking about the same thing here.

Software tools are any artifacts which can be used to assist the process of creating software. Thus I am limiting my consideration to tools which are used in the SDS and am excluding most of what the world considers "software tools," all those pieces of software that are used as tools in other processes. Note that "software" is an adjective modifying the process to which the tools are applied, not necessarily the tools themselves. Some examples of the kind of tools to which I'm referring are:

1. Debugging packages
2. Test case generators
3. Text editors
4. Compilers
5. Compiler generators
6. Configuration managers
7. Graphic model packages
8. Cost estimators
9. Project schedulers

Although this is an intentionally broad definition, in practice most software tools are also pieces of software themselves. Thus I am not concerned here with mechanical, job-scheduling boards or representations for software, even though all fit my definition. "Why?" you may ask.

There are a few mechanical tools (templates, for example) that may be useful in the SDS, but for the most part their use is clear-cut and we can safely leave their choice and application to the realm of the routine. Representations (particular notational forms for recording specifications, designs, test plans, and so on) are far from trivial, either in their choice or application. I would characterize them as tools, but am not considering them in this discussion for two reasons: First, most people in the field do not think of representations when you mention tools to them; second, they are best considered in the context of the methods which they support by providing a means of recording information developed by the method.[9.3]

One of the primary things one does in studying a complex system such as an SDS is to partition concerns into classes so that individual topics can be studied in a focused manner; in this case, I think it is useful to consider separately tools that support methods and tools that enforce policies, rather than try to consider everything together. For example, at a workshop[9.4] held to discuss needs and research directions for software development tools, three categories of tools were discussed: cognitive (corresponding to what I am calling procedures), notational (corresponding to representations), and augmentative (corresponding to the definition of tools that I am using). While there was good discussion and useful communication between the different areas (which is very important), one gets the feeling that more progress could be made by discussing a limited scope in more depth.[9.5]

I cannot totally exclude hardware tools from consideration here. There is no question that there are some (and more every day) pieces of hardware that in many cases are tools for the people in the SDS: workstations, ordinary terminals, portable terminals to permit one to remain in touch with a group when traveling, adequate processor and memory support for development activities, high-quality printers and plotters for producing hard copy, and so on. Especially in the area of workstations, terminals, and output devices, there are some important considerations to keep in mind in choosing and integrating them successfully into the SDS; while very important, those issues can best be discussed by others. I will only stress how important this issue is.[9.6]

Providing sufficient computing power (cycles and memory) for development work is also very important. Just as it is counterproductive to try to move a house full of furniture with a truck that is too small or moving men that are too weak to pick up the heavy items, trying to develop software in a situation in which the developers must endure excessive response times, or are not able to utilize proper support tools because of memory limitations, is foolish. Even though this is one of the earliest observations about the tools that are necessary for development,[9.7] it is still not universally heeded. For example, CRT terminals with full-screen editors, relatively mundane tools these days, are still not universally considered necessary to support programmers.

> *Cutting corners on basic computing support for development is always a bad policy.*

Another reason I am excluding hardware tools from serious discussion here is that typically they are interesting because of what they can "do." This implies an active element which in turn is either a program loaded in the hardware or a program that has been embedded in the hardware design. For example, the use of workstations that support "windows" is currently in vogue; windows, however, are primarily a software-created artifact. In either case, we are essentially concerned with the programmatic aspects.

Thus I am concerned here with pieces of software that can be used as tools by development personnel in the conduct of their roles in the SDS.

## A Simple Taxonomy

Software tools are recent enough phenomena that there are no widely accepted taxonomies or reference works yet.[9.8] Figure 9.1 presents a framework that you may find useful for thinking about tools. It is based on classification along two dimensions.

First, most tools today either help you prepare the workproducts produced by the SDS or help you manage the process that is producing them. While these two activities must be carefully interwoven, they are and will remain distinct; thus this distinction provides a good basis for categorization.

Next, whether we are looking at the management activity or the process of producing workproducts, we are concerned with analyzing information. Again, there is usually a fundamental separation between static and dynamic analyses. In the case of technical workproducts related to programs, this distinction is clear: The tool either helps us in analyzing the workproduct as a static object (its syntax) or in analyzing the probable results if the programs it describes are actually executed (its semantics).

In the case of management activities, this distinction is not made. However, there are reasons to believe it should be.

What few tools we have to support the management function in the SDS are only able to deal with current, definite information about the state of the software product being produced; actual configurations, costs projected on the basis of parameters measured at the current time. What we need are tools that in the realm of management provide the analog of dynamic analysis of technical workproducts; what will be the probable results if a particular set of decisions are made in specified ways, for example (essentially a decision support system for management of software development).

There are, of course, many other useful ways of categorizing software tools. You may see categories based on the form of representation the tool works with (typically, graphics or text), the type of processor it is to be executed on (personal computer, mini, mainframe), its mode of usage (batch or interactive), or the phase of the development cycle it supports (analysis, design, programming, testing). While these may all be useful, it is important to keep in mind some more fundamental dimensions that relate to the underlying nature of the SDS.

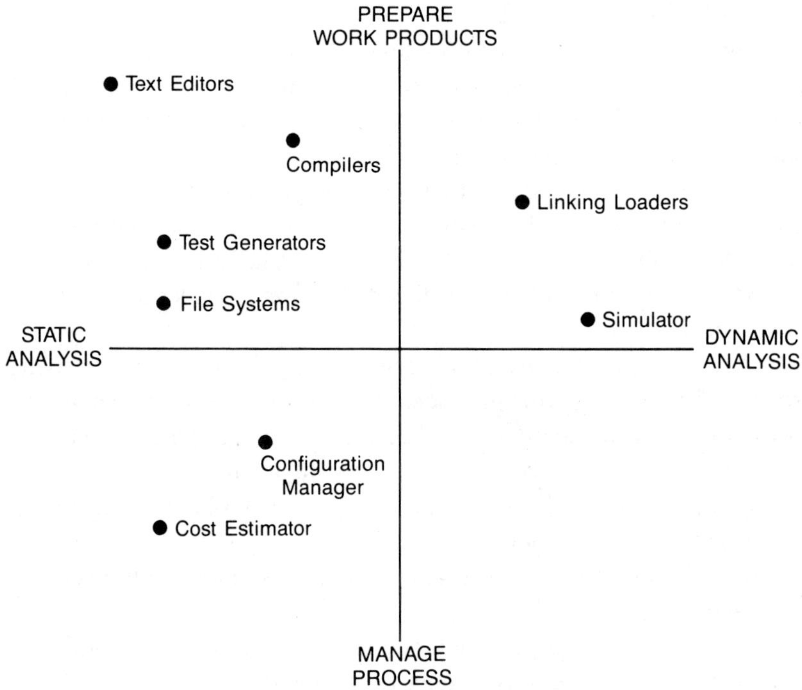


FIGURE 9.1 Basis for a Tool Taxonomy with Examples

## Who Do They Help?

Software tools should help everyone in the SDS.

At present, however, the farther you get away from the coding of actual programs, the fewer tools there are to help you. Thus almost no programs are produced without using assemblers, compilers, and loaders; with the advent of widespread interactive computing, the use of editors and filing systems is also almost ubiquitous. Tools for configuration management and cost estimation, usually both focused on program workproducts, are relatively common on large projects, but are not used uniformly. Support tools for the higher levels of design, requirements analysis, and project management are scarce and even less widely used.

This state of affairs has not escaped the attention of those concerned with the cost and quality of software.[9.9] Much of the advanced research and development in the mid-1980s in software engineering is directed toward providing more tool support. The gains from rather simple tools (such as a good editor or document preparation system) can be quite impressive, and this naturally leads people to try to build more and better tools, including ones that will support activities other than just coding. There are some problems, however.

On the one hand, there seems still to be far too much emphasis on developing better tools for the simple tasks (like preparation of code) and not enough on putting the ones we have now into productive use. This is understandable since to most people it is more interesting to develop something new (even if only slightly new) than it is to take something that already exists, polish it, and struggle with the difficult task of introducing it into everyday use.

On the other hand, some attempts to develop tools for more complex activities such as analysis, design, and management, are fighting tremendous odds against success because they are not based on a solid understanding of the processes they are trying to support.

## 9.3 Put Your Socks On First!

Automation in software engineering is often ahead of its time.

That is not to say that it is so advanced, but rather that some things are automated before they should be. That is, unfortunately, the case in many of the tool-building efforts that are currently consuming a great deal of energy and resources.

If the principles of a process (for example, the design of a complex program) are well understood, then a good tool can be developed that will not only aid the process but will help enforce its use. If the process is not understood, then a tool will very likely not help the process and may impose quite another process on the user. As one manager expressed it to me, "You get wrapped around the axle" looking at the tool and lose sight of the principles and objectives of the process that you set out to support in the first place.

An old, and trivial, example is the use of compilers. A compiler of a high-level language is a tool which supports the process of creating a program to carry out some function; compilers were originally developed to make it easier to express solutions to problems in computer code. If you look carefully, you will see that most compilers focus on the process of translating programs in one language into correct equivalents in another language; they are highly successful at supporting that process. They do not support directly, however, the process of *creating* programs. Only in trivial case does a compiler indicate to you that there is a semantic problem in your program (that is, a problem of meaning); they only tell you if there is a syntactic problem which would cause problems with the translation process that the compiler is trying to carry out. And in no case does a compiler tell you that you have misunderstood the problem in the first place.

We don't care that compilers don't directly support the process that they were originally intended to support since they do a very valuable job quite well and indirectly support the more creative process by relieving us of tedious details. That is well understood and no one is confused that compilers are somehow supposed to be supporting a more creative process.

This isn't always the case, however. Another example that is more bothersome is in the area of tools to support requirements analysis and specification. A popular and valuable process is to build graphical models of existing and/or proposed systems to use as the basis for communication between customers and developers; many tools are starting to appear that claim to support this process. Unfortunately, they may distort and mask the real process of understanding and communication that should take place since some focus attention on the gee-whiz aspects of the tool.

If one is building graphical analysis models consisting of many interconnected diagrams, each containing a number of symbols, there is no question that some assistance in drawing and keeping track of the diagrams, and the model they form, can be most helpful. Our current capability, however, is basically limited to providing an automated drafting assistant and librarian. The danger is that people will confuse the process of drawing diagrams (which is understood and can be supported) with the process of doing requirements analysis (which we don't understand very well).

For example, one of the things we do understand about the analysis process, which should take place at the beginning of a systems development effort, is that it must encourage in-depth understanding of the problem to be solved by the analyst. One of the advantages of the graphical modeling techniques is that they provide a way for the analyst to study the subject in an abstract and simplified form (the model he or she is building). It seems clear that drawing diagrams by hand forces the analyst to pay attention to detail relationships in the problem domain (represented by connections in the model); an automated tool that rapidly draws lines and boxes may remove this forcing function that literally pushes the analyst's nose in the details of the problem.

That there are tradeoffs (reduction of tedious and unimportant clerical tasks, for example) goes without saying. My point, however, is that we don't understand in any scientific or systematic way what the important factors in the process are and what their impact is. Building tools that just help with part of the process and perhaps displace or mask other, important, parts may in the long run reduce the effectiveness of the underlying process.

> *The gee-whiz aspect of tools can distract us from the process they are supposed to support.*

Prototyping is another area in which there is a danger of putting the horse before the cart. The idea of building a prototype of a system is an old one in engineering, and was brought to attention in software development by Brooks's influential book *The Mythical Man-Month.*[9.10] For various reasons, the idea of building "rapid prototypes" has become popular and a number of tools or methods for prototyping have been proposed. While prototyping can certainly be a valuable approach in some situations, some of the so-called rapid-prototyping tools have little or nothing to do with a process in which a scaled-down version of a system is built, its operation under actual conditions is *carefully studied,* and then a full-scale version built using the data that have been systematically collected from the prototype.

If these tools have some useful purpose, as they often do, fine. The danger, however, is that tools may be bought and placed into use by an organization under the assumption that they are going to support a prototyping process, only to find in practice that they don't. It is always the underlying creative process that we should be concerned with. While it will certainly be shaped to some extent by the tools we choose, we should first understand clearly what the process is.

The opposite effect in some ways is evident in the growing attempt to reuse software. While there are many possible forms of software reuse, a frequent objective is to be able to reuse small code modules in new systems with little or no manual modification. The process, in general terms, is well understood; the use of programs in a library is an instance of it. One of the major stumbling blocks to the widespread use of a reusability process, however, is the *lack* of appropriate support tools—librarians, modifiers, and system-building tools, for example. Here, our supply of tools is inadequate even though we have a relatively firm understanding of the process.

There is an empirical consideration that must be kept in mind, however. We can't tell precisely what kind of horse to use in many cases without hitching one to our wagon and seeing if it will work. In short, don't go to the other extreme and believe that no tools can be built until a process is thoroughly understood. As in all other areas of computerization, the act of trying to build a tool to support a process is by far the best test of our understanding of the process. Indeed, this is one of the primary motivations for the increased emphasis on empirical studies in computer research.

## 9.4 Who Makes The Choice?

I will leave to others to specify *how* one chooses software tools, although this chapter should provide some perspective on how to do it.

Many of the same types of considerations discussed above with respect to procedures apply to the choice of tools. In addition, since software tools are either packages to be purchased or involve (in most cases) significant expenditures for development, it is often easier to apply traditional management processes dealing with capital acquisitions. Most tools are so new on the software scene that we really don't have much experience with them yet.

I do want to comment, however, on the interaction between management and technical staff in choosing tools. Productive and effective interaction is essential, and rarely found.

Tool builders, programmers, designers, and even some technical management people are basically technologists. Their training and personal interests tend to make them interested in tools *qua* tools, tools for their own sake, rather than for what they can do to aid the overall SDS and the business/organizational objectives it is supposed to be achieving.

Managers, on the other hand, are either not technical, or more frequently, enough out of date that they cannot accurately evaluate the impact of particular choices on the technical processes they should support. In the realm of management tools, they are more knowledgeable, of course, but may not have the current technical knowledge to evaluate the implementation of a proposed tool.

> *There must be careful cooperation between management and technical staff in making any tool choice.*

As in many other situations in the SDS, there is a good analogy in medicine. A physician on the staff of a hospital is expected as a professional to make the primary choice of the tools he needs. However, when those tools cost a large amount or money or must be shared with others, either to distribute the cost or because several professionals will be involved in their using them (as in the case of a CAT scanner), then hospital management as well as the other professionals will be involved in making the decision. Indeed, if the purchase is of a very expensive piece of equipment which may institute a whole new system of treatment, the final decision is usually made by the management since it will directly impact the overall objectives and policies of the hospital.

The analogy should be clear. The professionals who will directly use a software tool should make the primary recommendations, but they should be guided by management that keeps an eye on the overall objectives of the organization as well as helps focus attention on the ability of the tool to support properly the processes of the SDS.

This rather simple procedure unfortunately becomes bogged down in many cases because of the closeness of research and application in the still developing field of software engineering. In the next chapter I will discuss some aspects of that relationship, but first I have one last observation about tools.

## 9.5 Invest in the Future

*Man is a tool-using animal . . . Without tools he is nothing, with tools he is all.*

— *Thomas Carlyle Sartor Resartus*

A recurring theme since the late 1970s is the need to treat software development like a manufacturing process, at least for purposes of capital investment in tools and training. I won't bore you with a repeat of the arguments here, at least partly because they seem so obvious that it bores me to go over them!

I do, however, want to support those arguments strongly in the context of the SDS view of development. In building any system, you must invest effort to create and tie together the parts. Tools are an integral and essential part of the SDS. Buying them, building them, or supporting the research necessary to build the next generation of tools are all ways of investing in the future of your SDS. Viewed as an investment which may take some time to pay off, but which will have some significant payback, it should be obvious that a sane and systematic approach to acquiring tools should be employed in most SDS settings.

CHAPTER

# 10

# Foreign Relations

CHAPTER

# 10

# Foreign Relations

*In foreign relations as in all other relations, a policy has been formed only when commitments and power have been brought into balance.*

— *Walter Lippmann U. S. Foreign Policy*

10.1 A Paradigm (introduction)

10.2 The Mother Country (computer science)

10.3 Nationalism (software engineering)

10.4 Uneasy Coexistence or Allies? (information systems)

10.5 The Promised Land (artificial intelligence)

10.6 Trading Partners and Visitors (customers and users)

10.7 Fellow Citizens (the rest of the organization)

United Nations/Saw Lwin

## 10.1 A Paradigm

As with countries, an SDS rarely exists in complete isolation. Even the most technical, inner-directed development group must use some concepts and ideas from computer science that originate elsewhere. In fact, the relationships between an SDS and the rest of the world are generally quite broad and important.

As everyone involved with software is well aware, the rapidly expanding and changing nature of all of the different subcultures that are interested in systems development often makes those relationships troublesome. People that used to be an integral part of the development group (for example, machine operators) are now typically part of another culture (operations); people that formerly were outside the development group (for example, users), may now be an important part of a development team (during requirements definition and acceptance testing). Shifting boundaries and even no boundaries at all will continue to be the norm.

In such an unstructured situation, it is often difficult for those just entering the scene, or those trying to manage the relationships, to understand the roles that different players typically take. My purpose in this chapter is to provide perspective on some of the roles and a simple paradigm for dealing with them: View the SDS as a country.

> *The relationships between an SDS and some of the surrounding groups and disciplines are rather like those that exist among nations. Different languages are often spoken, there is a good bit of provincialism, border skirmishes may break out, and wars are not unheard of!*

While I won't push this analogy too far (an exercise left to the reader), it does provide a model for describing relationships between groups.

As with relations between nations, two caveats are in order: First, you will usually be able to find other, perhaps diametrically opposed, viewpoints. Second, whatever the situation today, it will undoubtedly change!

## 10.2 The Mother Country

Systems development is an exciting and productive field partly because it draws from so many different fields and integrates them in new and interesting ways. Mathematics, electrical engineering, psychology, computer science, logic, management science, and others all contribute concepts, techniques, and tools. In that sense, there is no single mother country from which all of us in systems development have come.

For software systems work, however, computer science is indisputably the homeland. It is the source of much of the underlying, systematized knowledge about programs and their execution[10.1]; it extends our horizons about what is possible in software and about how to go about achieving it; it has been and remains the discipline that is the primary integrator of concepts from other areas for application to software; and it provides the basic education for an increasing number of the professionals working in SDSs.

In the early days of computing, software development and computer science were essentially the same thing. While there were some important pieces of work earlier, it has really been only since about 1960 that computer science has been a field of study with objectives, concerns, and techniques that differ to some extent from those of an SDS. In the same time frame, software systems development has started to stand on its own as a field with *its* objectives and concerns. In this way, computer science is like the mother country from which systems development derives much of its culture, philosophy, and religion; development, as a new country, has its growing pains while the mother country sometimes seems to not want to let go of its former colony, even though it is sometimes less than enthusiastic about its growth!

Taking a very narrow view for the moment, computer science (as a field) is concerned with creating a base of scientific, systematized knowledge about computers, software, and their use. While it is still rather far from completing that task in any but the narrowest of subdisciplines, that objective drives it and conditions its concerns.

In a pragmatic sense, that means that a "pure" computer scientist, someone usually to be found in a university or a basic industrial research lab, is concerned with doing science, not building systems. His or her output is journal papers, patents, experimental results, and prototype systems. Of course, in many cases, the computer scientist is not doing research that is all that "pure," so that the results may be close to a form that is immediately usable in a development situation.

For example, a prototype built by the computer scientist to explore the properties of a new algorithm for generating test cases may be immediately applicable with only minor alterations; on the other hand, it may turn out that the properties of the algorithm make it unusable for any but the most trivial situations. To the developer, this turn of events would cause an immediate loss of interest; to the scientist, this may be a perfectly acceptable result because it might suggest the next research path to be explored.

This difference in objective illustrates rather well the basic nature—and the problems—of the relationship between development work and computer science. Computer science can provide the answers to basic questions (for example, what are the theoretical limits on the behavior of a particular algorithm) and can explore next-generation (and beyond) tools and concepts for the organization and development of software systems, just as chemistry provides basic knowledge for use by chemical engineering. As such it must be supported, encouraged, and permitted to grow as any basic science.

Aside from the fact that computer science is only starting to mature and systems development is even younger, the major problem in the relationship is a mistaken set of expectations on the part of some on both sides, and a confusion of roles on the part of some computer scientists. Too often, development people expect computer science to provide immediate solutions to the problems facing an SDS. Sometimes the problems are not ones that computer science is prepared to deal with at all (for example, preparation of language translators for old languages for which the technology is well known); other times the problems are ones that will not be solved in a short amount of time (for example, how to effectively test complex programs); and almost always it is the case that there are not enough resources to tackle the problem.

What is needed is a clearer understanding by development people of what computer science can and cannot do. Coupled with this there needs to be more willingness by development people to solve their own problems using the knowledge that already exists, or else to help define clearly the research that needs to be done.

On the side of the computer scientist, greater willingness to help translate the research results into pragmatic information is needed.

This can take many forms—consulting, expository writing, seminars, personal interchanges. Further, the computer scientist must be ever alert to the need for basic research that comes out of the pragmatic work of development personnel.

The other problem with this relationship between mother country and new land is caused by the computer scientists. Too often, they either do not understand or else ignore the basic objective of computer science. The result is that they waste their time working on problems for which they have neither the resources nor the context (this is especially true in the area of development tools and procedures). Rather than working on basic research problems which will help us solve pragmatic development problems in the future, they try to solve today's, or even yesterday's, problems. An added concern is that sometimes the computer scientist expects his latest idea to be applied immediately and becomes very cynical about the pragmatic world when it isn't.

In extreme cases these attitudes and expectations (on both sides) lead to very counterproductive behavior in which the computer scientist refuses to work on anything which is even remotely connected to a pragmatic problem, while the developer refuses to read any journals or use any new idea that is associated with research. Both lose in this case, but fortunately, these extreme cases are not too common.

If the development person will maintain a realistic perception of what computer science can and cannot do and if the computer scientist will not expect instant acceptance of his ideas while at the same time focusing on the proper role of his field, then relationships between the two should grow to be more effective for both.

## 10.3 Nationalism

One view of software engineering, which I share, is that it is an attempt by the citizens of the new country to establish a culture distinct from that of the mother country—a sort of nationalism.[10.2]

I was trained as a computer scientist and at the university I focus my research on problems which will develop the kind of basic knowledge I was referring to above. While I consider that I am doing computer science research, I try to focus the research further so that it will eventually be applicable to the development of complex systems.

Some time ago, however, it became clear to me that software engineering was not computer science, if for no other reason than because of the basic differences in objective (development of systems in the one, development of knowledge in the other). Thus a separate, but closely related, discipline seemed appropriate in order to help focus education, training, and research. The relationship between computer science and software engineering is almost completely analogous to the relationship between chemistry and chemical engineering, physics and electrical engineering, or any basic science and an engineering discipline based on it, but including other knowledge and techniques as well.

The relationship between an SDS and software engineering should be clear. Software engineering is the field (body of organized and systemized knowledge and techniques) that is the primary supplier of the concepts, procedures, and tools for the SDS. Eventually, it should be the primary supplier of the technical people in the SDS; at present, however, there are too few formal training or education programs in software engineering for this to be possible. Further, it is software engineering that supplies many of the policies and much of the generalized information that are integral parts of the SDS.

So far, there do not appear to be any major problems with the relationship between most SDSs and software engineering. The relationship is new and seems to be well accepted on both sides. As long as the constructive aspects of the nationalism predominate, helping to focus energy on providing the necessary ingredients for quality SDSs, these two should be effective supplier-consumer nations.

## 10.4 Uneasy Coexistence or Allies?

The academic field of information systems takes a broad view. It is concerned with systems of any kind which collect, process, store, and distribute information, independently of whether or not they are implemented by computer-based systems. Further, they are often concerned with the relationship between an information system and the surrounding system that utilizes it.

The pragmatic counterparts of those interested in the academic study of information systems sometimes are not so clearly identifiable in industry. Yet the concerns are there and in some organizations they have led to the establishment of specific organizational functions and departments.

On the surface, it would seem that the field of information systems, or the people working in that area, would be natural allies of those in the SDS. After all, the SDS produces the computer-based systems that are often the engine of the information system. Such is not always the case, however.

The focus of many people working within the SDS is the technology, whereas the focus of many in the information systems areas (especially in the academic arena) is the organization that uses the information system. This would not be a problem, except that each side sometimes feels the other is insensitive to their concerns and perhaps even incapable of understanding them.

To aggravate the situation, either because of frustration with perceived shortcomings of the other or because of lack of confidence, it is not uncommon to find information system people doing what is simply software development work and SDS personnel becoming involved in information utilization issues that are unrelated to the nature of the information system they are supposed to be building. These incursions across borders and lack of respect for the other side needlessly lead to a state of uneasy coexistence in some cases or avoidance in others.

The systems view of development clearly indicates that there is always a larger system of which the SDS is only a part. In the case of the field of information systems, to the extent that it is concerned with issues that are complementary and supportive of what the SDS does, they should certainly be allies. Indeed, there is a strong need for the broad view that information systems offers and for the careful study and shaping of the interface between the information system and the surrounding system that utilizes it.

Even though most formal information systems are computer-based, this should not be allowed to monopolize the attention of those concerned. Unfortunately, the focus on the technology, rather than on its application, is not limited to those working in the SDS. People whose concern should be the broader information system sometimes seem to be as enamored with the technology as those who are supposedly the technologists; indeed, some technologists have very serious and deep concerns about the utilization of the technology.

When the SDS is properly organized with an appropriate set of objectives, it generally is not interfering with those concerned about the larger picture of information systems. On the other hand, most SDSs could do more to encourage those concerned with the larger picture. If this were done and the response were appropriate cooperation, then information systems work and the SDS could be powerful allies.

## 10.5 The Promised Land

A new player in the game of systems development has shown up: artificial intelligence (AI). While using computers to write programs was one of the very first tasks attempted by the pioneers of artificial intelligence 25 years ago, little further work had been done until recently.[10.3] Suddenly, the idea of applying artificial-intelligence techniques to some of the tasks in the SDS is heard at conferences, written about in magazines, and even found in a few software products.

In terms of my geopolitical analogy, some view AI as the promised land in which we will just speak our needs into a microphone and the intelligent, automated SDS will produce the needed programs in real time. That nirvana is about as close as most promised lands—and about as realistic.

That does not mean that AI techniques cannot be applied to some of the tasks that must be performed in the SDS. They can be and eventually some truly revolutionary changes may result; but that is for the long term.

In the meantime, there are some obvious candidates for the application of knowledge-based techniques to software development: configuration management, quality control, debugging, and project management. These and other concepts that are used in AI (but that can be found in other places as well) appear to have some strong application possibilities to the tasks of acquiring and representing specifications or judging the quality of a proposed design, for example. Limited forms of automatic programming in which executable code is produced from a set of high-level specifications are possible and basically just require a thorough job of turning research concepts into production methods.

*The promised land of totally automatic software development is a utopia that may not be reached in our lifetimes. But it does offer some limited improvements in the near term and much more significant improvements in the long term.*

The relationship between the SDS and the promised land of AI, then, should be pretty much like that between any utopia and the work-aday world in which most people live: Those ideas that work should be adopted as soon as possible; additional tasks to which the techniques of AI can be applied should be sought; and the promise of a shining possible future should not be allowed to detract or disturb the SDS from its immediate tasks.

## 10.6 Trading Partners and Visitors

*We are handicapped by [foreign] policies based on old myths rather than current realities.*

— *J. William Fulbright Speech in the U.S. Senate*

The customer that is buying the system the SDS is building is like a trading partner nation. There must be respect and reciprocity between them, honesty must be the watchword, and for the sake of clarity, the details of the arrangement between them should, as far as possible, be written down.

Customers come in many shapes, sizes, and flavors. They may be a specific external individual or organization, an internal group within the organization but not part of the SDS, a subpart of the SDS, an unnamed or mythical "customer," or some combination of the above. The role will change somewhat depending on the nature of the customer, as will the extent of formal relationships between the customer and the SDS.

The customer is critical to the success of most development projects. The SDS must have a relationship with the customer that permits appropriate objectives to be set, information for requirements to be obtained, in-process reviews to be carried out, and effective acceptance tests to be held. On the other hand, the SDS must make sure that the customer does not have the ability to intrude into the proper workings of the SDS and throw it out of whack. Striking that balance of cooperation is not easy. A senior manager of a sophisticated development organization, went to some pains to stress the following view of intelligent customers:

> Much emphasis is placed on the intelligence of the development organization. An overlooked, but perhaps even more important, point is that the customer must also be intelligent. The customer must understand and demand quality development. He must understand that the goal is to get a product out, not just obey a contract or a set of regulations.
>
> A good customer on a complex project must be willing to throw away the rule book and the contract in order to reach the objective of delivering a system. This flies in the face of some of the prevailing "wisdom" that dictates that one must not step outside the contract or the development guidelines. Indeed, that is good advice as long as it is kept in perspective. The perspective is that all of the rules and contracts are formulated to achieve an objective—building a quality system. It is certainly the case in most large, complex, state-of-the-art projects that not everything can be foreseen in advance; indeed, very little can be completely seen in advance. The result is that during the project as the development team learns more about the problem and the solution, they must be able (under appropriate controls) to change the rules.

The real issue, then, is to be able to control properly the changes to the rules, rather than worrying about the changes themselves. This metalevel of control, however, is rarely utilized except by the most sophisticated and mature organizations. Confirmation of the soundness of this attitude is found in the fact that studies of the Apollo moon landing program identified this same attitude as one of the key contributors to success.

Users of systems are often not the customers that buy the systems, except in the case of personal computers. For large, complex systems, relations between the users and the customers must be carefully distinguished since they may have very different—even opposing—requirements and views of the system.

For example, the customer (purchaser) of a financial management system for a large organization may be interested in obtaining the most functionality for the least expenditure; this may be best achieved by using a batch-processing system for some functions. The users of the system (the clerks, administrators, etc.), however, may be more interested in ease of use of the system, which may well be best served by having a completely on-line system.

Users, like customers, have a valuable role to play in the development of a system, especially during the requirements definition activity. The SDS must treat users like visitors to a foreign country—welcoming them and treating them with courtesy. The users, on the other hand, must respect the customs of their hosts.

This idyllic situation is sometimes clouded, however. Users are often customers too. Neither customers nor users know what they want in some situations. The SDS may think it knows best and fail to pay appropriate attention to either their trading partners or visitors; or, at the other extreme, it may always do whatever they want, abdicating all professional responsibility to guide customers and users in appropriate ways.

Enough has been preached about the importance of the relationship between the development organization and those most directly concerned with the success of the development: the customers and users. There is no particular magic or deep mystery involved; it is simply a relationship that must be carefully and constantly tended.

## 10.7 Fellow Citizens

No, I'm not starting a political speech. I'm referring to all the other people and groups in an organization that must interact with the SDS.

Above and beyond all the usual caveats about relationships among the members and parts of an organization, the SDS often has a special set of problems in this realm. It is often the new kid on the block; it typically gets special treatment in terms of space, salary, working hours, and other resources; and most incriminating of all, what it does may severely impact others.

It is this last item that is the key factor that must be carefully managed. Systems may delay or speed up work; lateness of delivery can be disastrous to a department that is dependent on the new system; not only individual jobs, but entire departments can be replaced by a new system. These, and many other, factors mean that the SDS is often sitting on a hot seat in a glass box with respect to their fellow citizens.

In the early days of computing, one rarely thought about the ways in which the system one was building would change its users and the whole environment in which it operates. Oh, of course it was clear that calculations would be much faster or that one could keep track of larger inventories—things that were directly replaced or touched by the computer. But one rarely thought of the system as changing an entire environment.

If there is one thing that the past 40 years (more accurately, probably, the past 20 years) should have taught us, it is that computer systems have an uncanny way of becoming an integral part of their environments so that they not only change the surroundings but are changed by them. Entire industries such as publishing or air travel have been altered by the existence of the computer, while others are starting to be impacted as computing technology becomes more sophisticated. Editors work in new ways, travel agents have new demands placed on them and need not deal with others, graphic designers must radically change how they work, all because of the computer's impact on their industry or profession.

This reality is sometimes more evident to the purchasers and users of computing systems than it is to those of us who create them.[10.4] There is a growing body of serious studies that outline some of these impacts; there is less, but some, study of the nature of the relationship between the SDS and its environment. It is this relation that I am suggesting must be carefully managed.

CHAPTER

# 11

# And They All Lived Happily

SIX FLAGS
MAGIC MOUNTAIN
COLOSSUS
SIX FLAGS
MAGIC MOUNTAIN
COLOSSUS

CHAPTER

# 11

# And They All Lived Happily

*The great end of life is not knowledge but action.*

— *Thomas Henry Huxley*
*Technical Education*

11.1 In the Final Installment (introduction)

11.2 So What? (perspective on the perspective)

11.3 How to Get and Sell Religion (hints for technology transfer)

11.4 Will John Marry Susie? (where are we headed)

Courtesy of Six Flags Magic Mountain

## 11.1 In the Final Installment

Will the strange ideas of Willard gain acceptance? Will the family members return to the fold and attend church? Will John marry Susie?

These and other compelling questions will be answered as our drama of complex systems development in the modern world unfolds. In the meantime, can we gain something from the episodes we have seen thus far? Can we take charge of our own destinies and avoid shame and bankruptcy?

Yes!

In this final chapter, I want to provide a brief perspective on the perspectives presented here, comment on technology transfer, and share with you a view of the future.

## 11.2 So What?

Look back over the previous pages and refresh your perception of what is here.

> *To paraphrase McLuhan, The System Is the Message.*

I have viewed development of software, indeed of any complex system, as an interacting system of objectives, policies, information, people, procedures, and tools. This software development system (SDS) is driven by a search for quality and is susceptible to many of the same kinds of problems that plague the end-product systems we build: inability to meet goals, mistakes, high cost, and out-of-control operation in extreme cases.

Yet it can also work smoothly, react to applied controls like a fine race car, and produce high-quality products on time and under budget. I have encountered SDSs that run smoothly and ones that are problem-plagued. The difference, as with computer systems, is usually explained by how well they are designed, implemented, and operated, not in their individual parts, but *as a system.*

There is no formula guaranteeing success and no general set of plans for an SDS. If you have read this book expecting to learn exactly what to do, then I can guarantee you are disappointed. On the other hand, if you were looking for some perspective on what you are encountering in the world of systems development, then what I have provided should give you a start in the right direction.

My perspective on this perspective is that it encompasses three things: a structure, some observations, and a set of judgments. The structure is the systems view of systems development. The model of the general SDS presented in Chapters 3, 4, and 5, and expanded in the following four chapters, provides a framework and viewpoint that will aid your understanding of the world around you.

The presentation of the model is laced with observations—mine and those of others—on a number of different development systems. The observations are varied in level and detail. Some are from the perspective of the "owner" of the SDS, while others are from the perspective of project managers or even individual technical team members. Some are one-line comments, while others take several pages to present.

As a scientist I am uncomfortable that we don't have firmer, more systematic confirmation of the validity of the model. Even a good solid survey would help! Ten years or so of academic research by management professors and graduate students should reassure me on this score!

On the other hand, as a consultant and businessman, I am convinced enough of the model's validity to stake my professional reputation on it and to found a business on it.

I expect that you will take the third element presented in this book—the judgments—for exactly what they are: the judgments of one person. My perspective, however, is that I am not alone in evaluating these observations in the way that I have.

So what you have here should be a reasonable companion for your journey into systems land.

Before you depart (or return) let me leave you with one more observation and one more set of judgments.

## 11.3 How to Get and Sell Religion

This was the title I used for my working notes to capture the essence of my conversations with a very senior person on the subject of technology transfer. I think it captures the essence of one of the important elements of building (or modifying) your SDS: you, and those around you, must first get the "religion" of systematic systems development and then you must sell it to others, so that everyone involved with your SDS is singing the same hymns.

Originally I planned to have a whole chapter on the subject of technology transfer. When it came time to write it, I decided it deserved either a few paragraphs or an entire book, but nothing in between! The book will have to wait, so let me share my observations on what works in technology transfer in the space of a small section.

Getting religion is, of course, a personal matter. What I have observed, however, is that for most people it falls into two major categories of motivation. The technical value of the systems approach to development, the increased quality of the product and the efficiency of the process of producing it, convinces many. This is especially true for technical people, for whom it is ample motivation once they see it demonstrated or try it for themselves.

*Approach technology transfer as you would a project.*

For others, especially those more oriented toward the business aspects of systems development, finances are the motivation. A systems view of development can lead to financial gains not only in the immediate performance of the development tasks but in the overall lifetime financial profile of the products produced. To paraphrase an old saying, most people are motivated by either technology or money.

Assuming you have religion, how do you sell it to those around you?

Technology transfer is a critical issue in our modern culture and seems to be especially needed in the area of software development. I am certainly not the first, nor the only one, to consider the process of technology transfer, although until quite recently very few were concerned with it in our area. As you might expect, there is considerable general literature and experience to draw upon, as well as a growing amount of experience, specifically in the software area.

The key factor is suggested by the theme of this book: systems development. Given that what you are trying to create is a system (for building systems), then it seems obvious that you should attack the problem in the same organized way that you would attack the building of a complex software system—with a careful requirements analysis and design, effective implementation, measurement, and controlled evolution over time. Indeed, that approach works.

As you might suspect, these simple observations on getting and selling religion can be detailed indefinitely. But not here!

## 11.4 Will John Marry Susie?

Will the systems view of systems development catch on and sweep the country like wildfire (to coin a phrase)?

When it comes to predicting the future, I have nothing more to offer than anyone else in foreseeing what a group of people will do. I am not sure that the "systems view" *per se* will come to be identified as the underlying structure of development organizations any more than it has become the permeating view in more general business organizations. For one thing, there are clearly a lot of political and market forces that must be taken into account in the larger picture, and the systems view is not always successful in this regard.[11.1]

But the question I have posed is not the name identification of a particular concept; rather, it is whether or not that concept will become a driving part of the complex of concepts used to organize and manage systems development. To this, I will give a resoundingly positive prediction: Yes!

For the foreseeable future (which means no more than five years in the fast-moving world of computing), essentially all systems development is still going to be done largely as it is today. It often takes at least that long for a new tool or concept in the systems development area to make its way from the laboratory into preliminary use (and longer for widespread use), and there is nothing currently working so well in the laboratory that it will completely revolutionize things when it is put into use.

Given that for some time things are going to be much as they are now, the best organizing concept by far is the systems approach. It is clear that in development we have a number of different elements to deal with; the activity is an objective-oriented one; individual pieces can be optimized, but experience teaches us that no one piece can be optimized so highly that it will result in performance superior to that of a well-tuned collection of competent components.

In short, I see no conditions in the near future that will negate the validity of the systems approach to systems development. Believing in the rationality of most technical undertakings, I conclude that the motivations of quality and money (which are really the same thing) will continue to motivate the use of the systems approach.

There will, of course, be many changes—and at a high rate of change. Better tools, especially ones with a modicum of intelligence embedded in them, will appear. Enhanced procedures, especially those with more formal or theoretical bases, will appear. Improved education and training for those in the SDS is already available if people would just invest in it. In short, we are on the threshold of some relatively dramatic increases in the capabilities of the components of the SDS; the resources that are being poured into their improvement will indeed help, although perhaps not always as much as is hoped.

The critical areas, as always in a system, will be in their integration and management. In the SDS, this means we must learn more about the policies that are best suited to tying the various components together and how to shape objectives to drive the whole thing. Surrounding the whole thing is the information that is generated by and used in the SDS. Understanding what it is and how to handle it is the key to all the rest.

It is humanly possible to do a decent job of all this—improving components, tying them together, and managing the associated information. If you do, and if you keep a healthy outlook on the whole enterprise,[11.2] then you can have the software you want without getting ulcers in the process!

# Appendixes

APPENDIX A

# Development Activities and Lifecycles

*It is circumstance and proper timing that give an action its character and make it either good or bad.*

— *Plutarch Lives*

In this appendix I want to expand on some of the basic development activities and lifecycles mentioned in the main body of the text. This brief discussion, however, should not be taken as a complete coverage of the subject.[A.1]

## Development Activities

Let's begin by reiterating the distinction between *stages* of development and the *activities* that are carried out in each. Common usage is to name the stages with the dominant activity of that stage (e.g., analysis, design, programming), but it is clear that many different activities may occur during a particular stage.

For example, during the analysis phase of development, we may build a prototype of part of the proposed system and actually execute it in order to obtain a clearer picture of what the customer wants. Thus it is probably best to view the stages of development as relating to the managerial concerns (schedules, budgets, deliverable workproducts, and so on) while viewing the activities as relating to the technical work being performed.

In Chapter 5, we presented a very simplified list of activities; in that vein, a more complete list of the technical activities that one finds in software development might include:

1. *Analysis*: Understanding something by separating it into component parts
2. *Specification*: Describing something by its external characteristics
3. *Design*: Devising an artifact that meets a set of objectives
4. *Programming*: Building a coherent set of instructions for a processor that will cause it to exhibit a desired behavior

5. *Testing*: Determining empirically if an artifact meets a stated set of specifications
6. *Verification*: Determining if a step in the development process has been correctly carried out
7. *Validation*: Determining if a description of a system, or the system itself, properly meets the expectations of the customer
8. *Evolution (maintenance)*: Making changes to an existing artifact

Note that these definitions are purposely broad, and not necessarily listed in chronological order. Thus the definition for testing includes testing specifications, designs, *and* code.

One can refine a list such as this, and there is some research interest in doing so in order to provide a firmer conceptual basis for tool and procedure development. Our interest here, however, is not in providing a thorough discussion of all possible activities, but in emphasizing the importance of separating what people do from the names given to certain stages of development.

As an example, let's look at one of the most glaring examples of confusion—evolution (usually called maintenance). A typical lifecycle model (such as the "waterfall model" described below) will label a single stage of development "maintenance"; there may even be entire departments named Software Maintenance and you will certainly encounter software professionals who will describe what they do as "maintenance."

But what goes on in a typical maintenance activity of a large system? Among other things, requests will be made to add substantial new functionality to the system. If accepted, and the function is a major one, then at least two kinds of analysis must take place: analysis of the requirements to make sure they are complete and well understood, and analysis of the existing system to determine the impact of making the proposed changes. (Some would argue that these, in fact, are differenct forms of analysis.)

Then the actual changes must be designed (they may involve thousands of lines of new code, for example), programmed, tested, integrated into the system, and the resulting enhanced system tested to make sure that it still performs the original functions plus whatever new functions have been added. In short, a number of activities have taken place.

The danger is that one may not properly understand and focus on the basic intellectual activities of development, independent of the stage during which they may be dominant. The result can be improper and inadequate control of the process, poor choice of personnel, and substandard support of the activities with tools, procedures, and training.

By analogy, suppose we organized the University curriculum into Introduction (year 1), Basics (year 2), Advanced (year 3), and Application (year

4), and assumed that only in year 2 was someone studying Basics of any subject. Then, among other distortions, course prerequisites and what we expected of students would be rather different.

### Lifecycle Models

There are numerous models of the "lifecycle" of system development. Some of these methods are descriptive (i.e., they describe what exists), some are prescriptive (i.e., they prescribe what steps should be taken), and some are normative (i.e., they establish a standard; for example, some of the DoD regulations that set out specific development phases that must be followed).

As concern for the software engineering process has increased almost exponentially, so has concern for having the "right" lifecycle model. This concern has some very positive aspects and some that may be counterproductive. On the positive side, the backbone of any systematic, visible software engineering process must be a clear set of workproduct definitions and an indication of what steps should be taken to create those workproducts; this is precisely what a lifecycle model is intended to do—and can do if used properly. Also, since most software is still developed today without the aid of *any* very well-defined lifecycle, almost any, properly used, is better than none.

The negative side of this concern over having the "right" lifecycle is that a lot of effort can be expended for little or no gain. It must be remembered that we are discussing *models*, not reality. Models, by definition, are an abstraction of reality. They can help us shape reality by helping us see the relationships between different aspects of development more clearly, and thus it is important that they be relatively accurate. However, since they are always simpler than reality (or should be!), we should not become too impatient when they seem not to capture everything we see in practice.

What is happening is that as people in a wide variety of situations realize the importance of the lifecycle that is being followed, they try to find better descriptions than the traditional ones. Several research workshops have been devoted to the "software process" (the complex of activities mirrored by lifecycle models) and The Eighth International Conference on Software Engineering, in 1985, had the software process as its focus. It is also very important to recognize that researchers are looking for entirely new processes for development (often automation-based) that may radically change our need for highly visible, intermediate workproducts, for example.

This is all to the good, but it means that our collective understanding of the characteristics of software lifecycles is changing rather rapidly. In such a situation, we must be prepared to cope with models that always seem inadequate; eventually the rate of change of our understanding will slow down, and then we will be able more easily to prescribe appropriate lifecycle models. (Fifteen years ago, great concern was expressed that we did not have adequate descriptive means to handle the large collections of on-line data that were just starting to grow; while we certainly do not have the last word yet, the situation with respect to data models is not nearly so fluid now as it was then.)

*Waterfall Model*

While there are no standard definitions or models of the software engineering process, the lifecycle shown in Fig. A.1, commonly called the *waterfall model*, is frequently used to describe the overall structure of the software engineering process. Many of us recognize some of the deficiencies in this model (distribution of activities not shown, iteration not clear, early testing invisible, prototyping not shown, and so on) but it nonetheless is a good description of the current *perception* of what software engineering encompasses. Because of its simplicity, it also has value for explanatory purposes.

There are two essential ingredients of a model: its component parts and the relationships between them. Figure A.1 basically only shows the temporal components of software engineering by major phase of activity. These major phases have been described in many places.[A.2]

*The PSC Systemeering Model*

As an example of a rather different model of development, let's look at one that originated in Finland.

It is generally accepted that several viewpoints or perspectives should be considered in the development effort. In the PSC systemeering model and its generalizations the *main perspectives* have been developed from general systems theory and semiotics.[A.3] In the most general form these are as follows (Z stands for the ideal-seeking, purposeful system we are developing):

- The *pragmatic (P) perspective* studies Z as an element in its environment $\overline{Z}$, paying attention to the needs of those having an interest in the outcomes of Z and $\overline{Z}$.
- The *input-output (I/O) perspective* studies the external behavior of Z i.e., the outcomes provided by Z and $\overline{Z}$, and the resources necessary to achieve these.
- The *constructive (C) perspective* examines Z as a system of functions and of resources responsible for the realization of those functions.
- The *operative (O) perspective* studies the internal behavior of Z.

(Originally the last two perspectives were combined, and the term semantic (S) was used for the second. The abbreviation PSC refers to this combination of the three main perspectives.)

The PSC systemeering process is subdivided into four main phases where each main phase is concerned with the *decision problems* of a certain

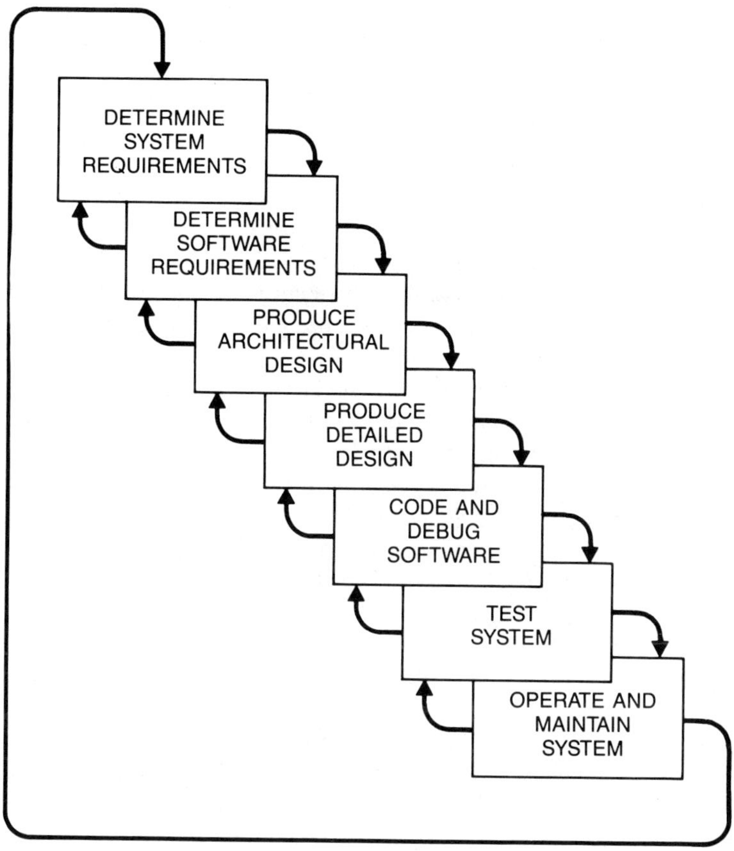


FIGURE A.1 Waterfall Model of Software Engineering (© 1981 IEEE with permission)

perspective. Solving these problems yields a set of models at successively lower levels of abstraction for each main phase. The highest level of abstraction is *pragmatic* (P), the second *semantic* (S), and the third *constructive* (C). Each main phase supports a *class of decision makers* and is accomplished by appropriate *experts* (systemeers and implementors).

In the pragmatic main phase, the information system is studied in terms of its *influence* on the environment and the influence of the environment on the information system. *All the phases consist of a design (and/or implementation) and test cycle.* In the P main phase, alternatives for an information system solution are evaluated using a criterion of the *net value of the effectiveness versus all the costs* incurred during the lifecycle. At this broad level the evaluation is qualitatively oriented. Effectiveness is a multidimensional criterion taking into account such factors as economic, social, technical, communicational, ecological, and managerial components between Z and $\bar{Z}$. The models selected for the proposed system at this level establish the solution space for moving into the S main phase and give the answers to the question pair "Why-How" on the highest level.

The development of alternative solutions is refined in the semantic main phase as the focus turns to an evaluation of the *information content* produced by the system in terms of users' needs. This refinement takes the alternative set chosen in the P main phase and develops alternatives at the next lower level of information system definition. The design and test criteria in this phase are more tangible than in the P phase. We evaluate alternative information sets in terms of *informativeness, accessibility,* and *adaptability.* These factors can in turn be stated as more explicit criteria for measurement. Using the lowest level criteria in this decision framework, the S-level decision maker estimates net value based on *cumulative user satisfaction* expressed as a function of these criteria *less the costs* of providing that level of satisfaction. The answers are obtained to the question pair: "What-How."

At the third constructive level of information systems development, the design and test responsibilities determine the structure and processors for the system. This identifies the man and/or machine components that will accomplish each function required in the information system to satisfy the information needs identified in the S main phase and the influences defined in the P main phase. At this level the decision criteria shift to the more quantitative *efficiency* factors. For instance, at the most general C-level evaluation, the application can be designed and tested in terms of the sum of design and implementation costs, operations costs, and maintenance costs. These factors and their lower level expressions provide the basis for selecting a C-level solution that achieves maximum efficiency for the *total cumulative costs* of the proposed information system during its lifecycle. Answers are obtained to the question pair: "How-How."

In the fourth implementation phase, the subsystems are totally implemented, the new system is tested from all the perspectives, and decision making concerns the use and operational quality of the development product. The completed information system is therefore defined as a set of models (and their descriptions) from all the main perspectives and the physical realization of these models.

In the PSC model of the lifecycle, the design resulting from a given phase is analyzed in a preliminary fashion using later-phase criteria and is even experimentally implemented in order to determine the *feasibility* of the given design. For instance, for the P main phase, the S-, C- and even B-level experimental implementations are tentatively developed by the systemeers to see if the P-level result is feasible in terms of the highest S-, C- and B-level criteria. After completing all levels of design in the P main phase, then the proposed information system is then tested in reverse order. The solution proposed in the P main phase is tested at the B-, C-, S- and P-levels respectively. This highlights the iterative top-down design and bottom-up test that is built into each phase of the PSC lifecycle.

Carrying the procedure one phase further, the solution developed in the S main phase is designed and possibly implemented in general and/or experimental terms at the C- and B-levels. The resulting S-level solution is tested successively in terms of B-, C-, S- and P-level criteria. This strategy indicates the *two-dimensional character of the PSC model.* For the P, S, C, and B phases through time, there are P-, S-, C-, and B-levels of design, implementation, and test within each. This feature provides a robust approach to information systems development.

I have included this top-level description of the PSC model (taken from a joint paper with its originator[A.4]) to illustrate that the traditional models of development we typically use are very weak in their descriptive power.

*Traditional Business Systems Development*

A composite of the traditional view of systems development phases has been defined as[A.5]:

*Situation review*—Identification of the problem or opportunity that presents a challenge to the user

*Requirements identification*—Determination of the information outputs that will alleviate the problem or capitalize on the opportunity

*Physical design*—Specification of the input, process, and storage modules that are required to produce the indicated outputs

*Program preparation*—Preparation of the instructions for the machine components of the information system

*Procedure preparation*—Preparation of the instructions for the people components of the information system

*System conversion*—Parallel or direct cutover from current to the new capability developed to replace it

*Utilization*—The ongoing use and maintenance of the information system to serve the purpose for which it was developed

Again, there are many variations on this theme. This particular model is included as illustration.

*An Evolutionary Model*

Lucas[A.6] has proposed an evolutionary approach to systems development in combination with "creative design" strategies. This view assumes user-initiated systems to which the systems department responds with prototype outputs to serve as a basis for mutual discussion of the user need. This stimulates ideas for other outputs. In this way the user and systems personnel engage in a collaborative problem solving dialogue. This dialogue is characterized by a series of design, program, and test cycles. As the system evolves to an acceptable level of user support, the user gradually assumes full responsibility for his or her application. Even when the application has matured, new ideas for further development emerge, but at a slower rate. In this approach, there is no final product or "finished" application. It is always an ongoing development effort.

### Comparison

The waterfall, traditional, evolutionary, and PSC models of the systems development lifecycle can be compared and contrasted. The four versions of the lifecycle are summarized in Fig. A.2. The phases of the traditional model appear in the left column. These terms are taken from the phase definitions above. The five phases of the evolutionary model appear in the middle of the figure. The inception and initial grouping phases correspond in part to situation review; part of the intention of these two phases precedes what is normally encompassed in situation review. However, because of its experimental nature, some aspects of the first three traditional phases are covered by the evolutionary model. Mutual progress covers the situation review through procedure preparation phases. Finally, conversion and maturity correspond approximately to the systems conversion and utilization phases respectively.

The distinctive feature of the PSC model is the coverage of *all* traditional phases in each phase of this approach. The P, S, and C phases all involve the program preparation through utilization phase on an experimental basis. This feature of the Lucas approach is built into the PSC model. The comparison also highlights the greater emphasis placed on the early systems development phases in the PSC approach. The rationale for this heavier relative investment is that more conscious decisions in earlier phases reduces the investment required to converge on the B-level solution.

The additional investment in the earlier phases is compensated for by reduced resource demands in the C, B, and utilization main phases. The top-down systematic reduction in uncertainty for the design and test of the information system following the PSC model results in little or no net increase in the total development cost with a significant potential saving in user frustration. Users will more likely obtain an information system that will adequately respond to the problems and/or opportunities they are confronted with. This comparison suggests the greater sophistication of the PSC model in light of the traditional and the evolutionary models. To coordinate and integrate the

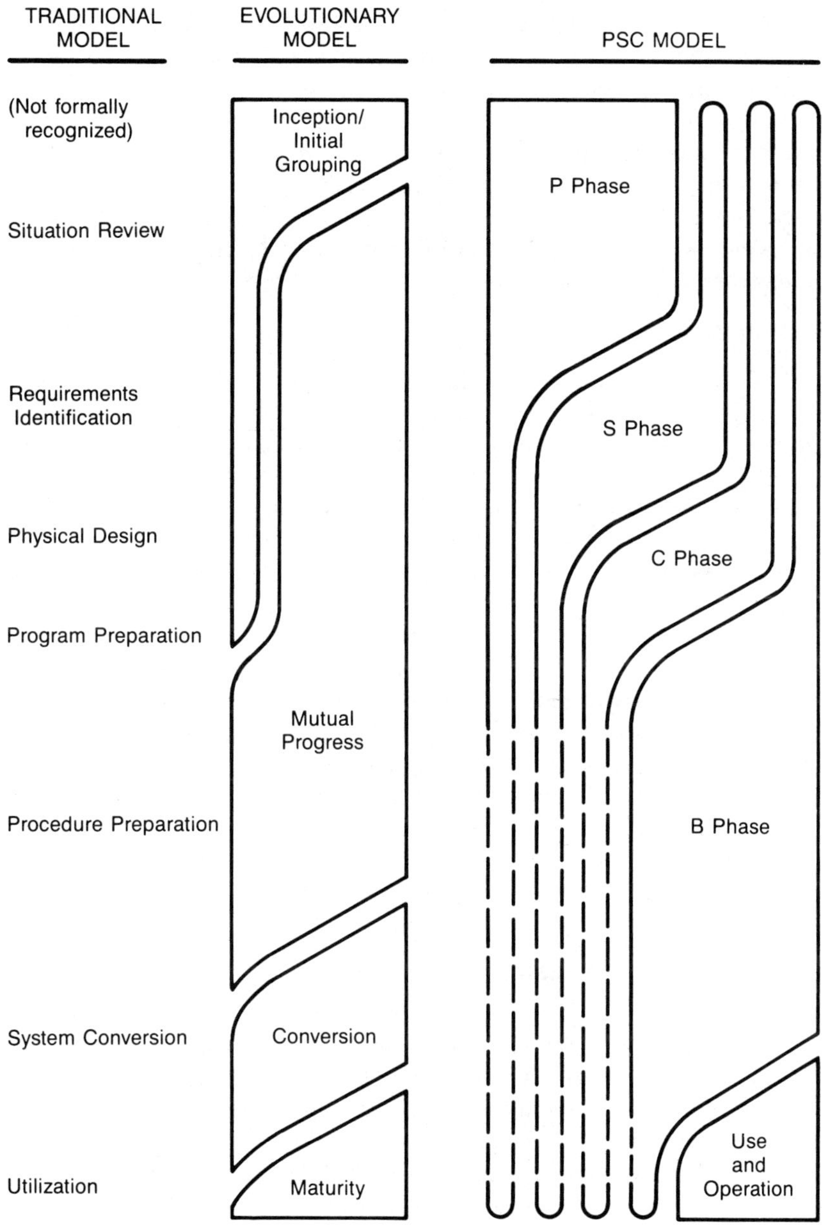


FIGURE A.2 Macro Level Comparison (© 1981 IEEE with permission)

work in the PSC approach requires a position that is more sophisticated than traditional systems positions: the role of *information systems architect.*

One of the factors that has led to a great deal of discontent with current lifecycle models is the fact that they tend to be very sequential and imply that development must extend over long periods of time. Extended development periods lead to real problems in a world in which the requirements for a system may change several times before the system is completed. This concern for shortening the development cycle (and the models that describe it), along with other factors, has led to the development of various system prototyping concepts and tools.

### Prototyping

Building a model of a complex artifact before building the final version (prototyping) is a well-established technique in traditional engineering. Recently, a great deal of interest has arisen in using prototyping in software development. While hardly a new idea, concern over the problems often encountered in traditional systems development coupled with the widespread acceptance of different modes of computing (e.g. interactive) and the emergence of some new tools (such as program generators and database query systems) has sparked this interest anew.

Prototyping is indeed a valuable tool for the software designer. Unfortunately, it must be used properly or it can lead to many of the same problems of loss of project control and of systems that are difficult to maintain. There is a good bit of confusion in the current literature on what prototyping really is, stemming from the desire of some to jump on a bandwagon and claim that their particular language or tool or method is the thing that everyone has been looking for! While we cannot provide a complete guide to prototyping here, it will be useful to discuss briefly the relationship of prototyping to the design process. Simply, we see three ways in which a prototyping activity can be productively used in software development:

1. *Preliminary prototyping*: In this traditional mode, one builds a functioning system that is substantially like the desired one. It is placed into service, studied, and then ultimately replaced by the final system. Typically, the "prototype" does not have a full complement of functions and error checks, may be implemented in an inefficient manner, and is used only by "understanding" users. The switchover to a full, well-built system that is based on the experience with the prototype is done on a definite schedule. An example is a quick and inefficient implementation of a compiler for a new language; once the language design is frozen an efficient compiler can be built.

2. *Concurrent prototyping*: This can be used to bring up a limited version of a system quickly while a traditional development process is employed to build the full system. Experience with the prototype may be used in the full system, although the emphasis is more on getting results to the customer quickly via the prototype and less on collecting information that will be relevant to the system design effort. For example, a management support system can be quickly put together using existing packages to provide needed information even though the report formats may be inconsistent and some features may be missing; while the prototype is supplying the essential information, a refined and complete implementation can be built.
3. *Decision prototyping*: This can be used at *each* stage of development where needed to help make decisions. Thus, at the functional specification stage, one might build a prototype of the user interface in order to get feedback from potential users on proposed specification; at the design stage, one might prototype several different architectures to determine which provides the most efficient implementation; during implementation one could prototype alternative algorithms to study their execution properties.

As better tools for prototyping are developed and as our understanding of how to use them improves, prototyping should become an integral part of many software development efforts.

### Conclusion

This brief discussion of lifecycle models has skipped over a number of important concepts, but it should provide you a clearer picture of the range of issues involved in understanding the development process.

APPENDIX B

# Notes

### Prologue

**Note P.1 (p. xix):** Some useful textbooks on software development include [Fairley, 1985]; [Pressman, 1987]; [Gilbert, 1983]; and [Abbott, 1986]. Full citations on all references will be found in the Bibliography.

**Note P.2 (p. xxv):** For example, [Feigenbaum and McCorduck, 1983], [Nasbitt, 1982].

### Chapter 1

**Note 1.1 (p. 5):** [Jones, 1986] lists 11 meanings for "lines of code." He discusses in detail the problems with using them as a productivity measure and shows how to improve measurements. Unfortunately, there is no accepted measure other than lines of code, due in part to the wide variation in what other types of workproducts are produced.

**Note 1.2 (p. 5):** See [Weinberg, 1971] for an interesting study of the impact of directions on the work of programmers.

**Note 1.3 (p. 7):** Our ability to design hardware (typically, a special-purpose chip) that implements entire functions or even complete applications without any software (in the sense of programs that must be loaded into a primary memory and executed) in no way changes the centrality of software. Indeed, the best way to look at special-purpose hardware is that it is software that is frozen, and software in which the cost of change will be very high. The common ingredient is the design of a set of functions and associated data. The mode of implementation (hardware or software) does not change the nature of the logical design task.

**Note 1.4 (p. 7):** See [Sayles and Chandler, 1971]

**Note 1.5 (p. 9):** Software representations are dominated by programming languages, for which there are multitudes of references. Serious consideration of representations for other forms of software (requirements, specifications, designs, etc.) is usually found in the context of a particular method for design or specification (for example, structured design) described in a book or paper about the particular method. A survey of a number of different representations can be found in [Martin and McClure, 1985] and [Peters, 1981]. [Jones, 1986, pp. 48ff.] discusses different categories of representation from the standpoint of power. A software engineering text such as [Fairley, 1985] contains descriptions of many representations in the context of their usage in development.

**Note 1.6 (p. 12):** Ada is a big step, technically, over languages such as FORTRAN and COBOL—and certainly assembly language—that were created before we understood (at least in an explicit way) most of the principles of large system construction that we now have. On the other hand, it is important to recognize that because of the time it takes to design a new language and get it into use on any large scale, there have been advances in our understanding of SEK that are not reflected in Ada. Further, there are many organizational/social factors surrounding the adoption of any new language, so that the adoption of this (or any other new software representation) proceedsvery slowly. There are by now many sources of information on Ada; I can recommend three: [Booch, 1983], [Cohen, 1986], and [Habermann and Perry, 1983].

**Note 1.7 (p. 14):** [Belady and Lehman, 1976] reports on work done around 1970 while [Lehman and Belady, 1985] includes later work.

**Note 1.8 (p. 26):** Software engineering in general deals with this, especially the technical aspects. See [Gunther, 1978] for a thorough and detailed treatment of the managerial aspects.

**Note 1.9 (p. 27):** See [Freeman, 1983b] and [Freeman, 1987] for a discussion of this viewpoint.

### Chapter 2

**Note 2.1 (p. 32):** [Pirsig, 1974] discusses the meaning of quality in the context of a semifictional motorcycle travelogue. Because the main character works as a programmer, there are some insightful comments about the nature of software and its documentation.

**Note 2.2 (p. 32):** See [Peters and Waterman, 1982]. The lessons they draw from studying many organizations apply to the software group as well as the whole company.

**Note 2.3 (p. 34):** See [Boehm *et al.*, 1973]. [Fairley, 1985] and [Jensen and Tonies, 1979] discuss some of the properties of quality, but do not carry the discussion much beyond what Boehm *et al.* first defined in 1973.

**Note 2.4 (p. 35):** The quality definitions given here are informal, matching common practice. One of the encouraging signs in the field, however, is the emergence of more rigorous treatment of some of these qualities; see, for example, [Leveson, 1984] and [Musa, 1987].

**Note 2.5 (p. 42):** See [Page-Jones, 1980].

**Note 2.6 (p. 42):** See [Fagan, 1976].

**Note 2.7 (p. 43):** See, for example, [Jones, 1986].

**Note 2.8 (p. 43):** See [Norman and Draper, 1985].

**Note 2.9 (p. 45):** The standard reference on software quality is yet to be written. [Dunn and Ullman, 1982] provide a useful introduction to some of the mechanics of software quality assurance, but it is important to remember that quality is the ultimate subject of much of software engineering. An excellent, general approach is described in [Crosby, 1980].

**Note 2.10 (p. 47):** The activity called "testing" in much software development is actually a combined activity of testing, repairing, and redesign of the system.

**Note 2.11 (p. 48):** See [Gleitman, 1981, pp. 212–214], and [Weinberg, 1971].

**Note 2.12 (p. 48):** See, for example, [Peters and Waterman, 1982].

**Note 2.13 (p. 49):** See the paper by Matsumato in [Freeman, 1987] for a description of one such factory.

**Note 2.14 (p. 50):** These are among the emerging trends identified by [Nasbitt, 1982] and readily visible to all of us.

**Note 2.15 (p. 51):** In science there is the concept of a paradigm shift [Kuhn, 1970] when the set of beliefs and general framework that scientists hold change radically in a short period of time. For example, until around 1965 geologists explained data on the basis of a set of beliefs about how the earth was put together. Then, in the space of a few years, sufficient evidence was amassed to convince most geologists that the plate tectonic theory provided a better organizing framework; since then, data are explained in these terms, sometimes rather differently than under the old paradigm. In software, the paradigm of "discovery design" that prevails now may well shift to a paradigm of "quality production."

## Chapter 3

**Note 3.1 (p. 57):** Copyright © *The Random House Dictionary of the English Language, College Edition* [Random House, New York, 1984, 1975]

**Note 3.2 (p. 59):** If you are new to the "systems way of thinking," I recommend you read C. West Churchman's *The Systems Approach.* As one of the fathers of the approach—and a pragmatic applier of it to numerous situations—his excellent introduction will provide insight and perspective on some of its uses. Even if you are an old systems thinker, you will find some interesting reading in it.

**Note 3.3 (p. 71):** Establish some measure of quality; for example, the number of complaints received per month or the number of errors found per 1000 lines of production code per week, or the ratio of estimated to actual development time for requests. You want a measure that characterizes the overall SDS, which may mean that you have to factor in several such measures with appropriate weights. Then estimate for a given improvement what it will cost to carry it through; again, the cost may be a combination of money, time, and intangibles.

Form the ratio of quality measure/cost and pick the ones with the highest ratio to start on first. For example, many organizations find that design and code inspections greatly improve the quality of their products. Training people to perform them typically is easy, doesn't take long, doesn't cost much, and takes effect quickly; so the payoff is high and the cost is low, leading to a high ratio.

In contrast, teaching all your designers to use a specific technique may have high payoff, but the payoff may not be realized for a number of years and it may take many months of training just to get them started. In this case, the low cost/quality improvement ratio indicates this would not be the highest priority item (if your objective is to get quick improvements, which it almost always is!) even though in the long term providing this training may be the most important thing to do.

This discrepancy between short-term and long-term benefits often traps us. The demand for quick results all too often pushes out the much more important long-term improvements.

### Chapter 4

**Note 4.1 (p. 89):** [Boehm, 1981, pp. 191ff] discusses how to recognize some classes of inappropriate software product goals. Appendix B of Boehm's book discusses a number of goals for the internal, software engineering aspects of the SDS.

**Note 4.2 (p. 91):** Some initial studies were done in 1969 and reported in 1971. See [Boehm, 1981, p. 404].

**Note 4.3 (p. 96):** [Jones, 1986] provides some industry-wide data and a number of references.

**Note 4.4 (p. 98):** See, for example, [Boehm, 1981] and [Jones, 1986].

**Note 4.5 (p. 104):** SADT is one of several techniques that go by the name "structured analysis" and that employ graphical models. More details on it can be found in [Fairley, 1985], [Ross, 1977], or in a forthcoming book by [Marca and McGowan, 1987].

The SADT diagrams in this book were drawn with the kind assistance of Michel Lissandre and staff, using the specification tool SPECIF available from IGL, Paris, France.

**Note 4.6 (p. 106):** Just as we may build different models of reality, we may have different underlying assumptions on which the models are built. My approach is based on the assumption that for the purpose of understanding its productive behavior, we may model an SDS as a collection of active elements (the parts) that take certain inputs and eventually produce certain outputs. This approach has worked for me in a number of situations and leads to examples and more detailed analyses that lead to useful insights.

For other purposes, however, different assumptions about the underlying reality may be necessary. [Kling and Scacchi, 1982], for example, use an assumption about data processing environments in order to understand why and how technical decisions are made; it holds that there is a web of interacting conflicts and basic behavior or action styles that explain what is going on. In an earlier paper, [Kling, 1980] outlines a set of perspectives one can take to understand what is going on; in those terms, my approach is that of the rationalist.

I don't wish to defend or condemn the assumption of rationality as a tool for describing organizations in general, since that is not my present concern. For our purposes here—making sense out of software development situations—I find the assumption that we can describe things as a rationally based system (the SDS) to be well suited. The basic evidence is that I can describe situations in terms of inputs and outputs and capture the things of interest (for example, whether or not a group is getting the information it needs to produce the required outputs). Further, it is clear that there are some distinguishable elements of such environments (for example, policies and physical tools) and that these elements, in fact, enter into the production of outputs from inputs (if you remove one totally, it will be noticed if it was, in fact, part of the system) and that they affect each other (a policy against buying new equipment will certainly be felt if the old equipment is unable to produce the needed outputs).

**Note 4.7 (p. 109):** See [Freeman, 1983b] and [Freeman, 1987].

**Chapter 5**

**Note 5.1 (p. 135):** The first usage of "evolution" that I know of was by Van Horn [Van Horn, 1980, pp. 209–226] in an interesting paper about the nature of software maintenance.

**Note 5.2 (p. 136):** [Lientz and Swanson, 1980] report around 20% for corrective maintenance in the type of data processing situations they studied. Whatever the actual number in your situation, it is almost always small. If not, you probably have some serious problems in your technical development activities.

**Note 5.3 (p. 138):** There are few books that specifically address evolution. Three that do are [Glass and Noiseux, 1981], [McClure, 1981], and [Zvegintzov and Parikh, 1983].

**Note 5.4 (p. 139):** See, for example, [Aron, 1974], [Aron, 1983], [Fairley, 1985], [Jensen and Tonies, 1979], [Pressman, 1987], and [Zelkowitz *et al.*, 1979].

**Chapter 6**

**Note 6.1 (p. 145):** Large projects normally use work-breakdown structures to divide the total task up into a number of smaller tasks. These tasks are typically organized into a network and elaborate schedules developed to show when and by whom each task will be performed, intermediate milestones (sometimes called inchpebbles) established, and so on.

One of the surprising positive points about employing this type of management tool is that it provides managers and technical people with something to talk about. Of course, knowing when something is due is a useful reminder to the manager, but perhaps of more importance is that the schedule provides a point of discussion.

It is then, within the context of a schedule discussion, that the manager (and the technical person) can learn what is really going on. Technical problems can be brought to the surface, interaction or other personnel problems can be identified, and support or system problems can be uncovered.

**Note 6.2 (p. 146):** People understand intellectually the difference between an activity and the tangible workproduct that is the result. Yet this difference is often not internalized. This is quite evident in many schedules that one encounters on projects which show very clearly that activity *X* will take place over time period *P*, but which indicate no result (workproduct) that can be objectively ascertained to have been created. In such a situation, the technical methods are not supporting the organizational need to track and report progress.

**Note 6.3 (p. 150):** See Chapter 3 of [Brooks, 1975] for a good discussion of team organizations.

**Note 6.4 (p. 151):** See [Mumford, 1981] and [Rudawitz and Freeman, 1981] for some specific approaches.

**Note 6.5 (p. 158):** Configuration management is a discipline long used in the creation of large, complex sets of equipment such as factory machinery or computer hardware. The issue is that in producing, and later servicing, such a configuration, it is important to know exactly what elements were used. (There are often slight changes made to equipment over the lifetime of its production, so that the particular unit installed in one configuration may differ a bit from the same type of unit installed in another configuration.) Configuration management, then, consists of the policies and procedures for defining and keeping track of configurations. See [Bersoff *et al.*, 1980].

## Chapter 7

**Note 7.1 (p. 166):** [Boehm, 1981], especially Section 33.6, which discusses in detail many of the aspects of people-intensive software production.

**Note 7.2 (p. 167):** See [Lowen, 1982].

**Note 7.3 (p. 168):** See [Wonder and Donovan, 1984].

**Note 7.4 (p. 174):** This is a subject that is only beginning to receive systematic attention. [Weinberg, 1971] is one of the first (and most cited);

[Curtis, 1985] is a more recent compendium in the same area. Also see [Kerola and Taggart, 1981].

**Note 7.5 (p. 174):** See [Peter and Hull, 1969]. [Boehm, 1981] also discusses some of the reasons why the Peter Principle is so often observed in the software world.

**Note 7.6 (p. 176):** See [Freeman, 1983a].

**Note 7.7 (p. 181):** See, for example, [Edwards, 1979], [Kerola and Taggart, 1981], [Lowen, 1982], and [Wonder and Donovan, 1984].

**Note 7.8 (p. 183):** [Semprevivo, 1980] provides a review of some of the social science research relevant to teamwork. He then discusses in concrete terms how to apply that research to the task of creating more effective systems development teams. As both a teacher and a practitioner of long experience, he has a unique and valuable perspective to offer.

**Note 7.9 (p. 184):** See [Gibbs and Fairley, 1986] for the current state of software engineering curricula. [Yates, 1985] discusses some general ideas on systems engineering.

**Note 7.10 (p. 185):** See [Freeman, 1986].

**Note 7.11 (p. 185):** See, for example, [Parker, 1978].

**Chapter 8**

**Note 8.1 (p. 192):** [Parnas, 1985], for example, argues that the continuous mathematics basis for all of traditional science and engineering is inappropriate for the fundamentally discrete nature of computing. Whether or not that is the case, it is clear that many of the classical intellectual tools are not as effective for describing and analyzing computing as we need.

**Note 8.2 (p. 194):** For example, see [Freeman, 1983] or [DoD, 1983].

**Note 8.3 (p. 196):** See, for example, [Bersoff *et al.*, 80] and [Babich, 1985].

**Note 8.4 (p. 201):** See [Jackson, 1975].

**Note 8.5 (p. 201):** See, for example, [Wirth, 1971] or [Ledgard, 1974, pg. 64].

**Note 8.6 (p. 201):** See, for example, [McGowan and Kelly, 1975].

**Note 8.7 (p. 201):** For more information on the technical procedures, see [Fairley, 1985] or [Pressman, 1987]; for quality assessment procedures, see in addition [Dunn and Ullman, 1982]; for managerial procedures, see [Gunther, 1978]. "Rolling estimates" are those that are "rolled over" and updated as specific milestones are reached and more detailed technical information becomes available on which to base estimates of future work.

**Note 8.8 (p. 204):** See, for example, [Page-Jones, 1980].

**Note 8.9 (p. 206):** An interesting example of this approach can be found in [Lehman, 1980]. [Lehman and Belady, 1985] provide a deeper coverage of their very valuable approach to understanding and controlling the dynamics of large systems.

**Note 8.10 (p. 207):** See [Marca and McGowan, 1987] and [Ross, 1977].

**Note 8.11 (p. 211):** See, for example, [Basili, 1985], [Jones, 1986], [Peters, 1981] and [Wasserman *et al.*, 1983].

### Chapter 9

**Note 9.1 (p. 218):** There are, of course, some extremely important tools which have been used for years; compilers and loaders and, more recently, editors and file systems. A few years ago a book [Kernighan and Plaugher, 1981] was published that described a number of tools for the programmer. However, the use of compilers is 30 years old and the routine use of complex loaders and other such tools is at least 20 years old; after those advances, there has been very little until recently. See [Zelkowitz *et al.*, 1984] for an insightful study of practices, especially tool use.

**Note 9.2 (p. 219):** See [Riddle and Fairley, 1980], Chapter 1, for a fuller discussion of these and other requirements.

**Note 9.3 (p. 221):** In fact, the core of the issue is the representation, so that it may be more accurate to discuss what *methods* are needed to produce a given representation.

**Note 9.4 (p. 221):** See [Riddle and Fairley, 1980]

**Note 9.5 (p. 221):** For example, a more recent collection of papers [Barstow *et al.*, 1984] focuses just on interactive programming environments (essentially the tool aspects thereof). This book contains descriptions of a number of tools; while most are still largely in the research stage, it does provide a sample of what was happening circa 1982. It also has an extensive bibliography.

**Note 9.6 (p. 222):** See, for example, [Yalamanchilli *et al.*, 1984] for a discussion of workstation characteristics and [IEEE, 1985b] for papers on current work in the field.

**Note 9.7 (p. 222):** See, for example, [Boehm, 1973b].

**Note 9.8 (p. 223):** See [Houghton, 1983] for a taxonomy and survey of tools.

**Note 9.9 (p. 224):** See, for example, [DeRoze and Nyman, 1978].

**Note 9.10 (p. 227):** See [Brooks, 1975].

### Chapter 10

**Note 10.1 (p. 235):** The [Newell *et al.*, 1967] definition of computer science is merely a reflection of work that already had a solid history at that point.

**Note 10.2 (p. 237):** See, for example, [Freeman *et al.*, 1976].

**Note 10.3 (p. 240):** See [Freeman, 1974] for a review of early work; [IEEE, 1985a] and *Expert* (a magazine published by the IEEE Computer Society) have a sampling of current approaches.

**Note 10.4 (p. 244):** [Kling, 1980] provides an overview of some of these impacts and cites much of the relevant literature.

### Chapter 11

**Note 11.1 (p. 251):** See [Kling, 1980] for an excellent discussion of other perspectives.

**Note 11.2 (p. 252):** For an irreverent, but largely true, examination of systems, read [Gall, 1975].

### Appendix A

**Note A.1 (p. 255):** The material here is drawn from [Kerola and Freeman, 1981], [Freeman and von Staa, 1984], and [Freeman, 1985].

**Note A.2 (p. 258):** See, for example, [Boehm, 1976].

**Note A.3 (p. 258):** See [Kerola *et al.*, 79].

**Note A.4 (p. 261):** See [Kerola and Freeman, 1981b].

**Note A.5 (p. 261):** See [Taggart, 1980].

**Note A.6 (p. 261):** See [Lucas, 1978].

# Glossary

The definitions given here are informal and pertain to their usage in this book.

**Abstraction** A representation of something that contains less information than the something. For example, a data abstraction provides information about some referent in the outside world without indicating how the data are represented in the computer.

**Abstract** Containing less information than reality.

**Ada** A programming language, developed under the leadership of the U.S. Department of Defense, specifically oriented to support modern software development practices.

**Algorithm** A precise set of instructions for carrying out some computation (e.g., the algorithm for calculating an employee's take-home pay).

**Architect** The person responsible for creating the structure in a system (e.g., its organization into major parts).

**Artificial intelligence** Software that displays "intelligence"; the subfield of computer science that works on the problem of creating "intelligent" programs.

**Cobol** A programming language oriented toward business data processing.

**Code** A computer program expressed in the machine language of the computer on which it will be executed i.e., the executable form of a program. More generally, a program expressed in a representation that requires only trivial changes to make it ready for execution.

**Compiler** A program that translates a program written in one language (e.g., FORTRAN) into another (e.g., machine language for an IBM 370).

**Components** Parts of a program or computer system.

**Computer** A piece of hardware that can store and execute instructions (i.e., interpret them and cause some action to occur).

**Configuration** A collection of items that bear a particular relation to each other (e.g., the data configuration of a system in which classes of data and their relationships are defined).

**Customer** A person or entity paying for a piece of software.

**Design** (*n.*) A plan for a program or piece of software.

**Design** (*v.*) To create a design; to plan.

**Development** A set of activities that are carried out to create a piece of software (e.g., design, programming, and testing).

**DoD** The U.S. Department of Defense.

**Engineering** A process of applying scientific and other information in specific ways to achieve technical, economic, and human goals.

**Evolution** Changes to a piece of software after its initial development; typically, this is repair of problems, adaptation to new conditions, and enhancement with new functionality.

**Feedback** Information from some process that is sent back to the entity carrying out the process in order that some variables of the process can be changed *"Feedback from the customers gave the development group several ideas on how to improve the systems they were producing."*

**FORTRAN** A programming language oriented toward scientific calculations.

**Function** A special duty or performance of a thing or a person (e.g., the function of the programmer is to create programs; the function of a compiler is to translate programs from one language to another).

**Hardware** Computer equipment, as opposed to the software.

**Heuristic** A rule of thumb.

**Interface** The boundary between two things, typically two programs, two pieces of hardware, a computer and its user, etc.

**Language** An agreed-upon set of symbols, rules for combining them, and meanings attached to the symbols that is used to express something (e.g., the Pascal programming language, job-control language for an operating system, and a graphical language for building models of a proposed piece of software).

**Lifecycle** A defined set of stages through which a piece of software passes over time.

**Maintenance** Changes to a piece of software after its initial development; also called evolution.

**Method** A way of doing something.

**Methodology** A collection of methods.

**Model** An abstraction of reality that still bears enough rese mblance to the object of the model that we can answer some questions about the object by consulting the model.

**Module** A unit of a software system, usually relatively small.

**Objectives** Targets for action, such that we can tell when they have been met (e.g., the objective of producing software that incurs no more than three fatal errors in the first year of operation).

**Operating system** The software that controls a computer system.

**Paradigm** A model way of doing something or of analyzing something *"The paradigm for doing design inspections was described in the course."*

**Parameter** A variable whose value may change the operation but not the structure of some activity (e.g., an important parameter in the productivity of a program is the language used).

**Phases** Individual stages of work on a piece of software (e.g., the testing phase).

**Policy** A rule of behavior (e.g., the policy specifying when design reviews are to take place).

**Procedure** A method or set of steps defining an activity; technically, a program that can be executed as a subactivity by another program.

**Process** Technically, a procedure that is being executed on a specific set of data; more generally, a procedure for doing something that is actually being carried out.

**Processor** That part of a computer capable of executing instructions. More generally, any active agent capable of carrying out a set of instructions (e.g., a transaction processor for modifying a database).

**Product** Usually, an entity to be sold; more generally, the result of some process.

**Program** A set of instructions for a computer, arranged so that when executed they will cause some desired effect (such as the calculation of a quantity or the retrieval of a piece of data).

**Prototype** A scaled-down version of something, built before the complete item is built in order to assess the feasibility or utility of the full version.

**SDS** Software development system; a system whose operation results in systems being produced.

**Software** Programs, data, designs for programs, specifications, and any of the other information that is relevant to a particular set of executable computer instructions (either existing or planned).

**Specification** A description of a program that does not provide information on how the program works; typically, a functional specification that defines *what the program does.*

**Structure** Framework: *"The structure of the program was very poor,"* means that the outline of the program, as represented by the major paths of its possible flow of control, was poor, which in turn usually means that it was jumbled, had many alternatives, that the connection between different regions of the program was unclear, and so on.

**Subsystem** A system contained within a larger system; usually the subsystem can "stand alone" (e.g., the programming subsystem in a development organization).

**System** A collection of elements that work together, forming a coherent whole (e.g., a computer system consisting of processors, printers, disks, etc.).

**Tool** Any artifact that can be used to amplify the power of a human being in developing software; usually refers to a tangible object such as a terminal or a program (e.g., a test-case generator).

**Transformation** A change of one aspect or form of software into another form (e.g., the transformation of specifications for a program into the design of a program that fulfills the specifications).

**Waterfall** The name for the "classical" software lifecycle, so named because the chart used to portray it suggests a waterfall.

**Workproduct** The tangible result of some activity (e.g., a program is the workproduct produced by a programmer).

**Workstation** A device designed to be the physical instrument on which a programmer or designer (or any other type of worker) does his or her work. A programmer's workstation, for example, might consist of a graphics screen, a powerful microprocessor with local memory, a set of support software such as a computer, an editor, and a debugger, and a network connection to a mainframe.

# Bibliography


[Abbott, 1986] Abbott, Russell J. *An Integrated Approach to Software Development,* John Wiley and Sons, New York, 1986.

[Aron, 1974] Aron, Joel D. *The Program Development Process Part 1: The Individual Programmer,* Addison-Wesley, Reading, Mass., 1974.

[Aron, 1983] Aron, Joel D. *The Program Development Process Part 2: The Programming Team,* Addison-Wesley, Reading, Mass., 1983.

[Asimow, 1962] Asimow, Morris. *Introduction to Design,* Prentice-Hall, Englewood Cliffs, N.J., 1962.

[Babich, 1985] Babich, Wayne A. *Software Configuration Management: Coordination and Control for Productivity,* Addison-Wesley, Reading, Mass., 1985.

[Barstow *et al.*, 1984] Barstow, David R., Shrobe, Howard E., and Sandewall, Erik (eds). *Interactive Programming Environments,* McGraw-Hill, New York, 1984.

[Basili, 1980] Basili, Victor. *Tutorial on Models and Metrics for Software Management and Engineering,* IEEE Computer Society Press, Washington, D.C., 1980.

[Belady and Lehman, 1976] Belady, L.A., and Lehman, M.M. "A Model of Large Program Development," *IBM Systems Journal,* vol. 15, No. 3, pp. 225–252, 1976.

[Bersoff, Henderson and Siegal, 1980] Bersoff, E. H., Henderson V. D., and Siegel S.G. *Software Configuration Management: An Investment in Product Integrity,* Prentice-Hall, Englewood Cliffs, N.J., 1980.

[Boehm, 1973] Boehm, Barry W. "Software and Its Impact: A Quantitative Assessment," *Datamation,* May 1973. Reprinted in [Freeman and Wasserman, 1983].

[Boehm, 1976] Boehm, B. W. "Software Engineering," *IEEE Transactions Electr. Comp.*, December 1976.

[Boehm, 1981] Boehm, B. W. *Software Engineering Economics,* Prentice-Hall, Englewood Cliffs, N.J., 1981.

[Boehm *et al.*, 1973] Boehm, B. W., Brown, J. R., Kaspar, H., Lipow, M., MacLeod, G. J., and Merritt, M. J. *Characteristics of Software Quality,* TRW Technical Report SS-73-09, 1973; North-Holland, Amsterdam, 1978.

[Booch, 1983] Booch, Grady. *Software Engineering With Ada,* Benjamin/Cummings Publishing Co., Menlo Park, Calif., 1983.

[Brooks, 1975] Brooks, Frederick P. *The Mythical Man-Month: Essays on Software Engineering,* Addison-Wesley, Reading, Mass., 1975.

[Churchman, 1979] Churchman, C. W. *The Systems Approach,* revised edition, Dell Publishing, New York 1979.

[Cohen, 1986] Cohen, Norman H. *Ada As A Second Language,* McGraw-Hill, New York, 1986.

[Crosby, 1980] Crosby, Philip B. *Quality is Free: The Art of Making Quality Certain,* Mentor, (New American Library), New York, 1980.

[Curtis, 1985] Curtis, Bill. *Tutorial: Human Factors in Software Development, 2nd Edition,* IEEE Computer Society Press, Washington, D.C., 1985.

[De Roze and Nyman, 1978] De Roze, B. C., and Nyman, T. H. "The Software Life Cycle—A Management and Technological Challenge in the Department of Defense," *IEEE Transactions on Software Engineering,* vol. SE-4, No. 4, pp. 309–319, July 1978.

[DoD, 1983] DoD Ada Joint Program Office. "Ada Methodologies: Concepts and Requirements," *ACM Software Engineering Notes,* pp. 32–50, January 1983.

[Dunn and Ullman, 1982] Dunn, Robert, and Ullman, Richard. *Quality Assurance for Computer Software,* McGraw-Hill, New York, 1982.

[Edwards, 1979] Edwards, Betty. *Drawing on the Right Side of the Brain: A Course In Enhancing Creativity and Artistic Confidence,* Houghton Mifflin, Boston, 1979.

[Fagan, 1976] Fagan, M. E. "Design and Code Inspection to Reduce Errors in Program Development," *IBM Systems Journal,* vol. 15, No. 3, pp. 182–211, 1976.

[Fairley, 1985] Fairley, Richard. *Software Engineering Concepts,* McGraw-Hill, New York, 1985.

[Feigenbaum and McCorduck, 1983] Feigenbaum, Edward A., and McCorduck, Pamela. *The Fifth Generation: Artificial Intelligence and Japan's Computer Challenge to the World,* Addison-Wesley, Reading, Mass., 1983.

[Freeman, 1974] Freeman, Peter. "Automating Software Design," in *10th Design Automation Workshop,* June 1973. Reprinted in *Computer,* pp. 33–38, April 1974.

[Freeman, 1983a] Freeman, Peter. "Fundamentals of Design," in [Freeman and Wasserman, 1983, pp. 2–22].

[Freeman, 1983b] Freeman, Peter. "Reusable Software Engineering: Concepts and Research Directions," in *Proceedings of the Workshop on Reusability in Programming,* September 1983. Reprinted in [Freeman and Wasserman, 1983, pp. 63–76].

[Freeman, 1985] Freeman, Peter. "Concepts for Understanding Design," internal working paper, ICS Dept., UC Irvine, March 1985.

[Freeman, 1986] Freeman, Peter. "Essential Elements of Software Engineering Education Revisited," in [Gibbs, 86].

[Freeman, 1987] Freeman, Peter. *Tutorial on Software Reusability,* IEEE Computer Society Press, Washington, D.C., 1987.

[Freeman and von Staa, 1984] Freeman, Peter, and von Staa, Arndt. "Towards A Theory of Software Engineering," working paper, ICS Dept., UC Irvine, 1984.

[Freeman and Wasserman, 1983] Freeman, P. and Wasserman, A. (eds) *Tutorial on Software Design Techniques,* IEEE Computer Society Press, Washington, D.C., 1983.

[Freeman *et al.*, 1976] Freeman, Peter, Wasserman, Anthony, and Fairley, Richard. "Essential Elements of Software Engineering Education," in *Proceedings of the 2nd International Conference on Software Engineering,* pp. 116–122, 1976.

[Gall, 1975] Gall, John. *Systemantics: How Systems Work and Especially How They Fail,* Pocket Books, New York, 1975.

[Gibbs and Fairley, 1986] Gibbs, N. E., and Fairley, R. E. (eds). *The Educational Needs of the Software Community,* Springer-Verlag, New York, 1986.

[Gilbert, 1983] Gilbert, Philip. *Software Design and Development,* Science Research Associates, Inc., Chicago, 1983.

[Glass and Noiseux, 1981] Glass, Robert L., and Noiseux, Ronald A. *Software Maintenance Guidebook,* Prentice-Hall, Englewood Cliffs, N.J., 1981.

[Gleitman, 1981] Gleitman, Henry. *Psychology,* W. W. Norton, New York, 1981.

[Gunther, 1978] Gunther, Richard C. *Management Methodology for Software Product Engineering,* Wilely-Interscience Publishers, New York, 1978.

[Habermann and Perry, 1983] Habermann, A. N., and Perry, Dewayne E. *Ada for Experienced Programmers,* Addison-Wesley, Reading, Mass., 1983.

[Houghton, 1983] Houghton, Raymond C., Jr. "Software Development Tools: A Profile," *Computer,* pp. 63–70, May 1983.

[IEEE, 1985a] *Transactions of Software Engineering,* Special Issue on Applications of Artificial Intelligence to Software Engineering, November 1985.

[IEEE, 1985b] *Proceedings of 1st International Conference on Computer Workstations,* IEEE Computer Society Press, Washington, D.C., 1985.

[Jackson, 1975] Jackson, Michael. *Principles of Program Design,* Academic Press, New York, 1975.

[Jensen and Tonies, 1979] Jensen, R. W. and Tonies, C. C. *Software Engineering,* Prentice-Hall, Englewood Cliffs, N.J., 1979.

[Jones, 1986] Jones, Capers. *Programming Productivity,* McGraw-Hill, New York, 1986.

[Kernighan and Plaugher, 1981] Kernighan, Brian W. and Plauger, P. J. *Software Tools in Pascal,* Addison-Wesley, Reading, Mass., 1981.

[Kerola and Freeman, 1981] Kerola, P., and Freeman, Peter. "A Comparison of Lifecycle Models," *Proceedings of the 5th International Conference on Software Engineering*, pp. 90–99, San Diego, 1981.

[Kerola and Taggart, 1981] Kerola, P., and Taggart, W. "Human Information Processing Styles in the Information Systems Development Process," paper accepted for the IFIP TC8 Working Conference on Evolutionary Information Systems, Budapest, Hungary, September, 1981.

[Kerola *et al.*, 1979] Kerola, P. *et al.* (eds). *Summary Report of the Systemeering Research Seminar of Tampere,* [Finland], Finnish Data Processing Association, Helsinki, 1979.

[Kling, 1980] Kling, Rob. "Social Analyses of Computing: Theoretical Perspectives in Recent Empirical Research," *Computing Surveys,* pp. 61–110, March, 1980.

[Kling and Scacchi, 1982] Kling, Rob, and Scacchi, Walt. "The Web of Computing: Computer Technology as Social Organization," *Advances in Computers,* vol. 21, Academic Press, New York, 1982.

[Kuhn, 1970] Kuhn, Thomas S. *The Structure of Scientific Revolutions, 2nd Edition,* University of Chicago Press, 1970.

[Ledgard, 1974] Ledgard, Henry. *Programming Proverbs,* Hayden Book Co., Rochelle Park, N.J., 1974.

[Lehman, 1980] Lehman, M. M. "Programs, Life Cycles, and Laws of Software Evolution," *Proceedings of the IEEE,* vol. 68, No. 9, pp. 1060–1076, September 1980.

[Lehman and Belady, 1985] Lehman, M. M., and Belady L. A. *Program Evolution: Processes of Software Change,* Academic Press, New York, 1985.

[Leveson, 1984] Leveson, N. G. "Software Safety in Computer-Controlled Systems," *IEEE Computer,* vol. 17, No. 2, February 1984.

[Lientz and Swanson, 1980] Lientz, Bennet P., and Swanson, E. Burton. *Software Maintenance Management,* Addison-Wesley, Reading, Mass., 1980.

[Lowen, 1982] Lowen, Walter. *Dichotomies of the Mind,* John Wiley and Sons, New York, 1982.

[Lucas, 1978] Lucas, H. C., Jr. "The Evolution of an Information System: From Key-man to Every Person," *Sloan Management Review,* 19, 2, 1978.

[Marca and McGowan, 1987] Marca, David, and McGowan, Clement L. *SADT: Structured Analysis and Design Technique,* McGraw-Hill, New York, 1987.

[Martin and McClure, 1985] Martin, James, and McClure, Carma L. *Diagramming Techniques for Analysts and Programmers,* Prentice-Hall, Englewood Cliffs, N.J., Englewood Cliffs, N.J., 1985.

[McClure, 1981] McClure, Carma L. *Managing Software Development and Maintenance,* Van Nostrand Reinhold, New York, 1981.

[McGowan and Kelly, 1975] McGowan, Clement L., and Kelly, John R. *Top-Down Structured Programming Techniques,* Petrocelli/Charter, New York, 1975.

[Mumford, 1981] Mumford, E. "Participative Systems Design: Structure and Method," *Systems, Objectives, Solutions,* January 1981, pp. 5–19. Reprinted in [Freeman and Wasserman, 1983, pp. 286–300].

[Musa, *et al.*, 1987] Musa, J. D., Iannino, A., and Okumoto, K. *Software Reliability: Measurement, Prediction, Application,* McGraw-Hill, New York, 1987.

[Nasbitt, 1982] Nasbitt, John. *Megatrends: Ten New Directions Transforming Our Lives,* Warner Books, New York, 1982.

[Newell *et al.*, 1967] Newell, Allen, Perlis, Alan J., and Simon, Herbert A. "What is Computer Science?," letter in *Science,* vol. 157, No. 3795, pp. 1373–1374, Sept. 22, 1967.

[Norman and Draper, 1985] Norman, Donald, and Draper, Stephen. *User Centered Systems Design,* Lawrence Erlbaum Associates, Hillsdale, N.J., 1985.

[Page-Jones, 1980] Page-Jones, M. *The Practical Guide to Structured Systems Design,* Yourdon Press, New York, 1980.

[Parker, 1978] Parker, Donn B. *Ethical Conflicts in Computer Science and Technology,* AFIPS Press, 1978.

[Parnas, 1985] Parnas, David L. "Software Aspects of Strategic Defense Systems," *American Scientist,* September–October 1985.

[Peter and Hull, 1969] Peter, Laurence J. and Hull, Raymond. *The Peter Principle,* William Morrow, New York, 1969.

[Peters, 1981] Peters, Lawrence. *Software Design: Methods and Techniques,* Yourdon Press, New York, 1981.

[Peters and Waterman, 1982] Peters, Thomas J., and Waterman, Robert H., Jr. *In Search of Excellence,* Harper and Row, New York, 1982.

[Pirsig, 1974] Pirsig, Robert. *Zen and the Art of Motorcycle Maintenance,* Bantam Books, New York, 1974.

[Polya, 1957] Polya, George. *How to Solve It: A New Aspect of the Mathematical Method, 2nd Edition,* Doubleday Anchor Books, New York, 1957.

[Pressman, 1987] Pressman, Roger. *Software Engineering: A Practitioner's Approach, 2nd Edition,* McGraw-Hill, New York, 1987.

[Random House, 1965] *The Random House Dictionary of the English Language, College Edition,* Random House, New York, 1965.

[Riddle and Fairley, 1980] Riddle, W. E., and Fairley, R. E. *Software Development Tools,* Springer-Verlag, Berlin, 1980.

[Ross, 1977] Ross, Douglas T. "Structured Analysis (SA): A Language for Communicating Ideas," in *Transactions on Software Engineering,* vol. SE-3, No. 1, January 1977, pp. 16-34. Reprinted in [Freeman and Wasserman, 1983, pp. 96–114].

[Rudawitz and Freeman, 1981] Rudawitz, L. M., and Freeman, P. "Client-Centered Design: Concepts and Experience," *Systems, Objectives, Solutions,* vol. 1, 1981, pp. 21–32. Reprinted in [Freeman and Wasserman, 1983, pp. 274–285].

[Sayles and Chandler, 1971] Sayles, Leonard, and Chandler, Margaret. *Managing Large Systems: Organizations for the Future,* Harper and Row, New York, 1971.

[Semprevivo, 1980] Semprevivo, Phillip C. *Teams in Information Systems Development,* Yourdon Press, New York, 1980.

[Taggart, 1980] Taggart, W. *Information Systems: An Introduction to Computers in Organizations,* Allyn and Bacon, Inc., Boston, Mass., 1980.

[Van Horn, 1980] Van Horn, Earl C. "Software Must Evolve," in Freeman, H., and Lewis, P. (eds), *Software Engineering*, Academic Press, New York, pp. 209-226, 1980.

[Wasserman, et al, 1983] Wasserman, A. I., Freeman, P., and Porcella, M. "Characteristics of Software Development Methodologies," in Olle, T. W., Sol, H. G. and Tully, C. J. (eds), *Information Systems Design Methodologies: A Feature Analysis,* North-Holland, Amsterdam, pp. 37–62, 1983.

[Weinberg, 1971] Weinberg, Gerald. *Psychology of Computer Programming,* Van Nostrand Reinhold, Princeton, N.J., pp. 126–132, 1971.

[Wirth, 1971] Wirth, Niklaus. "Program Development by Stepwise Refinement," *Communications of the ACM,* April 1971, pp. 221–227. Reprinted in [Freeman and Wasserman, 1983, pp. 533–541].

[Wonder and Donovan, 1984] Wonder, Jacquelyn, and Donovan, Priscilla. *Whole-Brain Thinking: Working From Both Sides of the Brain to Achieve Peak Job Performance,* William Morrow, New York, 1984.

[Yalamanchilli *et al.,* 1984] Yalamanchilli, S., Malek, M., and Aggarwal, J. K. "Workstations in a Local Area Network Environment," *Computer,* pp. 74–86, November 1984.

[Yates, 1985] Yates, J. E. "Systems Engineering: A Background," *Fourth International Conference on Systems Engineering,* Coventry, Lanchester Polytechnic, Coventry, England, September, 1985.

[Zelkowitz, Shaw and Gannon, 1979] Zelkowitz, Marvin V., Shaw, Allan C. and Gannon, John D. *Principles of Software Engineering and Design,* Prentice-Hall, Englewood Cliffs, N.J., 1979.

[Zelkowitz, et al, 1984] Zelkowitz, Marvin V., Yeh, Raymond T., Hamlet, Richard G., Gannon, John D., and Basili, Victor R. "Software Engineering Practices in the US and Japan," *Computer*, pp. 57-66, June 1984.

[Zvegintzov and Parikh, 1983] Zvegintzov, N., and Parikh, G. *Tutorial on Software Maintenance*, IEEE Computer Society Press, Washington, D.C., 1983.

# Subject Index

# Name Index